THEOLOGY
AND THE UNIVERSITY

an ecumenical investigation

edited by

JOHN COULSON

HELICON PRESS
BALTIMORE
DARTON, LONGMAN & TODD
LONDON

DARTON, LONGMAN & TODD LTD.,
64 Chiswick High Road, London, W.4

HELICON PRESS INC.
1120 N. Calvert Street,
Baltimore, Maryland 21202

© *1964 John Coulson*
First published 1964

Printed in Great Britain by Latimer, Trend & Co. Ltd., Plymouth
Nihil Obstat: Joannes M.T. Barton, S.T.D., L.S.S. Censor deputatus.
Imprimatur: ✠ Georgius L. Craven, Epus Sebastopolis, Vic.Gen.
Westmonasterii, die 16a Decembriis 1963. The Nihil Obstat and
Imprimatur are a declaration that a book or pamphlet is considered
to be free from doctrinal or moral error. It is not implied that those
who have granted the Nihil Obstat and Imprimatur agree with the
contents, opinions or statements expressed.

CONTENTS

PREFACE   *page* ix

INTRODUCTION   1
The Editor, John Coulson, Downside School

I. THEOLOGY AND THE UNIVERSITY

1. THE ECUMENICAL ASPECT   13
The Abbot of Downside, Dom Christopher Butler

II. AN EDUCATED LAITY—
problems and opportunities

2. THE CATHOLIC UNDERGRADUATE
   (i) *Dr Monica Lawlor, Lecturer in Psychology,
       University of London*   25

       Note—Religious Instruction in Catholic Grammar
             Schools (Hamish Swanston of the Birming-
             ham Oratory)   36

   (ii) *Herbert McCabe, O.P., Blackfriars, Manchester*   38

3. NEWMAN'S IDEA OF AN EDUCATED LAITY—
   THE TWO VERSIONS   47
   John Coulson

       Note—What is a layman? (Charles Davis)   63

4. THE CATHOLIC UNIVERSITY—THE AMERICAN EXPERIENCE   66
   Daniel Callahan, associate editor of The Commonweal,
   *and formerly Teaching Fellow in Roman Catholic Studies,
   Harvard Divinity School*

v

5. THE TEACHING OF THEOLOGY ON THE CONTINENT AND ITS
   IMPLICATIONS   78
   *Peter Fransen, S.J., Professor of Dogmatic Theology
   in the Jesuit Faculty of Theology, Heverlee, Louvain,
   and at the University of Innsbruck*

III. THEOLOGY—
its nature and practice

6. THEOLOGY AND ITS PRESENT TASK   107
   *Charles Davis, Professor of Sacred Scripture,
   St. Edmund's College, Ware*

7. THE EXISTING PRACTICE IN THE BRITISH UNIVERSITIES

   (i) Scotland—the Biblical tradition   133
       *J. K. S. Reid, Professor of Christian Dogmatics,
       University of Aberdeen*

   (ii) Oxford—the Anglican tradition   146
       *David Jenkins, Fellow and Chaplain
       of the Queen's College, Oxford*

   (iii) The place of a department of theology
        in a modern university   162
        *Canon Alan Richardson, Professor of Theology,
        University of Nottingham, Dean-designate of York*

   (iv) Roman Catholic participation
        in a modern university   173
        *Mgr H. Francis Davis, recognised lecturer
        in Christian Doctrine, University of Birmingham*

        Note—Theology and the new universities (Hilary
               Armstrong, Professor of Greek, University   188
               of Liverpool)

IV. THE CREATIVE CENTRE—
exercises in open dialogue

8. THEOLOGY AND LITERATURE
   (i) Natural Theology and its relation to poetry   193
       Dom Illtyd Trethowan, Monk of Downside Abbey
   (ii) Theology and Poetry—a reply   207
       *L. C. Knights, Winterstoke Professor of English,
       University of Bristol*

       Note—Literature and the Theologian (David
              Jenkins)   218

9. THEOLOGY AND PHILOSOPHY
   (i) The use of logical analysis in theology   220
       *Anthony Kenny, sometime lecturer in Philosophy,
       University of Liverpool*
   (ii) 'On making room for faith'—a Humanist's view   236
       *Stephan Körner, Professor of Philosophy,
       University of Bristol*

       Note—the Editor   247

V. NEEDS AND PROPOSALS

10. THE NEED FOR THEOLOGY FROM WITHIN THE SECULAR
    ENVIRONMENT   251
    Simon Clements, Walworth Comprehensive School, London

11. PROPOSALS FOR THE TEACHING OF THEOLOGY
    IN AN ENGLISH UNIVERSITY   268
    *Laurence Bright, O.P., Blackfriars, Cambridge.
    Editor,* Life of the Spirit

        Note—Kenneth Grayston, Deputy Head,
               special school of Theology, University of
               Bristol   273

INDEX   281

Preface

Since 1952 a group of priests and laymen have been meeting regularly at Downside Abbey; and they have, from time to time, augmented their meetings by the running of symposia on special subjects. So far, five such symposia have been organized and published, two of which have taken place at the Abbey of Bec in Normandy, in order more easily to secure the participation of continental scholars.

The sponsoring committee is as follows: John M. Todd (chairman), Dom Raphael Appleby (secretary), Laurence Bright, O.P., Simon Clements, John Coulson (editor), J. D. Crichton, Alexander Dru, John Foster, Dom Philip Jebb, Patrick McGrath, Ian McNeill, Neil Middleton, Dom Sebastian Moore, Dom Ralph Russell, Roger Sharrock, Lancelot Sheppard, Theodore Westow, Christopher Williams.

The books which have so far appeared are *The Springs of Morality*, *The Arts, Artists and Thinkers*, *Work*, *Problems of Authority* (edited by John M. Todd), and *True Worship* (edited by Lancelot Sheppard). Both the present symposium and *True Worship* were recorded by the B.B.C., and extracts were broadcast in the Sunday evening Home Service programmes. We wish to thank the B.B.C. and the Rev. Colin James, West Regional Religious Broadcasting Officer, for such happy and generous collaboration.

In addition to those reading papers, members of the sponsoring committee, and members of the Community of Downside Abbey, the following accepted an invitation to take part:

The Rt. Rev. Joseph Rudderham, Bishop of Clifton.

Professor Hilary Armstrong, Liverpool University.

Sister Edmund Campion, La Retraite, Weston-super-Mare.

Rev. Rupert Davies, Didsbury College, Bristol.

Rev. Kenneth Grayston, Didsbury College, Bristol.

Miss Cecily Hastings, London.

Rev. Michael Hollings, Catholic Chaplain to Oxford University.

Rev. Colin James, Religious Broadcasting Officer, B.B.C., Bristol.

The Very Rev. Gerard Meath, Prior Provincial, O.P.

Hugo Meynell, Esq., Leeds University.

D. Rice, Esq., Warden of Vaughan College, Leicester.

The Very Rev. Mgr. G. H. Tomlinson, Catholic Chaplain to London University.

Rev. Hamish Swanston, of the Birmingham Oratory.

Introduction

Theology can choose; it can remain dead and neglected, or take the pressure of the times and live; but if it chooses life it has need of three things: a university setting, lay participation and the ecumenical dialogue.

These are the conclusions to which, as by a convergence of witness, the contributors to this symposium arrived, not only in the texts of their individual papers, but by their collective testimony continuously reiterated during the discussions.

Our purpose was to take advantage of that movement within the Roman Catholic Church confirmed and encouraged by Pope John towards a theology which is ecumenical rather than polemical, in order that we might investigate whether it is now feasible for there to be closer collaboration between Roman Catholics and other Christians within the departments of theology in the modern British universities. These departments, by permitting the layman to take a course in religious studies as one of the subjects of his B.A. Degree, fulfil a basic condition for producing that educated laity the Church so much needs, since they enable the layman to pursue his religious studies in the same place, in the same manner, and alongside his secular and professional studies.

Although our aim was, therefore, to discover how the education of the Catholic laity in religion could be undertaken as part of their university education, we also came to understand more fully why it is better to think in terms of what Catholic theology might gain from the university, than to remain imprisoned within that ancient imperialistic metaphor of theology as queen of the sciences, and its derivative that theology ought to be a kind of glue that would enable universities to stick together their otherwise fragmented studies.[1]

[1] David Jenkins, p. 160.

1

Today, it is no longer universities but men that theology retains the power to unify.

This investigation had, of course, to be ecumenical; and this was, in the strictest and best sense of the term, what it turned out to be: Anglicans, Free Churchmen and Roman Catholics foregathered to work, and succeeded in praying together; they began by talking about theology, and found themselves doing it.

Because of its ecumenical nature this investigation may be read with profit by Catholic and non-Catholic alike; but the reader must be warned against two possible misunderstandings: this book is not a manifesto but the testing of an hypothesis before a tribunal of expert witnesses. And the greatest disservice which could be done would be for passages or papers to be wrenched out of their context for purposes of polemic: this is particularly a book which needs to be read as a whole, before a judgment of particular papers can be fairly made. The other misunderstanding is one to which all symposia are peculiarly liable: that papers repeat and overlap each other. In the present case, however, the reader must remember that the very success of our investigation depended upon our being able to bring about a convergence of witness from different (and traditionally conflicting) christian traditions; and a careful study of such repetitions or of differences (even merely of emphasis) may serve, moreover, as a useful means of measuring how much the ecumenical movement has achieved, and what may be the nature of its future problems.

I

The book falls into five sections; and its tone is set by the first paper. Starting with the principle that the first duty of the Church 'is not to safeguard the faith of the traditional Catholic, but to "teach all nations",'[1] the Abbot of Downside speaks of the ecumenical issues with the weight of one who has been an outstanding English contributor to the second Vatican Council. Theology in ceasing to be polemical has need of the ecumenical dialogue; and if this is to be more than a clerical hobby and is to receive the informed lay participation it requires, it needs a proper setting: this is to be found in the seed-beds of our intellectual life and leadership—the universities.

[1] p. 14.

II

In the second part a closer look is taken at what is implied when we ask for a laity better educated in their religion; and here, especially, the papers must be read in their proper context. Some are analytic and critical, and deliberately so: problems cannot be solved by pretending that none exists. The papers by Dr Monica Lawlor and Fr Herbert McCabe (and by Simon Clements in Section V) are the result of group study and consultation, and are concerned to examine the following questions: in what sense is the average Catholic undergraduate a religious person; and is it true that he makes less mark upon his university, and does less well than his non-Catholic contemporaries? Is he sufficiently prepared to cope with the environment of the open university; and ought his religious education to be more directly related to the needs of his university studies?

The concluding papers of this section move to a more general and historical approach. My own paper takes a closer look at the principles which Newman thought should apply in educating the Catholic laity, and at the claim usually attributed to him that they are best served by a Catholic university. Drawing on hitherto unpublished material, it goes on to show that, in later life, Newman changed his mind and reached the conclusion that a Catholic university was neither possible nor desirable.

Daniel Callahan, who has experienced Catholic and non-Catholic American university life, and was formerly an assistant to Christopher Dawson during his tenure of the Stillman chair of Roman Catholic studies established at Harvard in 1958, takes the question a stage further: is the 'closed' or specifically Catholic college or university with which American Catholics are familiar, producing the kind of educated laity who are required in the pluralist societies of today: and if not, why not?

Père Fransen combines a wide experience of European universities with a special interest in English affairs; and his paper is not only a first-hand description of the way in which theology is taught in some of the best continental universities, but acts also as the theological matrix for the other papers in this section. The needs of the laity for a fuller education in religion are further examined, and his conclusion —that there is no one absolute and obligatory Roman Catholic form for such provision[1]—has the further consequence: that the English

[1] p. 95.

opportunity for Catholics and non-Catholics to collaborate within an open department of theology has no parallel elsewhere and is therefore uniquely ecumenical.

III

It is with the third and following section, however, that many non-Catholics may choose to begin their study of this book, before moving on subsequently to the papers by the Abbot of Downside and Père Fransen.

The paper by Fr Charles Davis which stands at the head of this section is intended to be the theological master paper and to answer the following questions: what, then, is theology; and what does it demand? How far do our existing conceptions require to be amended; and what are the needs of theology peculiar to this, the century of the second Vatican Council? Fr Davis's answer is summarised in the opening sentence of this introduction; and his claim that the specific characteristic of a Catholic theology is that it is an ecclesial activity leads him to conclude that Churches in dialogue require a theology in dialogue. In the succeeding papers of this section, by means of an evaluation of the various British theological traditions as they exist within their respective universities, this dialogue is examined and rehearsed.

Professor Reid, a Presbyterian writing from within the Protestant and biblical tradition, explains the bases of his theology, the problems it faces, and the contribution which it can make to the university.

The Rev. David Jenkins shows how Oxford, by being obliged to take account of the changes in philosophical and historical methodology, has moved from its traditional position of being a closed, Church university to one of 'severe openness', in which teachers have ceased to be seminarians and become university theologians, with the paradoxical consequences that directly a denomination shows itself prepared to accept the openness of a secularised and neutral university, it is not only permissible but necessary that its teachers should make their denominational position as clear as possible. The apparent conflict between ecclesiastical authority and academic autonomy is resolvable when the ideal is seen to be an open department, but committed men.

Professor Alan Richardson has had considerable experience of how best to establish departments of theology in the modern university;

and his paper describes their origins and opportunities. Since the universities in which they exist were constituted to be neutral in matters of religion, Catholics can be accepted on equal terms with other denominations; and one cannot help but wonder what might have happened if the Catholics of a generation ago had turned their backs upon the battlements of Oxbridge and raised their eyes to Redbrick and its opportunities.

Two points of the greatest importance emerged from the paper and its discussion: that we must distinguish between the studies rightly required for the theologian proper (lay or clerical) and those designed to make laymen theologically literate. This raises the question of how much Greek and Hebrew might be required by the average educated layman who merely wanted to read religious studies as part of a general degree, especially as it is these courses which offer the best opportunity for that collaboration with neighbouring departments and the development of those new approaches in the teaching of theology for which all contributors asked.[1]

The second point concerns the need to teach such students, not only the content of theology but, if they are to apply it usefully in a secular environment, how to think about it. Both these points are further discussed by Fr Laurence Bright in his paper.

The final paper in this section is one of crucial importance for Catholics, as it is by the only Roman Catholic theologian yet appointed to be a full-time member of a department of theology in a modern university. Since 1947 Mgr H. Francis Davis has taught at Birmingham; and his paper faces squarely the question whether Catholic theology is of its nature to be distinguished from other christian theologies, and its teaching and study to be inevitably pursued, as in some continental universities, in parallel but separate departments. Mgr Davis's conclusion is that this is not the case, and that it is possible to satisfy the legitimate needs both of episcopal authority and of the autonomy proper to university studies; and where the ideal is that of an open department but committed men,[2] Catholics are welcome as fellow students and fellow teachers, having both something to give and to receive from studies thus ecumenically undertaken.

---

[1] v. Fransen, p. 95 and p. 103, and Richardson, p. 171 ff.

[2] v. p. 182 ff., Jenkins, p. 158 f., Richardson, p. 167 f., and Bright p. 278.

IV

The fourth section of the book may well appear to be the most perverse or the most stimulating, according to the reader's prejudice. Entitled *The Creative Centre*,[1] it attempts to demonstrate by example what happens when theology leaves the closed shop of its protected environment and walks abroad in the open market-place of the university. Here, we achieved our purposes—the spirits from the vasty deep came when we called for them; and for the full-bodied argument their papers provoked, the editor remains impenitently grateful. It was here, especially, that we ceased to talk about theology and started doing it, as we felt on the pulse what really happens when theology is placed in dialogue with critics of literature and with philosophers.

Dom Illtyd Trethowan was concerned to show that the value of literature for the student of theology is that the one assists the other, since in each case a similar activity of attention is required. His paper was written to invite a reply from Professor L. C. Knights; and as we followed Professor Knights's exposition of the poetry on which his reply was based, we understood what the layman would gain who came to see that his religious studies ought to be pursued to the same depth of sensitive and precise awareness 'of things in their depth and presentness', and of 'life coming to consciousness', as is required by the best university teachers of literature.[2] He would see how a theology that fails to take the pressure of its times and ignores the insights of literature becomes moribund, and poisons where it should nourish.

In discussion, the relevance of these issues to the deficiencies noted in the papers by Dr Lawlor, Fr McCabe and Simon Clements was quickly noticed and vigorously pursued.[3]

When disciplines which have long been strangers to one another are brought once again into relationship, certain difficulties particularly of language and comprehension are bound to arise; and some readers may find the notes on pages 218 and 247 useful as starting-points, particularly to the remaining papers in this section.

Anthony Kenny was asked to show how the methods of logical analysis, which form the basis of philosophy teaching in most British universities, assist in making theological thinking more precise and more applicable to the intellectual climate of our time; whilst

[1] *v.* Charles Davis, p. 108.
[2] Knights, pp . 217, 218.
[3] *See* pp. 33, 43, 263 f.

Professor Körner, from the standpoint of a humanist, undertook to show by what methods he was prepared 'to make room for faith'.

V

The fifth and concluding section is composed of two papers only. The first needs to be read in conjunction not only with those with which it was prepared (Dr Lawlor's and Fr McCabe's), but with those on Theology and Literature. It is written from within the secular environment by Simon Clements, a teacher in a comprehensive school in the East End of London. Its purpose is to show the need for theology from within that environment by examining how far those factors which render ordinary people deaf to theology are of cultural origin, and how far they are caused by the failure of theology to adapt itself to those harsh necessities of modern life by which the layman is inexorably confronted.

The discussion of this paper touched off a central issue: for what purpose do we educate in religion? To impart a body of knowledge, or to arouse a living response? The easy answer is 'both'; but what each member of the symposium had to learn for himself at each meeting and as it were for the first time was how difficult it is to remain 'open' and properly 'responsive', however much in theory we may desire to be so. Being 'open' means accepting criticism from unexpected directions, and realising that the questions we ask are usually more helpful than the answers we give, and that the teacher, whether he be in the infants' school or a university, a nursemaid or a theologian, achieves success at the very moment when he has made himself unnecessary, when—with the aid of 'the best that has been known and said in the world'—his pupil breaks through the dependence barrier of personalities and secondary authorities and comes at last to see things as they really are. What is true of the teacher is, as Pope John taught us, true also of the theologian, however eminent—that in so far as he makes a helpful response to those fellow members of the open society who are neither Catholic nor christian, he is beginning to create theology by moving from a notional to a real assent in matters of religion. For theology lives most fully when it is a theology *of* something—a good master, it may be; but it is an even better servant.

Simon Clements's paper is one man's voyage of discovery; its position in the book and the symposium is like the flax burnt in the face of a newly elected Pope—to bring us down to earth and to remind us of our responsibilities as we consider the proposals put forward in the final paper.

This paper by Fr Laurence Bright must, once again, be prefaced by that warning which applies to each paper in the book: it must be read in relation to what might be called the theological master-papers already referred to; and its proposals for the form which a theological teaching suitable for the laity might take in an English university must be seen not only as the result of Fr Laurence Bright's experience in teaching theology to the Catholic students at King's College, London, but as the outcome of much discussion and consultation between all the contributors to this investigation.

Without compromising the essentials of Catholic dogma, the proposals are intended to be ecumenical in spirit and to be strictly in conformity with the practice of British universities. They are based therefore on interrelated principles: that, as in the teaching of other disciplines, so in theology, equivalent emphasis should be placed on *how* to think and on *what* to think, in order that the layman can learn to relate his theological principles to the world in which he will have to live and to criteria other than his own. To this end and also for specifically theological reasons, the proposals envisage that the undergraduate layman should be taught by laymen *and* priests working in the closest partnership, and qualified both to teach and to research in the subject they profess.

From the manner in which these proposals were received, it may be asserted without reservation that our fellow symposiasts corroborated our initial hypothesis—that if, in Newman's words, the Church requires for its fullness 'the intellectual layman to be religious and the devout ecclesiastic to be intellectual', then in this country it is to the modern universities especially that she must turn.

This symposium, in its organization and publication, has been pre-eminently a labour of consultation and collaboration; and its merits can as firmly be ascribed to this happy fact, as its demerits to the shortcomings of its editor: the final decision in disputed cases has rested, as it should, with him; and his colleagues are in no ways responsible for his errors.

Although it might seem invidious to select any names for special thanks from so distinguished a body of contributors, each of whom without exception has given of his time and energy with a generosity for which we cannot be sufficiently grateful, I would like to thank my collaborator Fr Laurence Bright: our partnership—that of priest and layman—has shown me how true were the words of Newman when he spoke of such *conspiratio* as being of the essence of the Church; and I wish to record my deep personal indebtedness to him.

To the Abbot of Downside, the members of the community and to Dom Raphael Appleby, our host, I would like, on behalf of all the contributors, to express the thanks of those who, as they stood together at the last Mass of the symposium in the very room in which they had worked, argued and laughed together, discovered that they were the privileged witnesses to a moment of rebirth, as the form of the Church of the new diaspora was shown to them: it was an experience at once intellectual and religious, and a foreshadowing of what we have now committed ourselves to achieve.

JOHN COULSON

I

THEOLOGY AND THE UNIVERSITY

1. The Ecumenical Aspect

Dom Christopher Butler, Abbot of Downside

The following reflections confine themselves to conditions in this country. For obvious reasons, they deal mainly with specially Roman Catholic problems. And, as will be seen, they relate rather to theology than to religion as a whole. Further, I am required to pay particular attention to the ecumenical aspects of the questions raised; but I have not rigorously confined myself to this particular point of view.

At the present time, Catholics go up to our English universities and teach in them with the same freedom as the rest of the population. They have, of course, to qualify for entry on the same terms as everyone else; and this means that, to the extent to which some of our schools are academically less efficient than others, some Catholics may find themselves at a disadvantage in the stiff competition for entry. There are also some university colleges so positively identified with a special non-Catholic christian tradition that Catholics would tend not to seek admission to them—and perhaps would not be particularly welcome as members. It is even conceivably possible that, just as to be a Catholic is supposed to be a disadvantage to a conservative parliamentary candidate, so also it may in some cases be a disadvantage to a candidate for a college or university teaching post. But the point which is relevant to my reflections here is that ecclesiastical authority in no way discourages Catholics from seeking and pursuing a university education or career.

It was not always so. In the nineteenth century, when entrance to Oxford and Cambridge had become possible for Catholics, the bishops were most reluctant to countenance it. Instead, there was first the project of a Catholic university at Dublin and then an ill-fated attempt to provide higher education for Catholics under ecclesiastical control in London. The growing liberalism and secularism of Oxford and Cambridge were no doubt alarming enough;

but it may be that it was also feared that young Catholics would be perverted to protestantism. Whatever the reasons, the ideal of a Catholic university survived well into our own times. If one feels that it is a mistaken idea, this is not only because of the vast financial and practical difficulties which it involves, but also because it would mean that the Church was voluntarily interposing a barrier between herself and the culture of England. The first duty of the Church is, I suggest, not to safeguard the faith of the traditional Catholic, but to 'teach all the nations'. Moreover, it is questionable whether a policy of withdrawal, which in the nature of the case cannot be thorough-going, is the best strategy of defence.

The present policy of the Church, as is well known, is to allow Catholics to frequent the English universities, but to provide chaplains and chaplaincies for the Catholic undergraduates. These admirable institutions, comparable to the non-Catholic Pusey House and Latimer House at Oxford, need far more financial support and development than they have yet received. Intended in the first place for undergraduates, they frequently perform a service also for Catholic graduates and university teachers. They are, of course, usually outside the universities themselves (though I believe Keele provides a salary for the Catholic chaplain); but they are the only Catholic institutions at the level of the universities, with the exception indeed of Catholic societies like the Newman Society at Oxford or the Fisher Society at Cambridge—and these depend on the chaplains.

Meanwhile, the present century is witnessing one of the greatest transformations in indigenous christian outlook since the Counter-Reformation: the change-over from interdenominational rivalry and denunciation to what is called the ecumenical outlook; from controversy and polemics to so-called 'dialogue'.

Dialogue is not an entirely novel notion. The Catholic Church in north Africa, in the time of St Augustine, made an attempt to enter into dialogue with the Donatists, and there was a conference attended by representatives of both communions at Carthage in A.D. 410, under the chairmanship of a state official. It began awkwardly, because the Government, in summoning it, had called one group 'Donatists' and the other 'Catholics'; and the Donatists, anticipating the *Church Times* by about a millennium and a half, protested that it was *they* who were the true Catholics. From this untoward beginning the conference came to a discordant close. Again, there was real dialogue between the East and the West at the Council of Florence, and it was pursued with immense patience. The immediate result was excellent, and reunion was proclaimed. But when the Eastern negotiators returned home they were disowned by their own public, who preferred the turban to the tiara. Each of these experiments has its lesson for the modern ecumenist. Their rarity serves to emphasise the fact that, on the whole, it has for eighteen centuries usually been taken for granted on all hands that the correct reaction to divisions among christians is by way of polemical argument, abuse, denunciation, and the imputing to the other party not only of stupidity, disgraceful motives, and insincerity, but of every kind of moral corruption. (Exception must certainly be made, for example, for the Anglican-Eastern tentatives after the Stuart Restoration, for the discussions associated with Leibniz, and for the federation of the English Free Churches.)

All honour, then, to the Anglicans and Protestants who in 1910 launched what is now called the Ecumenical Movement. Their first concern seems to have been the scandal and waste resulting from competition between the denominations in the foreign mission field. There developed both a Life and Work movement, whose objectives were practical, and a Faith and Order movement to discuss doctrinal and ministerial issues. On the whole, it has been the experience of ecumenists that divisions between christians cannot be overcome by the facile device of disregarding doctrinal differences.

It is to the Eastern Orthodox that the credit is due for suggesting, after World War I, the formation of a World Council of Churches analogous to the League of Nations. But it was not till after the Second World War, at Amsterdam in 1948, that this idea was realised. Life and Work, and Faith and Order, have become subordinate elements in this great organisation. It is well known, but cannot be too strongly emphasised, that the World Council of Churches does not pretend to have achieved, even in miniature or embryo, a reunion of its constituent members. It exists rather to co-ordinate and promote trends towards greater christian unity and co-operation, with—in the minds of some at least—full visible unity as a possible ultimate goal. It is predominantly Anglican and Protestant in its membership; but while a number of Protestant bodies (especially some of the more 'extreme' or 'fringe' groupings) have declined to join it, there has been considerable Eastern participation.

Perhaps I should apologise for this cursory repetition of well-known facts. But it may be useful to have sketched in the background to some of the things I want to say later on. At this point, it may suffice to add, with reference to the work of the World Council of Churches, that there is little disposition among its best qualified practitioners to minimise the importance of doctrine; but there is a great determination to understand the position of those from whom one is divided, as also to lay stress on those factors which are held in common. Christians are aware today, as they had not been for many centuries, at least in the West, that there is a sense in which their mutual differences are less significant than the challenge to all of them in the unconverted world.

Although the ecumenical movement had awakened the keen and enthusiastic interest of a growing number of Catholics, including some eminent theologians, the Church for a long time not only refrained from seeking membership of the World Council of Churches but showed a great deal of reserve about the movement in general. There were signs of a thaw in an instruction issued about 1950, but the positive elements in it were so hedged about with cautionary language that it was not too difficult for a local hierarchy to use the powers, there recognised as properly belonging to it, in a restrictive sense.

As is well known, a dramatic change came about with the accession of Pope John XXIII. From the first he made it clear that the question of christian unity was one of his major preoccupations, and he in effect proposed the goal of unity as an ultimate, though not immediate, objective of the Second Vatican Council. He established the Secretariat for promoting christian unity, and in it made use of some of those who were already unofficially deeply concerned with the question. This Secretariat has been given the status of a Commission of the Vatican Council, despite the fact that the Council has had no share in the selection of its personnel. The Secretariat, whose President, Cardinal Bea, is one of the outstanding figures of the Council, has had an opportunity of doing vitally important work in the revision of the draft Scheme on Scripture and Tradition—a subject whose ecumenical implications hardly need to be emphasised by me. It is a matter of some interest, and a fact of some piquancy, that the ecumenical question was directly envisaged by no less than three of the draft schemes prepared for the Council beforehand—one is led to reflect that the subject of unity might better be dealt with by a single document.[1]

Pope John's personal initiative has in fact committed the Church to a new orientation as regards the ecumenical movement; all the more so, since it has awakened an enthusiastic response outside the Church. It can hardly have failed to influence Lord Fisher's brave and epoch-making decision to visit the late Pope while he himself was still Archbishop of Canterbury, and this in turn has paved the way for other historic visits to the Holy See. It will also have facilitated the acceptance given by so many christian bodies, and by the World Council of Churches, to the invitation to send observers to the Council. The presence of these observers was keenly felt by the members of the Council, and the proceedings inevitably took on a special 'ecumenical' colouring. The Council looks like endorsing by active concurrence Pope John's ecumenical initiative.

There can therefore be little doubt that ecumenism is a dominant issue for the Church and theology today. We have to learn the outlook and the methods of the ecumenical approach to the problem set by divided Christianity. And it is common sense that we should seek to profit by the experience of the ecumenical movement during the past fifty years. One truth that we should take to heart is that, while different christian bodies often use different words to describe much the same thing, they, perhaps even more disastrously, are liable to use the same words to describe different things. To overcome this difficulty we have what is known as the 'ecumenical dialogue': members of the different christian bodies have got to get together and talk to one another. Something can indeed be done by the written word, but actual face-to-face oral intercommunication has been found most desirable and fruitful. In the course of this dialogue the movement is building up its own technical terminology. Documents written in this somewhat unlovely jargon are less liable than others to be misunderstood—at least by other ecumenists.

Who, then, are to take part in the ecumenical dialogue? Is it the task of the ecclesiastical rulers, or of the theologians and scholars, or of the laity? At the present stage, it is at the level of theologians and scholars that it is probably proving the most successful. Discussion at the level of the hierarchy and of the heads of the separated bodies, useful and desirable as it is, can create its own problems—including

[1] *See* author's note, p. 22.

that of raising premature expectations among the general public. The Malines Conversations may serve to remind us that harm as well as good can be done by ecumenical efforts. At the level of the scholars and theologians a good deal has already been done, but much more participation by Catholics would be desirable. Catholics and non-Catholics meet in the Societies for Old and New Testament Study, in patristic and New Testament conferences, and in conferences such as those which have often taken place between Anglicans and English Dominicans. None of this causes much public stir in this country—except when, for instance, the Archbishops of Liverpool and York share a platform at a New Testament conference—and this is all to the good. As regards dialogue at the level of the laity, it is worth while to observe that (a) we can hardly prevent the laity from talking, and they will be more inclined to do so as the effect of Pope John's and the Council's ecumenical outlook make themselves felt; (b) it is important that the movement should penetrate deeply into the stratum of the laity; it could be positively dangerous to accomplish *rapprochements* at the upper levels which the laity were quite unprepared for—dangerous or at least sterile, as the Council of Florence may serve to remind us.

So we return to the question of the universities. As has been remarked, the nineteenth-century policy of forbidding Catholic attendance at them has been abandoned. There are dangers in such attendance, but it has been decided that we must incur those dangers, granted proper safeguards. Already, there is a large number of Catholic students in the English universities, and a considerable and (it may be hoped) growing number of Catholic teachers in them. Both at the undergraduate level and at that of the teachers, these Catholic lay men and women will inevitably talk with their non-Catholic associates.

Anyone who has been a student at Oxford or Cambridge, and I suppose the same is true of any of our universities—at least where there are resident students—will remember how we talked about everything under the sun and above it. Indeed, intellectual give-and-take between people of different views, outlooks and interests is, in the general opinion, a most valuable element in university education. It seems to follow that our Catholic undergraduates, if well-instructed and interested in their religion, will be likely to discuss religion and theology with their non-Catholic fellow-students. To dissuade them from doing so would be a counsel of despair. After all, as baptised and confirmed Christians they share in the apostolic vocation of the Church. And, from the point of view of their own faith, what could be more psychologically undermining than to discourage them from religious argument? Similarly, a Catholic don can hardly be expected to keep silent on the subject of his religion, which ought to be the most important thing in his life and the most commanding object of his intellect. In fact, Catholics at the university do talk about their religion. Perhaps they do it less than they should, but they are likely to do it more as ecumenism becomes more influential in the Church.

I have spoken of proper safeguards for Catholics at our universities; and I have mentioned the chaplains and the chaplaincies. They are of vital importance. But it must not be forgotten that these institutions are as a rule outside the university set-up. They can only influence Catholics, let alone non-Catholics, to the extent to which they are made use of. They are fishing from the bank of the pool. It seems to me to be beyond question that the situation would be immensely improved if Catholic theologians and philosophers were making their contribution *within* the university institution. It would enormously strengthen the position of Catholicism and of Catholics in the universities if there were Catholic dons whose primary and official competence was in one of these subjects, and if Catholic undergraduates were studying them. When a scientific question is raised in an undergraduate's room, it is the undergraduate who is studying science who is listened to with respect, if not always with agreement. As things stand at present, if a theological question arises, there may be a non-Catholic student of theology present, but there will be no Catholic student of theology who can put the Catholic position with its intellectual supports. *Mutatis mutandis*, much the same can be said of conversations in the Senior Common Room. It seems, therefore, to me that we want the presence of Catholic thinking at the universities at a level of scholarly and scientific precision, and also at a depth, comparable with that which is taken for granted in any of the existing university subjects.

I have been speaking of the presence of Catholic theologians and philosophers in the universities as a desirable safeguard for Catholics. It is an important point. But from the ecumenical point of view such presence is also desirable. The universities are the seed-bed of the intellectual life of the country. If the general ecumenical movement is to become a Catholic concern as well as being, which it has so far been almost exclusively in England, an Anglican and Protestant thing, then it is needful that Catholicism should make its presence felt within the universities as such, and should there initiate the dialogue which is to be carried on throughout our culture.

It is perhaps not necessary for me to say much about the practical issues that would arise if these views were accepted and acted upon. I have been speaking of a Catholic and religious need which would be met by the presence in the universities of Catholic theologians and philosophers. Like Fr Charles Davis,[1] I would not wish to minimise the value to the universities themselves of such a presence. And in fact, in so far as the need is ecumenical, it is common to Catholics and non-Catholic christians. At the same time, it has to be recognised that our universities are not Catholic institutions, and that they have a tradition which is hostile to any external control of their teaching. On the other hand, if it is conceded that the presence of genuinely Catholic theology in the universities is of advantage to the universities themselves, it must be recognised that such presence would not be achieved if the teaching which was given under this label was such as the Church herself would disown. Doubtless a practical solution of the underlying problem could be discovered without raising theoretical questions of principle. I wonder, by the way, whether anything could be found in the arrangements for teaching in the Scottish Catholic primary schools which could become a precedent for some analogous arrangement in the universities.

Reverting from these difficult practical problems to the ecumenical question, it is manifest that the presence of Catholic theology in the universities would afford magnificent opportunities for dialogue between Catholic and other Christian theologians. Hitherto, in this country, such dialogue has necessarily been rather occasional. Special conferences are called for ecumenical discussion, or Catholic and non-Catholic scholars or theologians meet at the annual sessions of the biblical societies. But, good as all this is, we need also a steady interaction of minds on minds; for this a university provides an ideal and normal setting. If Catholics would have much to give in such intercourse—not least the systematic approach in speculative theology which sometimes seems to be rather lacking in theology as it is currently conceived and practised in the English universities—they

[1] v. infra, p. 114 ff., For the case as stated by Newman, v. infra, pp. 49-53.

would also have much to receive. English non-Catholic scholarship has a wonderful record in the critico-historical field of biblical and patristic scholarship. This is a field in which co-operation ought to be easy in this country. Difficulties only arise here where one or both parties bring preconceptions with them into the field of scholarship, as Loisy did in his day, and as (so it seems to me) Bultmann and his school do today. The English approach, however, is on the whole empirical; and we can adopt that approach without any disloyalty, remembering that biblical scholarship has a function not only in dogmatic theology, but in the sphere of the *praeambula fidei*, where direct appeal to dogmatic presuppositions is illegitimate. But biblical study today is beginning to explore the new field of what is called biblical theology, and here too the opportunity for collaboration is great; here, we may be able to give as much as we receive. And it hardly needs to be added that we ought to be able to give much in the field of philosophy—though here too there is something that we might learn from the peculiarly Anglo-Saxon school (or trend) of linguistic analysis, even if we think that some of its exponents display a remarkable intellectual perversity.

To conclude, the weight to be attached to such considerations as I have here put forward depends on the importance which we assign to the English universities on the one hand and to ecumenism on the other. National concern for education has been progressing upwards from its nineteenth century concentration on primary education. Secondary education has already 'arrived', and technical colleges and universities are now well on the way. The Labour Party, at least, seems to be contemplating a great increase of universities by the end of this century. While one may have some anxiety about the maintenance of university standards in such a period of rapid increase, it seems past doubt that the cultural leadership of the country will come from those who teach or have been educated in them. If christian ecumenism is to exert its influence as something more than a clerical hobby, it ought to make expansion in the universities one of its chief targets. How important do we think ecumenism is? There are dangers in it, among them the danger that schemes for corporate reunion might be taken as a substitute for the loyalty of the individual conscience to the light which it has received or is receiving. This is a problem for all of us, whatever our present allegiance. It is especially acute for those who identify the Church which Christ founded with one of the existing christian communions. But indeed, the supremacy of the personal conscience is a principle which is common to all christians. On the other hand, humanity as a whole may well be moving towards a 'crisis of unity'. Under modern conditions, no iron curtains or differences of inherited tradition can for ever prevent that osmosis of ideas and spiritual movements which is linking the whole human race in a common predicament which demands a universal solution. In this crisis of unity the religion of the redemptive incarnation should have a decisive part to play. It is not easy to see how it can play that part effectively unless we christians are at least taking seriously the problems of our own divisions, and learning to view them in the light of the Gospel of charity.

Note.—Since the above paper was written, the Second Vatican Council has completed its second session, and references made to it in the preceding pages should be completed as follows. (1) The membership of the Secretariat for Unity has been enlarged, mainly with members elected by the Council itself. (2) The three separate treatments of the ecumenical question have been superseded by a single draft Decree on Ecumenism which is still under debate. (Cf., p. 16, *supra*.)

II

AN EDUCATED LAITY—
problems and opportunities

2. The Catholic Undergraduate (I)

Monica Lawlor

Catholics in this country have long been deeply concerned with the question of Catholic education; but we have perhaps paid rather less attention to the results of such an education than to the problem of securing it for the children of the Catholic community. Although political and financial necessity may well be responsible for such an outlook, this should not prevent us from considering from time to time what we are achieving at such cost. At a superficial level the answer is simple enough, we are providing a christian education in a christian community: one which is concerned with the moral and spiritual growth of the child as well as academic achievement. If, however, we want to produce evidence that our aims are adequately fulfilled it becomes much more difficult. What criteria shall we take? If we take the continued practice of religious duties as our criterion, we find that there are no adequate statistics to show whether the lapse rate among those who attended Catholic schools is less than among those who did not. Such a measure is in any case very crude as an estimate of the results of Catholic education, but to get even this measure would demand a very extensive, expensive and public piece of heart-searching.

The question is deeper than this: we want to know what sort of people we have educated, and how much and how effectively they contribute to the community at large. We also want to know if they are as well educated as most children academically and, if not, whether the other benefits they may derive from a Catholic education outweigh any deficiency. Apart from the real difficulty of assessing such subtle things as moral probity or social usefulness, there is the very great technical difficulty of gathering any kind of reliable information about a group as heterogeneous as the Catholic community—even our knowledge of its actual size is hazy.

When we want, therefore, to talk of the Catholic university student, we find ourselves very short of accurate information. Even the best efforts of the university chaplains and the Newman Demographic Survey are not able at the moment to give us more than a rough estimate of their numbers, let alone more pertinent information. Those students who have attended Catholic schools are more likely to be known to the chaplains, and it would be possible—given time, money and energy—to get information over the years about the proportion of those in Catholic schools who reach university or the final degree classes out of those who do; but at the moment no such information exists which covers more than a fraction of the university population.

We are therefore in a situation where we are forced to fall back on personal experience within the university, and on the general impressions gathered from people who are familiar either with the more actively Catholic students, or, as university teachers, with those they meet in the course of their work.

In what follows I shall be discussing such impressions gathered over a number of years of university teaching. As a psychologist I am well aware of the dangers of such generalisation and of the factors which, however inaccurate, are likely to create a reputation for a group. Nevertheless I am, by training, inclined to look for the probable genesis of attitudes and actions whilst the title of psychologist inevitably invites a certain amount of personal history-telling that may not be so invited by other academic labels. I have tried to include only such observations as I have found to be confirmed by Catholics who teach in other disciplines, colleges or universities than my own. In the main the Catholic students with whom I am most familiar come from Catholic grammar schools or small independent Catholic schools; and while there is no such thing as an 'average' student, certain common traits and attitudes emerge which are shared by at least many such students. In the subsequent paper, Fr McCabe is writing of similar students, and I find that his experience confirms my own.

Catholic students are distinguishable as a group; the effect of having been at a Catholic school is not negligible. While many people are of course profoundly affected all their lives by the type of schooling they received, I have the impression that among Catholic students the influence is deeper and more pervasive: they very seldom say of their schools, 'Oh! It was all right!'. It is more usual for a Catholic student than for most to view his schooldays as particularly important and inspiring, or quite the reverse. It may be this strong assessment of the school which leads many Catholic students to identify the Catholic school with the Catholic Church, since for many the Church is what the school was. The effect may well be calculated. I merely note that, if so, the success is overwhelming, for good or ill.

If we consider how these students differ from their contemporaries as members of an academic community, the only general conclusion seems to be that such comparisons are not particularly favourable to the Catholic student. Some things he will have in his favour, if he has been lucky, that others may lack. Perhaps the one which comes most readily to mind is that he may suffer less from limited imagination and deadly pedantry than other students. At their best Catholic students have a certain breadth of grasp and creativity which has often been washed out of those from ordinary grammar schools. It is this quality which makes the best Catholic students academically outstanding, because it lifts them out of mere competence into genuine creativity and originality.

They may also have a better grasp of their historical roots, a wider sympathy with things beyond narrow academic ambition, and it is perhaps worth noting, in a dull world, that they are not given to gloom, certainly not to steady gloom. It is often obvious that they have very considerable native ability, even though this may be untrained, and all too frequently unused, almost—one might say—unusable. All this means that the best of the Catholic students are most impressive, it is the rather too numerous 'rest' that may cause us to worry.

There is a general impression that, taken by and large, those from Catholic schools do rather less well than the average in public examinations from O level to first degree; although such an impression confirms my own experience I very much doubt whether this can be explained by any lack of intelligence. There are of course exceptions, just as there are cases whose relatively poor socioeconomic backgrounds account quite adequately for a mediocre performance at university. But the dim and the deprived would not constitute the sort of problem that prompts me to attempt this paper. Any and every university teacher will moan periodically about wasted talent and more frequently, though with less fervour, about its total absence; but Catholic students seem to be more frequently moaned over for the former reason than the latter. One inevitably asks oneself why the promise is never fulfilled, why the process of education remains little more than a half-fulfilled possibility. It may be that there is no problem, that they are all doing very nicely, but such evidence as we have does not suggest this, even if we start with the bare fact that Catholics are grossly under-represented in the student population,[1] and allow fully for the generally low socio-economic status of the Catholic population. In what follows, therefore, I am taking it for granted that there is a problem.

At least one reason for the comparatively poor performance of Catholics at university is that many of them show signs of having been inadequately taught. This is apparent both in their performance at entrance selection procedures and in their academic work. The teaching in Catholic sixth forms does not seem to be either so well organised or so deliberately aimed at the university as in the equivalent non-Catholic school. The range of subjects offered is frequently too limited, and students are often allowed to drop subjects too early. Where there is a shortage of suitably qualified lay teachers, sixth form teaching may well be done by people who, not being graduates of a British university, are unacquainted with the criteria demanded such as, for example, the emphasis on thinking for oneself.

The other ways in which comparative failure at university seems to come about are less obvious, less easily remedied, and in general more worrying, because they emerge more clearly from the religious presuppositions of the students in question, that is, from the fact that they are Roman Catholics. They are not confined to the Catholic student population, but they may be more characteristic of these as a group.

Perhaps the most important could be called the problem of authority. Its importance derives, at least in part, from the pervasiveness of the effects, and in part from the essential fact that adequate university work requires self-discipline and self-reliance. By self-discipline I mean the very simple things that a student must organise for himself, like getting up, arriving in time for things he either wants or is expected to go to, producing work on time, remembering what books or instruments he wants and where he is supposed to be, when. The broader demand for self-discipline arises because, in the majority of universities, and in the majority of specialist subjects, he has to

[1] See Newman Demographic survey report, March 1960.

organise his own work, and whether he does any depends on him. Compared with other walks of life the external sanctions brought to bear on university students are very limited; often lectures are not in any strict sense obligatory; although the tutorial system does demand the presence of the student and his essay, not every modern university has an extensive tutorial system. If he has sessional exams he is supposed to pass them. An arts student may have eight or nine lectures in a week, a tutorial once a fortnight, and an exam once a year. There are one hundred and sixty-eight hours in the week of which, on this reckoning, one hundred and sixty are organised by the student; if he lives in a hall of residence he may suffer the further demand that, for another fifty hours a week, he is supposed to be in the building and reasonably quiet. If he appears at no lectures, writes no essays and fails his exams, he will be asked to leave: this is the only real sanction to which he is exposed. The system is one which offers an opportunity rather than enforces a plan; people may attempt to alter the student's behaviour or outlook by a variety of verbal techniques from mild suggestion to Awful Warning, but the student is free in fact to ignore these.

This is the environment at the practical level. Now the requirements may strike the student as burdensome, his essay as a millstone round his neck, and his hall of residence as the near equivalent of borstal; people are rude to him when he is late, but he usually manages well enough. It is these simple requirements which many products of Catholic schools seem hardly able to meet: with delightful vagueness they come tomorrow for what happened yesterday, or somehow their watches stop more often than other people's: they are always very nice about it all, and deeply hurt if other people are not nice back.

This is one side of the coin. The other has the same origin, was moulded in the same mint. I have suggested that the overt commitments of the university student may be few, and there are some quiet, passive students who meet these and call it a day. If someone tells them to do something they comply, but that is it. Students like this seem to be the products, or perhaps victims, of strongly authoritarian systems. The 'so sorry I am late but . . .' types are those who, never having had to provide their own framework for living, simply flounder when the superimposed structure is removed; if this outer discipline or organisation has been complete enough they may emerge from it too lazy, too passive or too browbeaten to be really able to take responsibility for themselves, so they live in a state of perpetual chaos. Others, not so hopelessly disorganised, may yet be so lacking in initiative that they wait with folded hands until told what to do. This passive attitude can also be expressive of deep resentment which has found a socially acceptable outlet; it does not appear hostile, but it destroys both the authority and the victim with remarkable success in the long run. It is apparent that boarding schools more often achieve this effect than day schools, because they can exercise a more total control. Some students evidently come from schools where, at seventeen or eighteen, they are still being told how to spend virtually every hour of every day, when to wake up, when to go to sleep, when to talk, when to keep quiet, when to study, when to take recreation. Such a system may well be benevolent both in practice and intention, but carries within itself the seeds of dis-integration, which flourish when the authority is withdrawn.[1]

The effects of an authoritarian system of education have, however, aspects perhaps more destructive of intellectual endeavour than these, because they hit at the very heart of academic life. These are roughly comprehended in an unwillingness to think independently. This may take variegated forms; there is, for example, the specifically religious form, a simple 'we are right—they are wrong' approach to life. A student like this just assumes that he has the answers and other people the problems or the mistaken ideas. This is the Offensive/Defensive attitude that Fr McCabe describes in his paper; to what he says there I will only add that this is not an attitude you can keep up for long with any degree of intellectual honesty, and if something goes by the board it will usually be the honesty; 'after all,' as they so cheerfully say, 'never mind if the argument is phoney, provided it convinces.' If you let in the wet in this way, it gets around; and the same student will then want *the* authoritative book on this or that, ask for the line, and be prepared to plug it—an intellectual outlook that is death to thought. If the student's vocation is contemplative,[2] then to be valuable it must be an honest contemplation, and it de-mands an openness of mind which many of our Catholic students seem to lack, although of course they are not alone in this. For

[1] cf. Lewin, Lippitt and White, 1939, 'Patterns of Aggressive Behaviour in Experimentally-created "Social Climates".' *J. Soc. Psychol.* 10, 271–99.
[2] cf. H. McCabe, *infra*, p. 42.

academic work as we know it, a concern for the truth is fundamental —a concern which goes beyond merely registering what is correct, and for which only that which is seen to be valid is authoritative. A university community, although it may often fall short of this ideal, is bound to be a place where the obvious is questioned and the shibboleths crack.

The Catholic may feel himself torn between the 'truth' Catholic and the 'truth' scientific or historical; to remedy this he needs either a better theology, or to fill his mind so full of 'no parking' notices as to make his academic work narrow and unenterprising. He learns to recite but resists to the last ditch any real attempt to educate him, and he knows that in so doing he is living the virtuous life: a position from which neither cleric nor layman can shift him once he gets it really neat.

A different problem is raised by the student whose chief characteristic is an unworldly innocence, apparently carefully fostered and sometimes so extreme as to be positively frightening. This innocent child believes what you tell him because you are wise, benevolent, and there to be relied on—not quite, perhaps, because—horrid doubt— you may be numbered among the wicked, of whom he has heard rumours. These rumours unfortunately were too vague—he never met anyone who did not wear a label saying they were holy (except of course his less perfect school contemporaries) and he rightly doubts his ability to distinguish them readily unless they have red tights, a tail and horns. Such people have been sheltered from the world to a degree which makes the mind boggle; they often have a very rough time finding their feet in a university, coping on their own, making up their minds, and getting on with the rest of the human race without the guiding hand of Mother X or Brother Y. They are, to start with, very good and may stay that way, because everyone is too startled to disillusion them, and the university community is not on the whole an exploitive one. Others are not so lucky and quickly begin to regret paradise lost. Again they are ineffective as students, unless they can grow up quickly, and are lucky enough to find themselves in an environment which doesn't force too much on them too quickly; but there is a chance that they will curl up in sheer fright or go to pieces in one way or another, and so never really make much use academically of their time at university. This sort of immaturity may mean that they have enjoyed an unusual degree of security, and been the object of a very tender concern, but they have as little knowledge of themselves as they have of anything else, and their security is not that which comes from within and lasts a lifetime, but that which depends on constant outer support. Such outer support even the sheltered world of the university cannot provide, so that they are liable to be let down right, left and centre by those in whom they put their simple faith, and may become exceedingly bitter in the process. They are also liable to 'lose their faith' quite suddenly one day between lunch and tea for no apparent reason, much to their own bewilderment and that of others. To put it mildly these hazards and traumas not only take their mind off their work, but make it difficult for them to contribute much to the life of the university community.

There is another facet to this which is the 'lost innocence' type. These are reared in a similar environment, but have for a variety of reasons become very cynical, very early. They can ape innocence— they have been doing it for years. Some of these people are merely inaccessible, they have a sort of subterranean quality, as if their real selves went into hiding years ago and left a neat compliant shell on top, which they use for anyone who looks even vaguely like the innocent teacher of old. Others are deeply entrenched in double-think, capable of an unreflecting hypocrisy, and may be quite un-pleasant characters; equally they are quite untouchable, there is simply no way through the fog. They may have a capacity for de-ception, both of themselves and other people, which staggers the general run of people reared on a simpler ethic. Sometimes they are keenly combatant Catholics; they can recite the rules, they can say that 'it is all very wicked, but of course I do it all the same because, after all, what else can one do?' What is sad about such people is that, with many of those who have turned their backs more overtly on Christianity, they are plagued with guilt; and the very extremes to which they will sometimes go suggest a sort of despair, a need for punitive self-destruction. They never had a morality which worked, nor one on which reason could throw any light; it remains un-examined because it is unusable, and they are left with a pervasive sense of guilt and a few curious remnants of moral righteousness. They do not mind lying, but object to being called dishonest; forni-cation is inevitable, but contraception definitely wicked; abortion on the other hand is (as I have been told on more than one occasion) 'wrong but essential'. One thing alone is clear—that none of it makes sense. Typically, they register sexual sins, but have a very crude idea of morality beyond this. Yet they have heard of a moral system, and the idea does mean enough to ensure that they suffer in a way that a happy hedonist would not. The total impression is that such people are produced by a negative morality, which is at once too demanding and too arbitrarily fixed for them to accept it fully. It gives the student a well-developed sense of guilt, but if he lives within it he is cramped nearly to death, and if he lives outside it he is desperate. I have been talking about the more florid developments, but it is a frame of mind which originated when such people were very young, and when, in the interests of investing them with 'a sense of sin', someone succeeded in teaching them to recite a catalogue of frivolous or meaningless 'sins', and work up the appropriate feeling as a separate exercise.

Finally there is one other and perhaps more common failing among Catholic students which is probably particularly important in keeping them out of the top flight of university students, and this is their comparative lack of commitment. Commitment calls for something more than dutiful compliance, it demands a degree of self-involvement which must be in part an exclusion of other possibilities. The really successful university student becomes a physicist, a historian, or a philosopher rather than learning physics, history or philosophy. Now it seems that for many a Catholic there is a problem here—that of divided loyalties. Should he be a good christian or a good philosopher? Can he be both? Should he really dig himself so deeply into the things of this world? Is not his proper business to save his soul, to keep himself just a bit apart or distant from the threat of engulfment in the secular? You may be a nine to five worker with a bit of yourself, but not a successful student: this demands absorption. The scholar may find his work demanding or harrassing, but essentially he enjoys it, whether he formally acknowledges this to himself or not. This sort of commitment is not so much time-consuming (you can consume time quite as well contemplating yourself not working) as self-consuming.[1] Apart from the threat, with all its overtones, of the *world* implied in such a demand, most students do not see it as a 'good' to be aimed at. It also constitutes a challenge to change, and this may be the one thing the student has decided he should avoid.

---

[1] On the other hand it is worth noting that Catholic students do not on the whole suffer as much from a paralysing disillusionment as other students do—the disillusionment in which nothing seems worth doing, nothing worth while.

Many students have a well-developed sense of 'ought', and plenty of demands can be made on this; so they feel they ought to join the Legion of Mary, can hardly let the Sodality go by, then who's going to be secretary of the Catholic Society, not to mention U.C.S.; perhaps the Union needs their attention, then there's that course on Thomist philosophy, as well as the youth club they promised to help in a weak moment: what with one thing and another work has to take its place among the 'oughts'. Now work is hard, by definition, therefore good; but just when it gets interesting, it also gets less moral, and hence loses its priority. The exceptionally able student may suffer less in this way, he can do many things at once and, more used to finding his work interesting, can bear it better.

It is not merely this problem of divided loyalty that is critical, there may be a more general fear of getting involved, partly because of the theological overtones, and partly because past experience may have given a certain fear of involvement. This is part of the 'Please God make me a saint, but not now' attitude. The need to retain some privacy, some personal breathing space is felt too strongly for the student to be ready to look beyond it. The habit of saving one's strength may persist, although now it is the subject-matter of study which demands commitment rather than an arbitrary authority.

A lack of real commitment should not be confused with an unwillingness to work or a taste for riotous living—it is not a condition which can be remedied by restriction or moral exhortation. Critical to this state is a moral immaturity that can involve the whole personality; such an immaturity may well coexist alongside an anxious concern with the virtuous and much pious talk, both of which keep the real moral issues permanently out of sight. A negative view of sacrifice, with the emphasis on 'giving up', suggests a moral life which may be unbearably costly, and which is not merely difficult but actively destructive, if accepted completely; half accepted, it may suggest that the easiest way to be virtuous is not to become involved very deeply, so that when the inevitable sacrifice is demanded it may more easily be met. Such a view may be underpinned quite successfully by an emphasis on the merits of detachment. Too often a morality of this kind has been so effectively implanted that the student is unable to get beyond it. It has been established as a working norm by a steady abuse of the theological ideas comprehended in the notion of the christian life as sacrificial.

The same moral immaturity may produce a failure to grasp the idea of individual vocation which involves a commitment to the self, the willingness to become, rather than merely exist; there is no clear recognition that the good life is different for different people and that the individual has to make his own judgments. A person who feels he must emulate everyone's virtues and imitate all their good actions, or who, at any rate, talks in this way, gives one the impression either that he is adrift in the search for the good life, or that he is merely repeating dutifully some recollected but ill-understood counsel. Certainly students who think and talk in this manner are unlikely to see the moral implication of any deep commitment to what they are doing at the moment.

In this paper I have emphasised what is wrong with Catholic students or with the products of Catholic schools, more than what is right, because I feel that the dice are loaded that way. What I have tried to do is to see where the weakness is that affects their academic life and how it came about. The powerful influence exercised on these students by their schools is undoubtedly reinforced by their apparent feeling that in them they have had, in some sense, their fullest experience of the Church. Unlike the university, the school was a christian community and in one way or another it becomes a point of reference in later life.

We have in England no tradition of what, for want of a better word, I suppose we must call Catholic intellectualism;[1] nothing at any rate sufficiently substantial or widely known to provide the student with an exemplar of the christian intellectual life, with which he may identify himself, or to which he may naturally advert. Within the universities themselves Catholics have been few in number and generally quiet, almost anonymous; like many of the students themselves, they have for the most part only recently emerged from the shadows of social and economic disability. Beyond the towering figure of Newman, we have a series of lesser individuals whose isolated and often uncertain voices are scarcely audible. The christian community the student finds at the university may seem to him, at

[1] See Gilson's emphasis that 'piety is no substitute for technique', and his claim that to enable Catholic intellectuals 'to link together the science they have acquired with the faith which they have preserved, a technique of faith is necessary along with that of science'. By 'technique' he states that he means, not apologetics, but theology. 'The Intelligence in the Service of Christ the King' in *Christianity and Philosophy*, by Etienne Gilson, 1939. (Editor.) New York: Sheed & Ward.

least at first, to be both as extra-curricular as badminton or darts, and as an experienced reality strangely elusive compared with that from which he comes. Small wonder then that the student should look back to the known world of the Catholic school for his idea of the 'real' Church. What is sad is that too often the values of the Church thus experienced seem inimical to the demands of university life, and the student starts with a handicap which is difficult to overcome; it is also a handicap to which he may cling deliberately, because it seems 'right' for him to do so. The amount of wasted time, effort, talent and pain which this can involve makes the situation one we must not ignore, even if no easy remedies suggest themselves.

 NOTE

RELIGIOUS INSTRUCTION IN CATHOLIC GRAMMAR SCHOOLS

Many of the criticisms in the foregoing paper might seem to apply to students from all backgrounds or none, but what cannot be denied is that all religious education produces as well as resolves difficulties, and that Roman Catholicism, because of the rigidity with which its teaching is often imparted, produces problems of a distinguishable kind.

Since the majority of the undergraduates described by Dr Lawlor *probably come from Catholic grammar schools, it is useful to inquire further into the structure of the Religious Instruction syllabus taught in such schools.*

The following note is contributed by the Rev Hamish Swanston *of the Birmingham Oratory, Chaplain to the Upper School, St Philip's Grammar School, Birmingham:*

Despite the necessary and desirable difference that must obtain between different schools, probably most Catholic grammar schools have a syllabus for the teaching of the christian religion somewhat of the following pattern:

Year 1–3: A catechetics course which attempts to encourage a realisation of the Faith in scriptural terms by taking the boys through the Gospels, the Old Testament and Acts (probably in that order), while at the same time working through a manual of doctrine (the translation of the German Catechism perhaps, or the American *Quest for Happiness*).

4: The Catholic Schools' Religious Certificate (S.R.C.) examination (mainly doctrinal) and sociological questions.

5: The General Certificate of Education (G.C.E.) Ordinary
level in Scripture (a choice of syllabus, we take that based
on the synoptic gospels).

6–7: Here the pattern varies enormously, but probably all boys
do a course designed to discuss various problems in a
christian context, and some do G.C.E. Advanced level
Scripture in addition to this.

In general it is likely that the first three years will have four periods
of forty minutes each, and the rest of the school three periods each
week for religious instruction. There are schools which devote a
great deal more time to this discipline.

Such a description can mean little without some commentary on
the general attitude of those responsible for teaching such a syllabus:

(a) There is in most schools a realisation of responsibility for many
features of the situation described by Dr Lawlor. This is shared by
priests and laymen.

(b) Such a responsibility arises, at least indirectly, from the acute
shortage of laymen who are both willing and qualified to teach the
subject—in our school almost all the teaching of religious instruction
in the first four years is done by laymen. Clerics do the main teaching
in the upper school, because they are the only people who have had
an opportunity for adequate theological and scriptural training. We
have a philosophy graduate lay master who takes some Sixth Form
classes.

(c) The need for a thorough revision of the Sixth Form syllabus is
widely admitted. Thus the Catholic Colleges' Conference for 1963
has issued an outline of work for Sixth Forms intended to replace the
present syllabus. But a critic of the old syllabus is not likely to be
appeased with those revisions suggested. The new syllabus still pro-
pounds a view of the Church as primarily an authoritarian body, and
gives too little attention to the Church as a worshipping community.
Therefore many teachers are driven to devising their own schema.

(d) The main difficulty we face is the great sales-resistance of the
boys to anything other than apologetics. Apologetics can be treated
as a mild academic discipline with right answers. It can be kept
severely apart from life. The boys are convinced they know not only
the answers but even the questions. They ask only green herrings to

pass the period. To announce the New Testament doctrine of pre-destination to glory, or to rebuke an enthusiasm for the secret letter of Fatima is not enough. A master has to get them to see difficulties that cannot be dissolved by a syllogism or an appeal to an authority, to realise that Christianity is more than a set of required propositions.

(e) One method we have tried with moderate success is like that by which Simon Clements teaches literature (*infra* p. 256 ff.): the boys are given a well-written piece of prose or verse which deals with a problem that must occur to most thinking men—Justin on civilisation and faith, Newman on consulting the laity, Marx on industrial society, Sartre on the moral responsibility of the individual, or *Humani Generis* on speculative freedom within the Church—and it is hoped that by thinking and writing and talking about such an example of human intellectual endeavour the boys will be led to think for themselves and lean towards answers.

The aim of the seven years' course, and particularly during the last two years, is to develop christian intelligences by a progress through a series of real questions in a disciplined manner. It is evident that a great deal of care has to be exercised in choosing the texts and preparing the discussion, but we are convinced this is a properly directed effort. Those boys who stay on for a third year in the Sixth Form sometimes encourage us in this belief by the standard of their independent work on papers and projects agreed upon by master and pupil as the R.I. work of the year. We must be *patres et magistri,* and like all good parents and teachers raise up men who are our equals, whose thought and judgment and action we can respect as those of christians.

The Catholic Undergraduate (II)

Herbert McCabe, O.P.

This paper is based upon an experiment carried out by the Union of Catholic Students (U.C.S.) during the last three years. This has consisted in the issue of two small booklets of 'discussion out-lines' for the use of university students, called 'University Life' and

'I Live Now',[1] together with a series of conferences and meetings designed to explain the ideas behind these booklets and how they should be used. The booklets were written and rewritten in a series of meetings at which I was present, between the chaplains of several modern universities. The final text is not the work of any individual, so that when I speak about it, I speak with no special authority, and make no claim to speak for any of the chaplains, or for the group as a whole.

There have, of course, been any number of 'study outlines' and suggestions for group discussion in the past, produced by such Catholic organisations as Y.C.W., Y.C.S. (Young Christian Workers & Students) and the Sodality, as well as U.C.S. itself, but our work was meant to be quite different from all of these, and it is this difference that I now want to explain. I should also make it clear that we have had in mind throughout this work the student at the modern or 'provincial' universities. The problems for undergraduates at Oxford or Cambridge are in many ways different, and there seemed no point in trying to produce a comprehensive scheme which would cover both; but, as it turns out, the discussions have also been found useful at the older universities, although they were not produced with their situation in mind. The people we were thinking of were, then, 'first generation' students coming to a provincial university from a Catholic grammar school.

It is the general experience of those who work amongst students, whether chaplains or not, that Catholic students tend to be either defensive or offensive, and sometimes both. When I say they are 'defensive' I mean that there is a tendency to regard the university as a mildly hostile environment, as something to be rather cautious about. There are I think three causes for this. In the first place the majority of Catholic students are 'first generation' students. By this I mean that their parents have not themselves been university students. For the student's family, Catholicism is usually closely linked with certain conservative attitudes. In very many cases the family itself is new to middle-class conditions—Catholicism in England has until recently been almost entirely a working-class religion—and there is a natural concern for conformity and respectability. To such a family the university, seen mainly through press reports, appears as

[1] Available from the Catholic Action Service Committee of the Union of Catholic Students, c/o 21A Soho Square, London, W.1.

a challenge and a danger to their beliefs. This attitude of the family is often shared by schools with little past experience of sending students on to university. They have a picture of students with beards and C.N.D. badges constantly larking about, or getting drunk, or sleeping with each other. They are in fact under the illusion that the university challenges their way of life. This romantic picture of university life is, as we know, wildly and unfortunately untrue, but as a legend it helps to make the student entering on his first year feel that he is going into a strange environment, in which he would do well to watch his step. The second thing that makes him defensive is the training in defence he receives at his school. If he comes from a typical Catholic grammar school, he will have spent a great deal of his time during religious instruction in learning 'apologetics', he will have learnt ways of answering objections to the Catholic faith and means of proving by reason that certain things he believes are true. Because of this training he comes up to the university protected by a psychological shield. 'Out there' are people liable at any moment to challenge him about the infallibility of the Pope or the existence of God, he must be wary in his response to them, and above all he must be careful not to give away any points. He must check his own thoughts and words lest they should turn out to give an advantage to the enemy. So long as he sticks to the approved formulae he can pass from one part of the pattern to another with no difficulty at all, but he must be careful not to depart from the established usage; whatever anyone from 'out there' says must first be translated into punched cards in his own system, before seeing whether it can be accepted or rejected.

This is of course something of a caricature of the well-trained apologete, but any university chaplain will bear witness to the frightening degree of truth in it. Again and again the objection has come to U.C.S. that its booklets do not deal with 'the things that interest the students in this university'—can they not have some discussions dealing with contraception, the papacy, and other topics that they are actually faced with in day-to-day argument? The first barrier we have had to break down has been the desire to carry on in the university the discussions of apologetics which were such cosy fun in the sixth form. The discussions provided are described as 'too high-brow', 'too academic', 'not for the ordinary student'. Perhaps I ought to say here that, once the initial barrier is broken, the discussions have in general been a great success, but the barrier itself is of great interest. The matters dealt with in our discussions are 'too academic' for the single reason that they deal with theology.

This brings me to the third of the factors which put the Catholic student on the defensive/offensive: his innocence of theology. By this I do not mean that he is not acquainted with the traditional technical discipline of theology—of course he is not, any more than he is with astrophysics or quantum mechanics. But he is not familiar with the idea of theology, the notion of a personal, intellectual appropriation of his faith carried out in a believing community. The feeling that the faith is *his* faith, as well as the faith of the Church, is new to him. He does not, for example, go to the bible for personal intellectual enjoyment; he does not go to the bible at all.

The faith, for such a student, is basically something he has been saddled with. Like his family it is something he did not ask for but which, since he has it, he must as a point of honour defend. The defence of the faith by apologetic argument is indeed sometimes a means of staving off the awful prospect of a personal revaluation of the whole thing. The young man is arguing not so much to convince his 'opponent' as to satisfy himself that his armour is strong enough —strong enough to protect him from his own self-questioning. He is motivated not so much by a love of truth, still less by a love of his 'opponent', as by a terrible fear of disbelief. Supposing something went wrong with the arguments, supposing he were left without their support, supposing he were left standing on the edge of the abyss— surely he would throw himself in. He is in this condition because almost nothing has been done to nourish his faith. The whole apologetic apparatus has been a substitute for a genuine intellectual commitment to Christ. He dare not trust to his own faith because he has been taught to put his trust in other things.

The defensive attitude, which seems to me to be typical of the first-year student from a Catholic grammar school, expresses itself, as often as not, offensively. His business is not just the negative one of repelling arguments, he has also learnt that he must be 'an apostle': he must make converts. The theory is that once the people 'out there' have had their objections shown up for the shoddy intellectual muddles they really are, they will come flocking to listen to the clear convincing arguments of the apologetics books. The Catholic student is fairly trigger-happy—true, the pre-selected targets of his missiles usually died in the last century, but he has yet to learn this. The student apostolate has meant in the past very often a willingness to 'stand up for the faith', and it has not been recognised that the student has essentially a contemplative vocation—that his apostolate is contemplative.

My belief, which is shared in varying degrees by the other authors of these booklets, is that the first thing the student needs to do is to rethink his faith. He is to be positively encouraged to scrap the terminology and the categories of apologetics, and to discover the meaning of the faith anew. In so far as he makes this rediscovery in the company of, and with the help of, non-believers, this contemplative work will be an apostolate.

We started from the idea that a student beginning at the university enjoys a unique combination of factors favourable to a rediscovery of his faith. In preparing the schema for the first of these booklets, *University Life*, I had in mind five such factors:

1. The student is at an age when he wants to break free from his childhood. It will be welcome news that the faith is not infantile, and that he is free to break the images of the schoolroom. Experience has since shown that we may have exaggerated this factor. The booklet was designed for first-year students, but we have found that for many the need for freedom does not awaken until later.

2. He is entering into a new life. He has in most cases left home and come to live in a quite different environment, with new friends and new surroundings. We thought that this circumstance would make it a lot easier to understand the notion of Christianity as a new life.

3. He is entering into a community. University life, even in modern universities, is a community life such as a student will probably not have experienced before or experience afterwards. Understanding this community will help him to understand the notion of the christian community to which he belongs.

4. He is entering into a tradition. By this I do not mean he is entering into some venerable institution with ancient ceremonies and quaint customs. This is conspicuously not the case at modern universities. (From time to time efforts are made to ape Oxbridge customs, but these are hardly taken seriously, and are usually found incomprehensible by students.) By entering a tradition I mean simply that he is entering a community in which something is handed on.

What he receives is something passed on from a previous generation of the community, and something which is being continuously worked over by the present generation. The living tradition of scholarship seems one of the best available analogues of the christian tradition.

5. Finally he is entering a community which recognises certain values. The English universities characteristically respect intellectual freedom, value tolerance, and present a broadly liberal set of values from which the world may be criticised. In their turn the universities are tolerated, but regarded as rather too 'academic' and out of touch to be taken altogether seriously by the world. This again seemed to us an important analogue of the Church. Both the university and the christian community are askew to the world.

The general principle behind all these five points is that the university community presents an image of the Church. What the Church is in faith and through the sacraments, university life is, experientially: a traditional community united by bonds associated with common beliefs. This thought might, in most circumstances, be regarded as an interesting idea, a useful illustration of christian truth; but for someone called upon to grow up into university life it takes on a much greater significance. We are not asking the student to take a *look* at university life, and then see how it throws light on life in the Church; we are trying to help him to *live* the university life, to experience its meaning, and thus come to an understanding of the christian life. The understanding springs not from what is said about university life, but from the actual experience of entering into it.

The first task we set ourselves therefore is to help the student to enter into the university. We have stressed the differences between the student's new world and his previous life, and the need for accepting the break with the past. We have tried to awaken a sense of liberation and of independence which should come fairly easily to someone who has just left school—particularly a Catholic school; we have tried to make the student feel a sense of exhilaration and adventure in entering a new, wider, adult world. If this were established then we felt it could be used as a basis for understanding the theology of baptism. Becoming a christian means making a break with a narrower, constricted, less adult world and entering a new life. 'Our entry as adults into the new kingdom of Christ can be closely associated with our entry as adults into the student world. It is likely that the two will succeed or fail together' (Meeting 1). In this first discussion from *University Life* there is a deliberate (though unacknowledged) clash with attitudes which the student may be expected to have brought with him from school. The infantilism of much religious instruction and popular piety commonly leads him to think of the christian outlook as more limited and less adult than that of 'the outside world'. Though he would not say so in as many words, he pictures the Church as primarily protective and 'safe'. The real purpose of the discussion is to begin the fading of this picture. In general the value of the discussions is expected to lie, not so much in what is explicitly said, as in the slow shifting of assumptions and 'images'. It is for this reason that we have carefully avoided anything in the way of 'conclusions' to the discussions; instead, each meeting is supposed to end with the reading of a chosen piece of scripture. Our method, in fact, is the exact opposite of the conventional 'Gospel Enquiry'. This commonly begins with a reading from the scripture, which is then analysed and applied to our ordinary experience, the final result being some practical conclusion. We have reversed this procedure. We begin with an examination of some aspect of university life—not at all with a view to 'judging' it, or seeing how we can apply christian standards to it, but with a view simply to understanding it so that we can more fully enter into it. The second movement is to see the christian revelation as a depth within this human experience, and the final act is to read from the scriptures without any comment at all. It is hoped that the previous discussion will have helped the student to see for himself a new meaning in the scriptural passage. Of course the two commonest weaknesses in practice have been that the first part of the meeting runs to moralising instead of understanding, and the scriptural reading is omitted altogether. These are just the defects which we should expect, since the whole value of the course of discussions can be measured by the degree to which the attitudes behind such defects are gradually overcome.

At this point it will help to consider the details of a particular meeting. Meeting No 5, for example, is called 'Eating and Drinking'. The previous four meetings have been devoted to establishing a sense of community: we have discussed the newness of university life, the freedom and responsibility it implies; the importance of the community has been shown by a discussion of loneliness, and it has been stressed that the university community is not essentially an organised, authoritarian institution like a school, but a group of friends. For Meeting No 5, all those taking part are asked to read beforehand a couple of short passages, one from Charles Davis's book *Liturgy and Doctrine*, the other from Durrwell's *The Resurrection*, both about the eucharist as a common meal. At the meeting, attention is first drawn to the new significance of meals in university life. You now choose your company at a meal: eating and drinking are experienced as symbols and incentives to friendship. The discussion brings into prominence the function of meals as a social institution. In the second movement it is simply taken for granted that the Mass is a common meal, and the students are asked to discuss ways in which the Mass might more clearly appear to be what it is: 'Do you get the impression at Mass that we are all united? Does the Mass unite us as a meal does? How can it produce this effect? What changes would you suggest?' They are asked to read accounts of the meals of the risen Christ with the apostles, and to discuss their significance. The meeting ends with a reading from I Cor. 11.

As it happens, this turned out to be one of the occasions when what we might call the 'bland assumption technique' came unstuck. We had realised, of course, that to speak of the Mass without reference to sacrifice, and without explicit mention of the difference between the parts played by priest and people would clash with what the students had been brought up to expect—it was this clash, whether brought up explicitly in the meeting by the students, or simply having its effect in their minds, that constituted the value of the meeting. We had realised that in this sense the meeting would be novel; what we had not expected was that it would be quite unintelligible to some. We discovered that for a fair number of students the idea of the Mass as the common meal of christians was completely unfamiliar. We also found it necessary in the final revised edition to make explicit reference to the Mass as sacrifice, since the omission of this led in practice to a good deal of irrelevant discussion.

There is not much point in summarising the contents of the two booklets, since they are in any case very short, and I have tried to explain the idea behind them: that entering into experiencing and understanding university life can be a unique opportunity for entering into and understanding the christian revelation.

Such an approach involves a very considerable shift of viewpoint for a student who has been educated at an average Catholic grammar school. This is both its difficulty and part of its value. The more effectively the student can dissociate his faith from the limiting background of childhood, the healthier in practice it is likely to be. No doubt in later years the student will be able to recognise a value even in the infantile religion of his schooldays, but this is for the future; his immediate need is to escape from it into something more personal and more adult. It was with this need in mind that the two booklets I have been describing were produced. To quote from the Introduction to *University Life*:

> This booklet is not a course of instructions or a programme of action. ... We offer these outlines for meetings as tentative suggestions for ways in which you might tackle the problem of entering into the university and of entering fully into your christian life. We believe that these two discoveries can be the same. The new experience of university life and the experience of the newness of university life, can be a starting point for a realistic understanding of the new life in Christ which is the centre of christian revelation.

Both the preceding papers testify to an important principle developed by other contributors, notably Charles Davis, p. 131 infra, that, since theology is 'an ecclesial activity' and a matter of sentire in ecclesia, to acquire a social maturity is to lay a foundation for theological maturity, and vice versa.

Even in universities which are rapidly expanding and have too many non-residential students, this principle holds, since the sense of community has to be realised anew by all its members; and a christian placed in such circumstances might very well discover that the best way in which he could understand and respond theologically to his university community would be in the act of helping to create it.

3. Newman's Idea of an Educated Laity—the two versions

John Coulson

One of the most profitable approaches to Newman's work is to see it as an attempt not only to justify, theologically, the participation of the laity in a Church, which its critics have seen as an almost exclusively clerical monopoly, but also to explain why that Church has a duty in these present times to see that its laity is, both theologically and intellectually, highly educated.

Throughout his long life, education remained Newman's preoccupation: 'From first to last,' he says in 1863, 'education has been my line'; and it is usual to regard his lectures to his embryonic Catholic University, published as *The Idea of a University*, as the definitive statement of his position. From researches into the archives at Birmingham Oratory I have come to the conclusion, however, that this is no longer wholly true, and that in one important respect—that Catholic laymen could only be properly educated in a Catholic university—Newman changed his mind.[1] By 1867, for example, we find him referring to the Catholic University as a 'speculative perfection'; and it is my purpose to find out whether Newman changed his mind on grounds merely of expedience, or because his theological convictions in the sixties and seventies were different from what they had been in November 1851, when he accepted the invitation to become Rector of a Catholic university, which Dr Cullen, the new primate of Ireland, all hot from Rome, wished to see established in Dublin.

When Newman undertook the formation of this university, which was not intended to be confined to the Irish, but to be the English-

---

[1] Material hitherto unpublished is indicated throughout by means of a * and I wish to express my thanks to the Rev Stephen Dessain, of the Birmingham Oratory, for so kindly permitting me to publish it.

speaking equivalent of Louvain, he was still only a recent convert, having been received in 1845, ordained in Rome two years later, and returning to England to establish the Birmingham Oratory in February 1848. His prestige was untarnished, but his understanding of the empirical reality of the Church was notional.

His aim was simple: in his own words, it was 'to import Oxford into Ireland', but he soon learned that to the average Dubliner he was 'a mere page of history . . . they have heard my name, but they have no association with it'. But the apathy by which he was confronted had deeper and more political origins: British injustice and Irish incapacity to remedy it had produced what one patriot called in the very year of Newman's arrival: 'a paralysis of national feeling'.

Not only did this destroy the likelihood of a class coming into existence for whom a university education was possible, but most people believed that what was wanted was not so much an educated Catholic laity as a politically united Ireland, and that, in the words of Frederick Lucas, the editor and founder of the *Tablet*, 'in this island where people are mixed, and society is mixed, education must be so'.

Newman's other difficulty was the personality of his patron, Dr Cullen, the Archbishop of Dublin, who until the age of forty-six had been rector of the Irish College in Rome, was a determined opponent of mixed education, and saw the establishment of a Catholic university as a political move against his opponents within the Church; he seems to have been too long in Rome to have been able to adapt himself to local conditions; he judged Irish political aspirations by Roman standards; his narrow views were strictly adhered to; and in negotiations he preferred a system of clandestine manœuvres punctuated, after the Roman fashion, by periods of unnerving silence and delay. Newman noticed that he treated him not as a colleague, but as a servant.

It is important to see the argument of the first part of the *Idea of a University* (originally published separately in 1853 as *The Scope and Nature of University Education*) against this background. Newman complained that all his greatest works, with the exception of *The Grammar of Assent*, arose as responses to particular problems and situations, but such immediate stimulus always seemed to bring out his powers to their fullest, and it is this very empiric and occasional quality which makes him so very fresh and readable. These lectures are not a series of messianic utterances at the highest and safest levels of generality, but attempts to resolve a series of awkward questions, each pointing in a different direction, and to produce a coherent argument which will operate and succeed on many fronts. There were Catholics who saw no real difference between a mixed education at Trinity College, Dublin, and what the Catholic university could provide; and for them Newman had to show the advantages of a religious education over that which was purely secular or religiously indifferent. But there were others for whom a liberal education as defined by Newman and practised in England was a schooling in intellectual pride and an invitation to dabble in heresy and infidelity. 'The prelates,' Newman said, 'regard an intellectual man as being on the road to perdition'; and a seminary or convent type of education was far more in keeping with Catholic tradition as it was then understood, than an institution modelled on the lines of what one Irish Dominican called 'Oxford College'—and run not merely by converts, but—what was worse—by convert laymen.

In order to remind you of the strength of the case which Newman was subsequently to modify, it is difficult to avoid going over ground which is already familiar, namely the argument of the *Idea*.

Although the pursuit of liberal as distinct from useful knowledge is its own justification and is, therefore, an end in itself, it is a dynamic and dangerous acquaintanceship, not a passive reception of ideas. A successful liberal education, by developing that power which enables us to seize the strong point in any matter we are considering, accomplishes an enlargement of mind; but an unsuccessful encounter destroys, enfeebles and dissipates. 'You must be above your knowledge,' Newman reminds his audience, 'or it will oppress you.'

Newman's analysis is based upon a principle of limitation, or as he calls it, abstraction. The mind is incapable of grasping its world at once and as a whole; we abstract parts from that whole in the manner of a short-sighted reader; we progress by degrees and circuitous advances. These partial views or abstractions, as Newman calls them, are what constitute the various sciences or subjects of our knowledge; since they are the results of abstraction, they have to do with the relations of things rather than with the things in themselves. This knowledge is probable, hypothetical and partial, yet by its nature it seeks to explain the whole of which it is part, and continually to encroach upon the territory of some other subject matter and some other method of analysis. Examples of such totalitarian tendencies on the part of specialists can, of course, be cited indefinitely, from the Marxist reduction of ethical problems to economic causes, to that confusion of aesthetic with moral categories which was so prominent a feature of the *Lady Chatterley* trial.

'It seems', says Newman, 'that the human mind is ever seeking to systematise knowledge, to base it upon a principle, and to find a science comprehensive of all sciences,' and that sooner than forego this gratification, we prefer the completeness and precision of bigotry to 'a fluctuating and homeless scepticism', and that we will always 'put up with an illusion when we cannot get a truth'.

The point at issue, then, is not whether our knowledge should be unified, but how that inevitable process ought best to be undertaken; and the first shock Newman gave to some of the more narrowly pious members of his audience was his deliberate avoidance of the easy denominational way out of the difficulty. Knowledge is unified by an insight possessed by all men, irrespective of creed, the use of which 'constitutes a sort of science distinct from all of them, and in some sense a science of sciences'. Yet the academic man is exposed to a particular danger: the roots of his judgment lie far deeper than his chosen field of study, and he is, in this sense, only half a man; so that once he fails to be able to give an account of how the various aspects of himself are interrelated, that power of judgment and comprehensiveness, which it is the purpose of a liberal education to foster and impart, weakens; and what we dimly feel, we cannot resolutely communicate.

What can happen to the individual can happen in turn to his university, if it permits practices to develop which weaken it as a community, and if it allows the web of its teaching to become unravelled. Then it becomes, in Newman's phrase, 'a sort of bazaar, or pantechnicon, in which wares of all kinds are heaped together for sale in stalls independent of each other'.

Newman makes it clear that what all successful education has in common is the ability to grasp the idea it is attempting to embody, to define its type, to establish its criteria, and to clarify its motives. If you cannot assume this degree of common agreement, then all you will produce is mere specialists or victims of mass communication:

illiberal men and illiberal communities. 'Excellence,' says Newman, 'must have a centre.'

Such an education produces 'the gentleman'; and Newman uses the term descriptively rather than evocatively, as much in order to show what a gentleman is not, as what he is. This man who, in a celebrated passage in the *Idea*, is spoken of as being as simple as he is forcible, too clear-headed to be unjust, and as brief as he is decisive, is also spoken of as possessing that effeminacy of feeling which tolerates religion, not because it is true, but because it is venerable, beautiful and useful. Somehow the type lacks a certain initiative, a certain moral drive. His qualities, says Newman, may look like virtues—at a distance; but when he is faced with the sombre permanent problems that emerge periodically from the dark recesses of our ape-like consciousness, the gentleman is unprepared, and—if one may use the phrase—uncommitted: he has discovered the limits of a liberal education: 'Quarry the granite rock with razors, or moor the vessel with a thread of silk; then may you hope with such keen and delicate instruments as human knowledge and human reason to contend against these giants, the passion and the pride of man.'

Thus, the distinction between intellectual and moral excellence which enables us to grasp the difference between Nature and Grace is the recurring note in all Newman's writing about education. It is this which enabled him to understand the Catholic objections to a university conceived on the liberal, alien, Oxford pattern, and to say: 'Philosophy, however enlightened, however profound, gives no command over the passions, no influential motives, no vivifying principles. Liberal education makes not the Christian, nor the Catholic, but the gentleman.'

It is, of course, true that the philosophical insights that are sharpened by a liberal education, since they are innate, are religious in implication—this is the argument from the illative sense—but they can as easily lead to simple scepticism as to religious belief and Newman's answer to the question—what, then, are the grounds for giving religion a place in the university?—are firmly empirical and rest solely on an appeal to the observable facts of history.

Throughout his history, man has concerned himself with the problem of a supreme Being—God. A body of knowledge has grown up to which we give the name of theology, and any curriculum of liberal knowledge, or university professing to take all knowledge for its

province, denies the significance of such an existing body of knowledge at its own risk. This, as far as the university is concerned, is
what Newman means by theology: 'the science of God, or the truths
we know about God put into a system'. Nor must theology be allowed
to interfere with the freedom of the individual sciences in their own
sphere, and the theologian must remember that not even theology can
'be excluded from the law to which every mental exercise is subject,
namely, from that imperfection which ever must attend the abstract,
when it would determine the concrete. Nor do I speak only of
Natural Religion, for even the teaching of the Catholic Church is
variously influenced by other sciences.' Thus theology must find its
own way and exist on the university's terms and not its own.

Yet the peculiarity of its subject matter has certain irresistible side
effects, since theology, treating of things as they are related to their
creator, is bound to impinge on other sciences, and individual subjects will have one character when viewed in the context of theology,
and another viewed out of it.

We can now see how Newman answered the great questions with
which he started. Ought Catholics to support a Catholic university?
Yes, says Newman, if the Catholic university really is a university,
since 'if the Catholic Faith is true, a university cannot exist externally
to the Catholic pale, for it cannot teach universal knowledge, if it
does not teach Catholic theology.' Thus, for Catholics, the study of
religion is not a mere trimming, a mere matter of dispute between the
bishops and the government, but a condition of their general knowledge; and to blot it out is 'to unravel' (for them) 'the web of university teaching'. Newman also answers the question: what is the
difference between the education appropriate to a gentleman and
that appropriate to a Catholic layman? Both, in receiving a liberal
education, will have learned to think for themselves; but the religious
education of the Catholic will have reinforced those powers of judgment, where they are weak, and by helping him to understand how
the various aspects of his knowledge and himself are interrelated,
will save him from falling into a simple scepticism. His assent to the
truths of religion passes over from the notional to the real. Thus a
Catholic who has received a liberal but religious education is less
narrow and is possessed of a vitality or moral earnestness greater
than that of the mere gentleman; since by the aid of his theology he
has come to see his world as a whole; it is no longer dull, monotonous

and unprofitable, but—with the vision of the people of the middle ages—it is seen as a various and complicated drama, with parts and an object, and an awful moral. To such a man religion brings its own enlargement: 'an enlargement, not of tumult, but of peace'.

We should however be making a great mistake if we thought Newman's *Idea* to be a mere matter of paper reform. The meeting of liberal and moral values, of philosophy and theology, which he desires is a vigorous collision of mind with mind in the hard give and take of a university community, for theology gets on to terms with the other subjects of the curriculum not by an intellectual act *in vacuo*, but by surviving these collisions and inter-penetrations. Newman's stress is upon the university not as an ideal but as an *embodied* idea: the very title *Idea of a University* is itself an indication of Newman's approach, since the term 'idea' in his theology stands not for a mere concept, but for a principle with a life of its own and a power to develop into as yet non-existent forms and institutions: the very germ of a dynamic community, that ability (as Whitehead puts it) to embody high ideals in great institutions which was the achievement of the Benedictine centuries.

Newman's case for the Catholic university is, therefore, at once deeply theological and firmly empirical; and its definitive expression is in his first sermon preached after the opening of the university Church in April 1856:

> I want to destroy that diversity of centres, which puts everything into confusion by creating a contrariety of influences. I wish the same spots and the same individuals to be at once oracles of philosophy and shrines of devotion. It will not satisfy me, what satisfies so many, to have two independent systems, intellectual and religious, going at once side by side, by a sort of division of labour, and only accidentally brought together. . . . I want the same roof to contain both the intellectual and the moral discipline. Devotion is not a sort of finish given to the sciences; nor is science a sort of feather in the cap, if I may so express myself, an ornament and set-off to devotion. I want the intellectual layman to be religious, and the devout ecclesiastic to be intellectual.[1]

We have already seen something of the unpromising setting for Newman's great experiment, but there were even more fundamental objections. His fellow Catholics were unable to distinguish between a university (which had been asked for) and a college (which was really intended): in Newman's words, 'the office of a Catholic

---

[1] *Sermons preached on Various Occasions,* fifth ed. (1881), p. 13.

university is to teach faith, and of colleges to protect morals.' The clergy, however, if they were interested in intellectual studies at all saw them as a means of enforcing moral discipline; they could understand an education that had to be beaten into minds vitiated by original sin; they could, as Newman puts it, enter into alliance with the useful knowledge places; but their separation of intellectual from moral values was so radical that they seemed committed to the contradiction that where intellectual effort is not subversive of faith, it is indifferent to it. Thus either they had to deny the principle that all knowledge is influenced by faith, or assert that the process of intellectual development can be safely reduced to a mere technique, a something passive and neutral (which it never is) rather than dynamic and challenging (which it always has been). Behind these wrongheaded views was an assumption that made their adoption perfectly intelligible: it was that the realms of faith and reason are discontinuous, and that we must educate, therefore, upon the principle of an opposition, deep and unbridgeable, between nature and grace. Within the Roman Church such an education has always been narrowly denominational and entirely clerical in scope and control; under the régime it produces, the laity are indeed to be regarded as boys eternal, or—in the words of one of Newman's friends—'as a mass of suspects, supposed to be brooding on nothing but revolution, and only kept together by motives of fear and by the external pressure of a clerical organization'.

That this is not an exaggeration can be seen from one of the questions on university education circulated in England on behalf of Propaganda in 1864: it was: 'Ought the principle to be admitted that the laity should be more highly educated than their clergy?'

Newman's method of dealing with such objections is typical of his approach as a theologian. First, he answers them on their own terms at the empirical level, and then relates them to the theological principles which are being denied or disregarded—in this case the necessary function of an educated laity within the Church. Thus, if a university is turned into a convent, it will not work: great minds need elbow room, but so do lesser minds. If a university fails to reflect the world into which the layman must go, he will be driven to seek for his university in that world; yet to educate the clergy and laity on a separate system of principles will not merely increase the gulf between them (which in Ireland, Newman noted, was fearful), but it will encourage the Church to shrink within itself and to become in appearance an almost exclusively clerical concern. To demand from the laity, Newman says in his essay *On Consulting the Faithful in Matters of Doctrine*, nothing more active than a *fides implicita* will terminate 'in the educated classes . . . in indifference, and in the poorer in superstition'.[1]

This was not all, however. The narrow-mindedness that could discourage or deny the laity its traditional rights of active participation within the fullness of the Church was itself substituting its own theological abstractions for the fullness of Christian Revelation. What was needed was that the Church should put forth itself in all its fullness—a fullness which is not in the priests alone, but only in the *conspiratio* of priests and laity.

This is what Newman means by a masculine religion. It is one which is based upon the interaction of Nature and Grace, and not upon their irremediable opposition. It is a return to the primitive Benedictine ideal—a growth, rather than a structure; a restoration, rather than a visitation, correction or conversion. It is to reunite things which were in the beginning joined together by God, and have been put asunder by man. Such was the method of Newman's own patron, St Philip Neri, who relied not on protests and warnings, but on 'the counter-fascination of purity and truth'; and as Newman makes clear in one of his university sermons, it was the method of St Paul, 'the least magisterial of all teachers and the gentlest of all rulers'. 'For him,' says Newman, 'Grace did but sanctify and elevate Nature,' leaving him in the full possession of all that was human.

Thus Newman's idea of a Catholic university is that of a community—taking all knowledge for its object, autonomous in its administration—and constituting thereby a middle station in which priests and laity can meet, a point of equilibrium between clerical and lay education, where these partners in the Church 'may learn to understand and yield to each other', in order that they may 'act in union upon an age which is running headlong into infidelity'. This was Newman's ideal in the 50's. During the next decade, he was to discover that the conditions within the Church were precisely the reverse of that equilibrium between clergy and laity necessary for the establishment of a Catholic university.

[1] *On Consulting the Faithful in Matters of Doctrine*, edited with an introduction by John Coulson (Geoffrey Chapman, 1961). New York: Sheed & Ward.

C

Clergy and laity were so often at loggerheads that those laymen, such as Acton and Simpson, who attempted through journalism and writing to make a contribution to the life of the Church, were regarded with a suspicion that readily attached itself to Newman, when he attempted to give the theological grounds for such activity in his essay *On Consulting the Faithful*. As usual, Newman was fighting a war on several fronts: the intrigues by Faber and the London Oratory, by those who wanted to turn his own Oratory school into a conventional public school; growing suspicion of him at Rome as being, in the words of the mad Monsignor Talbot, 'the most dangerous man in England', had such an effect that even when Kingsley's attack upon him, and his reply in the *Apologia* in 1864, gave him a standing he was never entirely to lose, he was still regarded with suspicion until the end of the 60's.

Not only did he, in his own words, shrink from a society which had been unjust to him, he changed his mind about the Catholic university.

In November 1866, he described the Church as 'sinking into a sort of Novatianism—the heresy which the early popes so strenuously resisted. Instead of aiming at being a world-wide power we are shrinking into ourselves, narrowing the lines of communion, trembling at freedom of thought, and using the language of despair and dismay at the prospect before us, instead of, with the high spirit of the warrior, going out conquering and to conquer.'

In a revealing correspondence in March 1867 with Sir Justin Sheil, a magnificently robust old Catholic, Newman spoke of the Catholic university as 'a speculative perfection, which cannot be carried out in practice',* and of himself as on the whole not against young Catholics going to Oxford. Until Manning's appointment as Archbishop in 1865 the attitude of the bishops to sending Catholics to the English universities had varied. Ullathorne, if left to himself, would have established a Catholic Hall at Oxford in the 60's, and many Catholic institutions, Downside among them, affiliated to London University for external examinations in the 40's; but Oxford, because it was the home of the Anglican establishment, was anathema to Manning and the convert Ultramontanes; and a series of increasingly stringent prohibitions bedevilled the discussion of university education for Catholic laymen until 1895, when laymen were at last allowed to go to Oxford and Cambridge—some twelve years after the comparable permission to laymen in Italy.

If the Catholic laity had had but a quarter of the robust independence of Sir Justin Sheil, things might have been very different. Replying to Newman, Sir Justin speaks of 'the fanaticism . . . of Dr Wiseman and Dr Manning', and goes on to say: 'I assume to myself an absolute independence in the management of my secular affairs, in which I include education.' He dismisses as ridiculous the notion of 'foreign prelates and Jesuits of Propaganda'*—that faith and morals would be jeopardised by an Oxford education. But this was very much a minority view: on two separate occasions, in 1864/5 and 1866/7, Newman was prevented from going to Oxford, even at his own bishop's request, to found an Oratory, in case his presence there should encourage Catholics to defy the bishops and send their sons to Oxford.

Yet, as Newman said, 'necessity has no laws'; and he was even suspicious of the theological status of the prohibition; but where else could these young men be sent? It was soon to be no longer a matter of the fate of two hundred old Catholic families but of the urgent necessities of a newly emerging Catholic middle class.

In 1874, Manning's solution, and the one he had persuaded Rome to recommend, was officially adopted: the establishment of a Catholic university college in Bayswater. It lasted four years. The academic staff was distinguished but not autonomous; and the laity continued, as in Dublin, to be held at arms-length. The aim of the institution was to ensure that its pupils were 'vigilantly protected from all contact with the intellectual errors of National Education'.

It was assumed that Newman would support this fresh attempt at a Catholic university, but in a letter to one of its sponsors, the President of Oscott, he says bluntly: 'I should not propose a Catholic university, for I think our present rulers would never give us a real one'—and he adds—'nor a Catholic college at Oxford.'*

Newman's primary condition for a Catholic university had been the full participation of the laity in teaching and governing; and, as Fr McGrath[1] points out, his constitution for the Irish university implied as little dependence upon external authority as possible. Yet for the clergy to concede power to the laity involved an understanding of and sympathy for that very theology of consultation put forward in *On Consulting the Faithful*, for which Newman was delated to

[1] *Newman's University: Idea and Reality* by Fergal McGrath, Longmans, 1951, pp. 381–2, 384.

Rome. It also involved conceding as a matter of principle, rather than of expediency, rights to the laity in the temporal sphere, which were then (1870) being disputed. Manning and his supporters, for example, had petitioned for the Temporal Power of the papacy to be made a doctrine *de fide*.

Yet the principle of academic autonomy is implicit not only in the government of Newman's university, but in the liberty of a teacher to pursue his subject to its limits; theological primacy in theory must be won in fact, and theology becomes, if it can, the queen of the sciences on the university's terms and not its own. This is what Newman meant in speaking of the philosophy of the imperial intellect; its purpose is to discriminate rather than to simplify, to understand rather than to condemn. The educated Catholic has nothing to fear from the world of liberal values by which he is encompassed, since truth cannot contradict truth; but it is a truth which can be achieved only 'by many minds working together freely', and failure to observe this principle in, for example, a Catholic institution for Higher education would have two fundamental consequences.

The theology taught would become unreal (although in essence correct and true), since its methods and vocabulary would have no relation to the intellectual standards, methods and needs of the secular climate of opinion. An education in such a purely notional theology would produce neither educated priests nor devout laymen, but dissociated personalities, neither properly educated nor effectively devout.

Where intellectual education is subservient to a rigid and inflexible theology, intellectual standards drop, since questions cease to be open, and emphasis falls upon the correctness of the answers rather than upon the integrity of the method used, and the legitimacy of the answers it provides. Newman records an amusing encounter with a Jesuit who wished 'to indoctrinate the lay youths in philosophy'; and amongst his papers for February 1872 is a brief and almost illegible note on what a Catholic university is not. It is not 'a place to get up petitions for the Pope's temporal power, and be *deposed* if a man won't sign it, or to print in its Gazette the Pope's dogmatic Bulls, or *docete gentes* in Mathematics, or oblige a dissector ever to be bringing in Providence'.* Newman's second thoughts pose two major questions. When a Catholic institution succeeds academically, can that success best be evaluated in terms of the number of teachers (usually laymen) educated in non-Catholic universities which the particular institution has been able to employ, and are the lower academic standards sometimes associated with more exclusively Catholic institutions or universities, the result of not observing this practice and the principles it pre-supposes?

The second major question is would it be to the long-term advantage of theology, if it were studied in an open or neutral university, rather than in a specifically Catholic one; and is a Catholic university ever possible in a country such as our own? In order to take all knowledge for its object, a university must reflect the society in which it grows, because only thus can it provide that inclusiveness which alone makes possible the enlargement of mind that is the hallmark of its graduates. In a university the primary emphasis must be, therefore, intellectual; where, for whatever reason, an institution cannot or will not reflect the intellectual diversity of its society, it remains—if it is Catholic—a seminary; nor, if this is recognised for what it is, need we deplore it. A seminary or school, where the emphasis is on moral rather than intellectual development, is a necessary stage in education; but we can only escape the latent tautology if we realise that a Catholic society produces a Catholic university primarily because it is a society, and not because it is Catholic: in a mixed or non-Catholic society, Catholics are able to produce only seminaries or contributions to an existing university.

That this is a reasonable interpretation of Newman's later thinking can be seen from his willingness, in spite of personal disinclination, to found an Oratory at Oxford, if he were asked. But profound reservations are to be seen in his letters of this time. 'By mismanagement,' he says, 'the whole question has got into that tangle, that it can't be satisfactorily solved,'* and if a Catholic Hall were established, he feared it would encourage what is nowadays called the ghetto-mentality: 'Catholics in Oxford will be few and then despised, or many and then feared and hated.'* In 1863 Newman thought the point of principle turned on whether Catholics could be taught by Catholic tutors, but a note added in 1875 shows that he considered the dilemma too great even for this solution, since he now concluded that 'a College at Oxford, so isolated as not to have the influx of Oxford opinions, was an impossibility.'*

Although the effects of the Vatican Council were a further aggravation, in a letter to Lord Howard of 27 April 1872, Newman shows that his mind had slowly but decisively moved to what I have called the *second* version of his idea of the educated laity:

> On the whole I do not know how to avoid the conclusion that mixed education in the higher schools is as much a necessity now in England, as it was in the East in the days of St. Basil and St. Chrysostom. . . . In a large university, there are good sets and bad sets; and a youth has a chance of choosing between them. In a small, exclusive body there is no choice; and one bad member ruins for a time the whole community. *Thus the open university, when complemented by a strong mission, may be even safer than a close Catholic college.* * (My italics)

Here is Newman's change of mind. But before inquiring into its theological grounds, it is important to note that it marks a reversion to his position before he received the command to pioneer the Irish Catholic university. Newman had then favoured a mixed education as being dictated by necessity, but he had changed his mind in deference to the judgment of the Holy See. In his first lecture in the *Idea of a University* he had said that 'over and above the attribute of infallibility which attached to the doctrinal decisions of the Holy See, a gift of sagacity had in every age characterised its occupants,' so that if the Pope intended a Catholic university in Dublin, it was bound to succeed—a statement which, published in the first edition of the *Idea*, was deleted in later ones. Experience taught Newman to distinguish sharply between the Pope's infallibility and his sagacity,[1] namely, his ability to decide what was expedient for the Church at any particular time. His earlier point of view is also to be found in that lecture (section 3), and in 1867 he appears to have sent an amended version of this passage to Rome, entitling it 'on necessary exceptions in fact to the rule that education must not be mixed'.* It was not well received.

Newman's grasp of a problem is always, as I have attempted to show, fundamentally and essentially theological, and the change in his attitude to the education of the laity was all of a piece with the development of his understanding of the Church's ingression into the temporal order. As he grew older, his attitude became more deeply ecumenical; and his affection for old friends and for Oxford in particular caused him to be increasingly pained by the alien aspect which

[1] John Henry Newman, *Autobiographical Writings*, ed. Henry Tristram, Sheed and Ward, 1957, p. 320.

the Catholic Church seemed deliberately to turn towards his fellow countrymen: 'Catholics did not make us Catholics,' he said, 'Oxford made us Catholics.' His vision went beyond that of his English opponents, Manning, Ward and Talbot, who had done so much to discredit the Church in English eyes—'the political, ultra-devotional party', as he called them—to a view of the Church which had become, as it were, three-dimensional, and which received its most profound expression in the Preface to the third edition of the *Via Media* of 1877. By then he had come to see Christianity as 'at once a philosophy, a political power, and a religious rite'. This corresponds to the three offices of Christ as prophet, king and priest. Although in order to survive, Christianity had to be embodied in a 'polity', 'of which the essential idea is union and subordination',[1] its health and greatness depend on these three offices or functions being in equilibrium, since each aspect is liable to a characteristic abuse: theology can degenerate into rationalism, devotion into superstition, and the exercise of power into ambition and tyranny.[2]

Of these dimensions of the Church, theology, being as it is 'commensurate with Revelation', is the fundamental and regulating principle and, as such, 'has created both the Regal Office and the Sacerdotal'.[3]

It is possible to suggest that the conditions for the successful establishment of a Catholic university occur only when these aspects of the Church are in equilibrium;[4] and the nineteenth century was a period of extreme disequilibrium. Newman saw the great need of the Church as a renewal of theology which, by being made relevant to the times, became alive and able to combat the rising tide of infidelity; but this could be achieved only within a university which really was a university, since 'truth is the guiding principle of theology and theological enquiries',[5] and truth can be achieved only by 'many minds working together freely'. Newman said that his willingness to return to Oxford in an age, when 'the Pope himself is not a theologian', and theology had in consequence 'gone out of fashion', was to show 'a side of the Catholic religion more theological, more exact'; and it is evident that he looked to a revived theology as the means of

[1] *The Via Media of the Anglican Church*, the Third Edition, 1877, p. 345.
[2] ibid., pp. xl, xli.
[3] ibid., p. xlvii.
[4] *University Sketches*, ed. George Sampson, p. 234.
[5] *Via Media*, p. xli.

effecting, by curbing the power of both sides, a proper *conspiratio* of laity and clergy.

Without such a theology a Catholic university was impossible, and as far as the education of the laity was concerned, Newman concluded that the best policy was that which 'will commit the Church least'.* I believe that he came to this opinion because the temporal autonomy required for a university, a freedom not only to *think* but to *act*, belongs to the legitimate sphere of lay initiative, so that a university must not only be supported by the laity, it must be run by them: this is what establishes an equilibrium between laity and clergy, always provided that a university is not constituted, in its *idea*, on anti-Catholic principles, by requiring, for example, conformity to test acts or alien principles. Since, however, our own society has grown increasingly open and pluralist, so have our universities; and in a society in which Catholic values are neither officially nor positively attacked—as they are, for example, in Soviet Russia, or might have been considered to be in early nineteenth-century Anglican Oxford—the need for a Catholic university does not arise. Those of us in this room—humanist, non-conformist, Anglican and Roman—by recognising the values which unite us, admit to what Maritain calls 'a community of analogy . . . which makes possible a genuine human co-operation', for the best policy is not only that which commits the Church least, but that which, in overcoming the Church's alien aspect, shows that the educated layman, far from fearing the world of liberal values by which he is encompassed, is, in some special way, their guardian.

Are we then to abandon the discussion of a Catholic university as a waste of time? No, since this is to forget that Newman was a reasonably orthodox Platonist. The *ideal* of such a university, in its unity and wholeness of the moral and intellectual perfections, is the pattern on which we educate; the value of studying the *first* version of Newman's *Idea* is that, in telling us about the ideal Catholic university, it tells us about the structure of the ideal Catholic society, so that when, for example, we pray for the conversion of Russia, we know better what we are intending.

The value of understanding the *second* version of Newman's *Idea* of the educated laity is that we come to see that Catholic theology ought to form part of the syllabus of an open university, not only

* *v.* p. 47[1] *supra.*

because it is a legitimate field of study in an institution taking all knowledge as its object, but because, for the Catholic layman, his further theological education ought to take place in the same place and at the same time as his further intellectual education. But perhaps the most fundamental reason is that the study of theology would itself benefit from a policy which would inevitably encourage what Newman called 'a better sort of religious sentiment'.

— NOTE —

WHAT IS A LAYMAN?

Today, the distinction between clergy and laity made, for example, by Newman may appear to be theologically too rigid, to be derived from a particular set of cultural distinctions appropriate only to the time in which he was writing, and to conceal a further distinction between ordained and unordained members of the clergy. On closer inspection, such distinctions seem to suffer the death from a thousand qualifications; and Fr Charles Davis *has summarised the latest thinking on this matter in the following note:*

The question, 'What is a layman?' is difficult to answer because it can be asked from different points of view. The basic distinction in this matter is between ordained ministers (bishops, priests and deacons) and the other members of the community, who are designated as lay people. The distinction is one of function, but the ordained minister is not merely assigned a function by the community; he receives a sacramental consecration by the action of Christ and a grace of office. Nevertheless, the ordained minister personally has no privileged access to Christ and his mystery in regard to spiritual union; on that level all christians are equal in status. So, the distinction between ministers and laity remains fundamentally a distinction of sacramental function. Possession of a ministerial function within the christian community does not as such demand a complete withdrawal from secular tasks. The married priests of the Eastern Church and the instances there have been of priests who devoted their lives to science or other secular pursuit, indeed the example of Paul in continuing his job as tent-maker, show this. Pastoral necessities will normally dictate some withdrawal, but the christian ministry does not demand a withdrawal from the world by its very nature.

This leads to the remark that the distinction between clergy and laity is not the same as that between the ordained and the unordained. Others besides the sacramentally ordained belong to the clergy, and in earlier centuries this wider extension of the clerical state had considerable importance in practice. But more than this, in its concrete form the difference between clergy and laity is the result of various historical factors, both social and cultural, and is far from being a matter of unchanging divine law. If the distinction between ordained and unordained is part of the sacramental structure of the Church, the distinction between clergy and laity belongs to the sphere of changing sociological fact within the Church.

The laity are also defined in relation to religious, understood as those who withdraw from the world in order to achieve a fuller dedication to God; the withdrawal is a means not an end. If it is easy enough to distinguish the laity from those who are religious in the canonical sense of the term, it is not so easy to do so when this distinction is given a wider scope. Attempts have been made to define a distinctively lay situation and lay task. It is said, for example, that a layman is a christian who remains in his existential human situation in this world and lives his christian life in that situation, without embracing a new state or situation as a result of his christian profession. Living within an ordinary human situation, he has the task of christianising the world and secular pursuits. But if we take this as a definition of a layman, are the members of Secular Institutes lay people? What about full-time lay catechists or Catholic Action leaders? Where exactly are we going to draw the line in determining whether a man's existential situation comes to him independently of his christian profession? Suppose a man devotes a substantial part of his life to a distinctively christian task, while continuing to practise his ordinary profession? There are a multitude of borderline cases where the distinction is very difficult to apply.

It is also worth noting that the law of celibacy means that in the Western Church the secular priest is also in some sense a religious. A vocation to the ministry and a vocation to celibacy are of their nature distinct vocations on the side of the candidate. Thus, the law of celibacy for all priests means in fact a decision of the Church authorities to ordain to the ministry only those who have, as well as a call to the ministry, a certain vocation to the religious state, understood in the wide sense as a withdrawal from secular life with its tasks and duties. This double calling of priests in the present discipline must be kept in mind in arguing theoretically about what is or is not distinctively priestly.

In brief, the complexity of distinctions necessary in this matter makes it a delicate business to divide tasks into properly priestly and properly lay. Above all, the present form of the distinction between clergy and laity within the Church must not be taken as the only conceivable one.

In the light of the foregoing, and in view of the embryonic state of existing teaching about the function of the laity within the Church, Newman's emphasis upon the need for partnership between clergy and laity would seem not only the most expedient course, but that which is most likely to encourage the right theological developments and distinctions. The notion of such a partnership arises where the work to be done cuts across the existing roles assigned to clergy and laity—the teaching of religion in schools and universities, the formation of lay societies to assist the Church, or the formation of groups to bring problems to the notice of the hierarchy, such as nuclear warfare or the 'just' war. Where the roles of clergy and laity cannot readily be distinguished, the need is for a greater partnership rather than for less (otherwise clericalism and anti-clericalism are the result); and this need arises as the areas of dechristianisation widen, deepen and grow more impervious to the traditional methods of christian teaching. In the last analysis, as Rahner[1] points out, those who can best christianise the world today are those who have made it in the form it is, and keep it so—the laity; this is the irrefutable basis for their claim to be taken into partnership.

[1] Karl Rahner, S.J., *Theological Investigations*, vol. II, (London: Darton, Longman and Todd, 1963; Baltimore: Helicon, 1964) pp. 319–52. See especially p. 349 (cited above), and pp. 320–1, 336 (on the overlapping of some lay and clerical roles).

4. The Catholic University: the American Experience

Daniel Callahan

The subject of this paper poses some immediate problems. Ideally, one might like to be able to discuss the idea of a Catholic university in the abstract, adverting from time to time to the American experience to provide some useful illustrations of one way in which it has been realised in practice. Unfortunately, as they so often do, historical and sociological facts stand in the way. The Catholic university in America cannot be understood apart from the social and ecclesiastical histories and present-day reality of American Catholicism. It is far more the result of those histories, and of that reality, than it is the product of educational theoreticians. Another difficulty is that American Catholic higher education comes in many varieties; it is exceedingly difficult to generalise about it, much less to employ any single norm to judge its success or its shortcomings. Despite the dangers, it is impossible here to escape generalisations; and it is, of course, impossible to escape history.

But before attempting to generalise about the American Catholic university today, let me attempt a brief description of its history and the social context of that history.[1] The first thing to be borne in mind is that during much of the seventeenth and eighteenth centuries American Catholics were proscribed by law from holding public office, from voting and from opening Catholic schools of any kind. Nor were they, so far as I am able to determine, free to attend Harvard, Yale or Princeton; those colleges were all established under

[1] The best formal history of American Catholic higher education now available is Edward J. Power, *A History of Catholic Higher Education in the United States* (Milwaukee: Bruce, 1958). Throughout this essay I will use the expressions 'Catholic university' and 'Catholic college' interchangeably. There is, of course, a distinction between the two types of institutions, but it is one which is not especially germane to my approach.

Protestant auspices, their main purpose being the training of Protestant ministers. Thus any of those early Anglo-American Catholics who desired an advanced education had to go abroad—usually to France. By the time of the American Revolution, however, the climate had changed. If Catholics were still suspect to many of their Protestant neighbours, they at least soon gained full legal and political rights; and their loyalty during the Revolution helped to make them socially acceptable, as did the fact that they shared a common language and a common ancestry with most Protestants. But they still remained a distinct and small minority, and, with the exception of a few small Catholic academies established in the late eighteenth century, they had no educational facilities of their own. Of particular importance, the non-Catholic colleges still remained, in practice, closed to them.

From the very first, then, the early clergy and bishops were faced with an urgent problem. If the faith of the Catholic was to be preserved and strengthened, then education was of primary importance. Since non-Catholics were unwilling to make their schools acceptable to Catholics, there seemed no choice but for Catholics to create their own facilities. Toward this end, the first bishop, John Carroll, made Catholic education his main concern; and among the very first steps he took was the establishment of Georgetown Academy, outside Washington, in 1789. That Academy, which was soon taken over by the Jesuits, became the first American Catholic college. Thereafter, American Catholic education slowly increased in scope and strength. While priority was given to grammar schools, there was a gradual increase in the number of colleges throughout the nineteenth century, and their number continued to grow during the first half of the twentieth century.[1]

In the course of the nineteenth century, however, much of the social acceptance which the Anglo-American Catholics had been able to achieve for Catholicism just before and just after the Revolution was lost with the influx of the great waves of Irish immigrants who began arriving after the 1830's. Most of the blame for this change must be laid at the feet of the established Protestant majority

[1] There are now 278 Catholic colleges and universities in the United States with a total of approximately 340,000 students. Approximately 10 per cent of these institutions are universities. There are, it may be noted, approximately 500,000 Catholics enrolled in non-Catholic colleges and universities

who rejected the immigrants as much out of resentment and fear of their 'foreign' ways as out of a distaste for their religion. As the century progressed, Catholics tended to turn inwards upon themselves, to become defensive and insular. Not all of them were this way, but enough to cut Catholics off from the mainstream of American intellectual and cultural life. Ghettoism, whether in a real or a figurative sense, reigned supreme. If this was understandable and a common reaction of rejected minorities in any society, it was still very damaging to Catholics themselves.

It was certainly damaging in the sphere of Catholic higher education. For it meant that the Catholic colleges were looked upon as much to protect the student's faith and morals from the dangers of society as they were to provide a solid education. In addition, the faculties of these colleges had comparatively little contact with the faculties of non-Catholic colleges. Slowly but surely, the Catholic intellectual world became a self-sufficient one. As if to confirm its self-sufficiency, there began to appear in the 1920's Catholic academic societies: The American Catholic Philosophical Association, the American Catholic Historical Association, and so forth. During this long developmental period, still another reality became painfully apparent: there was no general plan for, nor any general coordination in, the development of American Catholic higher education. Colleges proliferated at a rapid rate, very often duplicating one another and sometimes competing with one another. It is thus possible today to find as many as five Catholic colleges in the same city (e.g., Boston, New York, Chicago)—all of them struggling, few of them co-operating with one another. Hence to the reality of a Catholic intellectual ghetto was added that of vast financial problems. And rarely if ever during these years of development did anyone conceive of the Catholic college as the place where an intellectual élite would be trained; it was considered necessary only that their graduates have some advanced knowledge of Catholic theology and philosophy, and a general education at least no worse than that to be had in secular colleges. As for the members of faculties, it was rarely required that they be outstanding scholars or even have aspirations in that direction. The important thing was that they be good teachers and examples of spiritual and moral rectitude.

Not surprisingly, as the Catholic college system grew by leaps and bounds, one could here and there detect a certain ambivalence among

American Catholics toward them. On the one hand, there were those, perhaps the majority, who took the greatest possible pride in them. If they were not turning out conspicuously great men, that was not the only thing that counted. They were turning out men (and later women) who could hold their heads up with pride—if not in the higher echelons of American life, at least at those secondary levels of society which are no less important. They were fine, patriotic Catholics. What more could one want? But there were those who did want more. By the 1920's there were those who began to wonder why there were so few Catholic scientists, scholars, and civic leaders. Was it actually necessary that, regardless of the standard of measurement one employed, Catholics should fare so poorly? But no sooner were these questions raised than an excuse was ready at hand. The fault— it was said—did not lie with Catholics themselves, nor did it lie in the theory or practice of Catholic higher education. Instead, it lay in the obvious fact that Catholics had been an immigrant minority: they had started out under the poorest kind of circumstances; it was a miracle that they had colleges at all. Sociology, in short—along with the saga of immigrant history—came to the rescue. More, of course, could be done; but that would take time, patience and a more favourable social situation.

Such was the pattern of Catholic self-criticism up through the middle of the last decade. At that point, in 1955 to be exact, the influential Catholic historian, Monsignor John Tracy Ellis of the Catholic University of America, in Washington, D.C., published a paper in the Jesuit quarterly *Thought*. It was called, simply enough, 'American Catholics and the Intellectual Life'.[1] In his article, Monsignor Ellis updated the statistics on the absence of Catholic intellectuals in America. As his predecessors on this subject had done, he paid tribute to the self-sacrifice of American Catholics in creating a massively large system of Catholic colleges; and he pointed out the solid historical reasons why there were so few Catholic intellectuals and scholars. That done, however, he then departed from the usual script. Despite the traditional excuses, he said, 'The chief blame, I firmly believe, lies with Catholics themselves. It lies in their frequently self-imposed ghetto mentality which prevents them from mingling as they should with their non-Catholic colleagues, and in

---

[1] Monsignor Ellis's article has also been published in book form: *American Catholics and the Intellectual Life* (Heritage Foundation, Inc., 1956).

70   THEOLOGY AND THE UNIVERSITY

their lack of industry. . . . It lies in their failure to have measured up
to their responsibilities to the incomparable tradition of Catholic
learning of which they are the direct heirs. . . .'

With Monsignor Tracy's article the floodgates were opened. Within
the space of a few years, articles by the score and a number of
important books appeared from all sides.[1] No longer was very much
heard of the immigrant struggle, and the self-congratulations which
Catholic educators had earlier showered upon themselves gave way
to an intensive self-analysis. But now the analysis turned on Catholic
shortcomings. There were too many colleges; too few good ones.
There was too little emphasis on intellectual excellence, too much on
manual theology and philosophy. There was too much emulation of
some of the less inspiring aspects of American secular higher education—an emphasis on business courses and athletics, for instance;
there was too little on the standards of excellence maintained by the
great American universities—experimental programmes for the
specially gifted, adequate time and funds for faculty research and
publication, freedom from puerile restrictions and censorships for
undergraduates, to mention only a few things.

These were some of the broad criticisms—and yet some of the ones
more tolerable and amenable to reform measures. But there were
criticisms which bit much deeper. Thomas O'Dea in his *American
Catholic Dilemma* spoke articulately for many when he said that a
genuine intellectual life among American Catholics was hindered by
formalism, authoritarianism, clericalism, moralism and defensive-
ness. One could perhaps improve libraries, reduce teaching loads,
select better students. But how could one bring about a total change
in temperament, a totally new way of approaching the intellectual
life? Obviously something more than money was needed. What?

That is the question which American Catholic educators have been
asking themselves ever since Monsignor Ellis abruptly brought to an
end decades of blindness to the actual quality of Catholic intellectual
life. Since that time things have not been the same. The public debate
and agitation have subsided, but the hard work is now going on.
Precisely because this work has just started, it is impossible to pass

[1] Among the more notable books: Thomas O'Dea, *American Catholic Dilemma*
(New York: Sheed & Ward, 1958); Justus George Lawler, *The Catholic Dimension
in Higher Education* (Westminster: Newman Press, 1959); Leo R. Ward, C.S.C.,
New Life in Catholic Schools (St. Louis: Herder, 1958).

judgment on American Catholic higher education. On the whole the Catholic colleges remain inferior. They are inferior to the great American non-Catholic colleges and they are inferior when measured by any but the most modest goals which the Catholic colleges themselves would like to achieve. At the same time, the reaction to the recent self-criticism of Catholic educators indicates a capacity for renewal and exploration; no institutions which have the capacity to pass an unfavourable judgment upon themselves can be prejudged. We can only wait and see what happens.

None the less, it is possible to ask whether a genuine reformation of American Catholic higher education is *probable*. It is certainly conceivable, but is it *likely*? To answer this question it is necessary to ask a more basic one. Will American Catholic educators be able to learn profitably, first, from the historical experience of American Catholic higher education, and, secondly, from the experience of the non-Catholic academic world?

Let us look at the first part of that question. It appears to me that the American Catholic experience shows that it is impossible to have a first-rate university when it is cut off from the mainstream of American intellectual life. The Catholic university can only be a meaningful university if it is a full partner in the national, pluralistic academic community. In the past, the Catholic university was conceived as an alternative to the non-Catholic institution. If the theory was understandable, it still meant that the Catholic academic world became a closed circuit. The result was an ingrown academic life. Catholics neither contributed much to the pluralistic intellectual community nor did they take much from it. Even when Catholic scholars did attempt to confront those problems which exercised the non-Catholic intellectual community, they usually did so too late to make any useful contribution to the discussion. Thus even today when Catholics, with energy and sincerity, do try to take their place, they suffer the handicap of a great time lag. They cannot fully keep up because they have too little contact with non-Catholic intellectuals and currents of thought to enable them to be in at the start of trends, movements and changes. They can only act and respond after the fact.

No less important, it appears that the traditional American Catholic university approach to theology and philosophy has had some disastrous consequences on Catholic intellectual life. This approach can be characterised by describing the main assumption which has motivated the teaching of these subjects. The assumption is that the Catholic Church has, in the course of its long history, developed a definitive and detailed body of thought and doctrine which should be passed on intact to the student. Thus in both philosophy and theology, students have been provided with textbooks which attempt to codify and systematise the 'truths' of Catholic thought. Unfortunately, this venture has had three harmful effects. First, it has meant that the students themselves generally find their theology and philosophy courses the most boring and least stimulating;[1] and, even worse, the ones which appear to have the least relevance to their lives. Second, since these courses normally are taught in an atmosphere precluding the exercise of a student's critical intelligence, they tend to stultify the development of a critical intelligence in all areas of his academic work.[2] Third, it does violence both to the nature of theology and to that of philosophy.

Fortunately, many Catholic educators recognise these deficiencies —I am saying nothing new here. Yet I am not sure that they have even begun to arrive at a solution. One result, for instance, of the critique of college textbooks in philosophy and theology has been a number of attempts to develop better ones. Perhaps this is a worthy goal; but it still seems to presuppose that the best thing for students is a textbook—a systematic secondary source. One might suppose that the experience of the past would have shown that a careful reading of primary sources would be much more profitable and stimulating for students. But that has rarely been tried; hence, the tendency is to refine old methods instead of attempting to begin afresh.

Let us look now at the second part of my question. Will Catholic educators be able to learn profitably from the experience of the non-

---

[1] In this respect, the fact that a large proportion of those teaching theology are not trained theologians is a further handicap to stimulating student interest. Nor are matters helped much by the common requirement of Catholic colleges that all their students shall do a four-year, compulsory course of theology and philosophy—a provision which often exhausts the interest of many students, as well as placing a tremendous manpower burden on university administrators.

[2] It is very uncommon for critical essays to be assigned in either theology or philosophy courses; there is thus little opportunity for research or speculation. The inadequacy of many Catholic university libraries, the burdens of heavy teaching loads which leave little time to read essays, and a strong tradition of dependence upon lectures help to explain, if not to justify, this deficiency.

Catholic academic world? The main fruits of this experience seem to me to be the following: that a competition among conflicting points of view is productive of a vital intellectual ferment; that students do far better work and gain more from their education when they are stimulated by their teachers to be critical and independent in their judgments; that a sharp distinction between faculty research and teaching is untenable; that institutional traditions and practices should be re-examined constantly and immediately rejected when they no longer serve their original purposes. Other points could be mentioned, but these will suffice.

They all point, however, in one direction: the more open a university the more likely it is to be a creative, live and productive one. If pluralism is, in the first instance, a necessity in the secular university, it turns out as well to be an asset in the intellectual order. In theory, one might expect that the most creative university milieu would be one in which all faculty members shared the same ultimate goals and worked, in their diverse ways, to contribute to its achievement. This has been at least one important assumption, I would suppose, held by those committed to the denominational university. In practice, however, it seems to work out in just the opposite way: the greater the babel of tongues, the more dynamic the university. In American Catholic education today it is generally assumed that a new, more comprehensive vision of goals and ends is needed. Yet, oddly enough, those universities which seem to have the most impact on the American intellectual climate are those which are very scant on institutional vision but very strong in urging each individual to create his own vision—or get along without one at all, if he so chooses. The secular university, paradoxically enough, seems successful precisely because it cares so little for ultimate values and so much about creating here and now the concrete conditions conducive to personal freedom.

There is, of course, some basis for a Catholic rejoinder about the purported 'success' of the secular university. Even if one grants that they establish the intellectual trends of the nation, produce the most creative scholars, and turn out the future leaders of the body politic, what do they contribute to the spiritual welfare of mankind? What do they have to say about God? These are pertinent questions—but only if their intent is not to evade the problem of quality in Catholic education. Unfortunately, however, many American Catholic educators have an ambivalent attitude towards the most eminent American secular universities; they both envy them for their achievements and scorn them for their secularism. Yet it may well be the case that it is their secularism which helps to account for their achievements. Or, to put the matter more precisely, it may well be the case that the 'openness' of the non-Catholic university accounts for their achievements; and that it is not necessarily the case that to be 'open' is tantamount to being 'secular' in the pejorative sense of the term.[1]

Here we immediately encounter the central dilemma of contemporary American Catholic higher education. Can there be such a thing as an 'open' Catholic university? The non-Catholic universities have afforded a practical demonstration of the value of the 'open' university. They provide a neutral ground on which men of all persuasions can meet, talk and, normally, wrestle with one another over their personal versions of the truth. They are committed to nothing ultimate—except, of course, to the 'truth' (which is resolutely left undefined). But for the Catholic university, it appears, such neutrality would be impossible. By its very nature—as it is understood today—the Catholic university is committed to christian values. It is not, and cannot be, neutral about the Word of God revealed in Revelation nor about the Church's authoritative teachings on the meaning of that Revelation. On the contrary, the Catholic university has, at its very basis, the duty of attempting to incarnate this commitment in all its work: in its teaching role, in its scholarly role, and in its civic role.

There is, it seems indisputable, something magnificent and eminently logical about this conception of the Catholic university. But it also appears, inexorably, to rule out the kind of creative neutrality which accounts in great part for the achievements of the secular university. Moreover, when one has ruled out the possibility of a radical critique of one's fundamental commitments, does this not close the door on that spirit of untrammeled inquiry which marks the secular university? These are very difficult questions to answer. To be sure, it is quite possible to reply, and very correctly, that a commit-

[1] It is possible to say this while observing that, in practice, few non-Catholic universities provide adequate courses in theology or religion. For the most part, those universities which have active departments of religion are heavily weighted on the side of Protestant thought. Few provisions are made for Jewish or Catholic students in the ordinary curriculum (see note on *Theology and the new universities, infra, p. 188. Editor*).

ment to christian truth is not bondage but the essential condition of genuine freedom. But this is a theological reply; it points the way, but does not in itself provide a blueprint for the Catholic university. In practice, on occasion, the commitment is present, yet the sense of freedom which should accompany it is not. Why should there be this discrepancy?

The American Catholic experience provides some reasons. In the first place, lacking solid scholarly respectability, the Catholic university often appears to seek social respectability. It has neither the self-confidence nor the solidity of great age to chart its own course regardless of public opinion. Hence the initial impulse is always toward the safe approach to any challenge. Unsure of its own position in American life, it seeks to avoid controversy—to avoid those radical analyses of men and institutions, *mores* and fads, which must always be the work of intellectuals. More than that, the Catholic university seems to strive for impeccable respectability within the Catholic community as well. Until very recently at least, American Catholicism has been a conservative and timid Catholicism. This has meant that university administrators have been subject to Catholic pressures towards conformity and passivity; they have had to worry about upsetting the bishops, the parents of their students, their lay and clerical trustees and financial supporters. They have had neither the will nor the fortitude to chart their own course as they see fit. For the administration in particular, this has meant that care and caution have become the course of wisdom. Seek the truth—but do not alarm the bishop, do not unsettle the students, and do not become known as hotbeds of radicalism.

Secondly, the relationship between clergy and laity in the Catholic university has been an ambiguous one. In the non-Catholic university, there would be no special difficulty about faculty criticisms of university policy—these would be expected and tolerated, subject only to the ordinary dangers of criticising men in high places. But in the Catholic university, the faculty today is predominantly lay and the administrators (excepting a few rare cases) priests. In such circumstances, the faculty critic is in a doubly difficult position: a criticism of university policy is tantamount to lay insubordination towards the clergy. Even when that is not at all the intent of the lay faculty, and even when the administration itself tries not to see it in that light—even, that is, under the most charitable circumstances, it is difficult to keep the scent of anti-clericalism out of the air. Often enough, unfortunately, it is in fact distinctly present. The net result is often a sense of great strain on the part of both clergy and laity. Not only, it seems, do clerical administrators feel themselves forced to protect their educational authority, but they also feel constrained to protect their priestly dignity and status. Whether intended or not, the clerical administration of the university often appears to the lay teacher to be a closed and inviolate province; and the lay teacher often reacts with bitterness, ceaseless private gossiping and silent rage at his exclusion from those high decisions which affect the life of the university. It is needless to elaborate why this kind of atmosphere does not encourage the full flowering of christian freedom; and it is as debilitating to the clergy as to the laity.

Thirdly, the Catholic university in America has been infected with one of the great diseases of post-tridentine Catholicism: the belief that the Church is best served by a public image of perfect internal Catholic unity and harmony. The Church, of course, is one and unity is of its essence. Yet this does not mean that Catholics cannot or should not differ with one another, or that all problems have been solved perfectly once and for all. Yet this is the myth that the Catholic university is prone to perpetuate: by its dislike of controversy among its faculty members, by its presentation of a bland and pasteurised theology to its students, by its fear of the outspoken professor or the wayward, sceptical student.

Perhaps these three causes of a lack of full freedom in the American Catholic university are endemic to every Catholic university, regardless of national peculiarities. I cannot make any judgment on this point. But I am certain that in America they account for part of the failure of the Catholic university to achieve its own goals, and its failure to be taken with full seriousness by the non-Catholic community.

To say these things does not, however, answer the question whether there can be such a thing as an 'open' Catholic university. So far the experience of the American Catholic university in this respect is not encouraging; but the fact that this question is now beginning to be asked provides some ground for optimism. But, in the end, it will only be asked directly and forcefully when the Catholic university begins to gain poise, independence and self-confidence. If one takes the Church universal as one's model, then it seems apparent that the most difficult dilemmas of our age are being confronted. By this I do not mean that this confrontation is necessarily widespread; instead, I mean that one can find scattered men and scattered groups dealing boldly with particular issues.

The first task of the American Catholic university will be to create an atmosphere open to all that is taking place in the Church—the taking seriously of even the most danger-laden minority positions to be found among concerned Catholics. If even that much can be accomplished, the American Catholic university will be well on its way towards creating a readiness to respond with energy and creativity to those immense developments taking place outside the Church. To be 'open' is to be Catholic; it is only through the failures of Catholics—their fears, their uncertainties, their quest for respectability—that there now appears to be an inherent contradiction in the idea of an 'open' Catholic university.

5. The Teaching of Theology on the Continent and its Implications

Peter Fransen, S.J.

M y aim in this paper is to speak as simply and directly as I can about my personal experience of theological teaching on the continent; such an approach has the merit of first-hand contact with a living reality, even though my experience has necessarily been of limited extent.

On the continent there are roughly five different institutional forms for teaching theology: the state university, the ecclesiastical university or institute, the more private religious faculties, the diocesan seminaries and religious colleges, and the various higher institutes for the teaching of theology to laymen. In each case I should like to say something about their historical background (at least so far as it is needed for the understanding of their actual status) and to analyse their peculiar problems.

And first of all what we might call the state universities. In the Middle Ages a university, called a *studium generale*, was a real corporate body, similar to a guild with its apprentices and masters. After a long struggle the universities achieved their own juridical status and a real independence of the royal power, the local town authorities, or the diocesan jurisdiction of the bishop. *Universitas* was a name first given to an association of students—their masters joined them after a certain time—in Bologna and Paris during the thirteenth century. In Bologna the *universitas* was an association of foreign students who wanted to defend their rights against the particularist policy of the free town, Bologna, which cared only for its own citizens. In Paris the arts students moved outside the limits of the old city, to the *rive gauche*, to avoid the narrow-minded jurisdiction of the Chancellor of the Cathedral, who was until then the only person in Paris who could bestow the title of master, with the *licentia docendi*, the right to teach and to open a school. In this struggle for freedom they were defended from the very beginning by the Pope, which explains how the old universities, especially the university of Paris with its famous faculty of theology, came under the partial jurisdiction of the Pope. In 1231 Pope Gregory IX conceded to the *universitas magistrorum et scolarium parisiensium* the Bull *Parens scientiarum*, which became the fundamental charter for the medieval universities all over Europe.[1]

In the following centuries even with the growth of royal absolutism and the development of the central and centralising authority of the state, the universities all over Europe never completely lost their own academic authority. This situation was fundamentally changed after the French Revolution and the reorganisation of the state by Napoleon. In the Roman Catholic countries, where the anti-clerical reaction of the liberal parties was strongest, as in France, Belgium and Italy, the old universities, together with the new ones which were founded during the nineteenth century, were fully secularised, often anti-clerical, and came completely under the centralising authority of the state, as a special department of the Ministry of Education. The heavy financial burden of modern scientific research has subordinated the universities to the state, which alone has the financial power to support them.

The separation of state and Church led to the abolition of faculties of theology in these universities, and the subject was no longer considered as one which should be taught there. However, this was not the case in the northern Protestant countries, as in the Netherlands and Scandinavia, where either the state, or the city, as at Amsterdam, maintained a faculty of theology in their university.

Furthermore, in the German-speaking countries the universities not only maintained a faculty of theology—and in the *Länder* with mixed religion even a double faculty, one for Lutheran, another for Roman Catholic theology—but they kept something of the old tradition of academic freedom, at least in Germany. In Austria the old centralising tradition of the Vienna administration deprived the universities of a great part of their academic autonomy. This was not

---

[1] H. Rashdall, *The Universities of Europe in the Middle Ages*, Oxford, 1893, 3 vol. Christiane Thouzellier, 'L'enseignement et les universités', in: *Histoire de l'Eglise*, Vol. 13, 'Le mouvement doctrinal du IXe au XIVe siècle', Paris, 1951, II, chap. IV, pp. 341–86.

the case in Germany, where the ideas of Wilhelm von Humboldt, who founded the university of Berlin and reformed that of Breslau in 1810, were strongly in favour of an autonomous and corporate body of scholars.[1] Only Germany has kept something of the old academic freedom of the Middle Ages in the state universities, not only for university professors, a title which in Germany is highly esteemed socially, but also for the students. In Germany and Austria the students are allowed within certain limits to travel from one university to another, where they can be matriculated for one or more semesters. This personal choice is naturally determined by the reputation of the professor, or of the university where they choose to stay for a few months. This system retains another aspect of the old tradition, in which each student selected one of the professors, who then became his personal guide, his master and tutor, and even his judge.

These faculties of theology are integrated into the general structure of the local university with its own traditions and customs. They retain a certain independence of the local diocesan jurisdiction and even of papal authority, at least in not being controlled by the Congregation for Seminaries and Studies, and therefore are not obliged to follow the regulations for ecclesiastical studies as defined by Pius XI in the Apostolic Constitution *Deus Scientiarum Dominus*, published on 24 May 1931, together with the Ordinations of the Congregation for the Seminaries and Studies, of 12 June in the same year. They possess their own academic traditions concerning the direction of studies, the organisation of lectures, and all the various academic exercises and examinations. They are influenced by the German university tradition of the nineteenth century. The ordinary professor expounds a particular topic he has chosen himself as subject for the semester. The teaching of the subject as a whole is often left to his assistant. There are many possibilities for personal discussion and work in the so-called seminars, which frequently possess their own library and rooms.

Because in previous centuries no laymen would ever have dreamed of reading theology, these faculties were only open to clerics, that is, to future priests, who frequently had to follow a few years of normal ecclesiastical training in the various diocesan or interdiocesan seminaries, before entering a university. I was told that many German

[1] W. von Humboldt, *Gesammelte Schriften*, vol. 10, Berlin, 1903.

students, disliking the atmosphere of a seminary, themselves organise their own theological studies in the particular faculties they favour, and present themselves to a bishop to be ordained at the end of their studies. This became possible when many faculties decided to accept lay students, men and women, and adapted their conditions for matriculation to the modern situation. In a few of them they have begun to have laymen as professors of theology—a new situation in the western Roman Catholic Church. The well-known faculty of theology at Paris has always been reserved for clerics, secular and regular. In Germany it is now possible to meet a woman or a married man who is a doctor of canon law or biblical theology. This is an important development which, although still rather limited, could have a real influence on the development of theological studies as a whole. Further development seems to be limited by the fact that the salary of a professor of theology, intended for a cleric leading a celibate life, is insufficient to maintain a family; and it would seem therefore more of a social and financial handicap than any other which prevents laymen from following this scholarly vocation.

The academic standing of these faculties depends of course on their own tradition, and at the same time on the amount of money available for inviting outstanding professors from other universities to teach in their own. I was told in Vienna that as soon as a professor became famous he was immediately snatched up by the University of Munich, which can offer him a higher salary.

We have seen how the German universities and faculties of theology have retained something of the mobility, the academic autonomy and freedom which made our universities in the Middle Ages into centres of culture and scholarship. I want to emphasise the importance of a certain academic freedom for the development of studies, because it seems to be something our time most needs. Scholarly activity, even in theology, which requires a very good library, is becoming so expensive that the need for concentration and organisation makes us forget the more important need for freedom of thought and work.

Discussion of the faculty of theology at Innsbruck in Austria will allow me to pass from the state university possessing a faculty of theology of its own to the various kinds of ecclesiastical university and faculty founded by the Church. In as much as they are independent of the state and not subject to the Ministry of Education, they are often called 'free universities'.

Innsbruck is rather a hybrid form of theological faculty, which at the same time belongs to the state and follows the Ordinations of the Congregation for Seminaries and Studies. It is the largest and most international faculty in the German-speaking world, comprising this year five hundred and twenty students, where Munich and Munster have about four hundred students each.

Since, on the continent, the modern state secularised the older universities, such as the Sorbonne, abolishing the faculty of theology, the Church has had to found and build new universities and institutes for higher religious education. Sometimes this could be done in collaboration with the state, as at Louvain in Belgium and at Nijmegen in the Netherlands. But where this was impossible, as in France, because of the very strong anti-clerical feeling of the government at the beginning of this century, the Church was forced to found various 'Catholic Institutes', as they are called in France, using the money of the laity. The lack of money is their principal weakness.

The Belgian and Dutch solution seems the best, wherever it is practicable. The teaching of theology does not need the very expensive scientific apparatus, the laboratories, the institutes for scientific research, the medical clinics, necessary to every modern university. But I am convinced that no real theological work can be done without a very good library, supplemented when possible by further specialist libraries, as in the case of the German seminar libraries. I am sure that theology is more akin to the positive sciences than to speculative philosophy.[1] Purely speculative theology leads very easily to a closed system of thought full of pointless discussions, and becomes a boring caricature of itself when systematised in a handbook of theology.

Theology is the systematically expressed knowledge of the divine revelation itself, and the first task of any theologian is therefore to listen to the Word of God. This Word of God has to be found principally in the bible. Therefore theology is impossible without a sound and extensive knowledge of exegesis and of biblical theology. The Roman Catholic also has the certainty of hearing this Word of God further expressed and witnessed to in the living teaching of the Church. This witness is not restricted to the authoritative teaching of the hierarchy in the Councils, whether ecumenical or local, or in

[1] P. Fransen, *Divine Grace and Man*, New York: Desclee, 1962, 18–40, and 'Three Ways of Dogmatic Thought', *The Heythrop Journal*, 4 (1962) 3–24.

papal and episcopal documents, it is also to be heard in the voice of
the whole Church in communion with the episcopate and the see of
Rome, that is in the teaching of theologians and of the living Church
all over the *Catholica*, as St Augustine called it.

If this is true, the study of theology cannot be limited to one part
of the Church. From this it follows that a minimal reading knowledge
of the most important ancient and modern languages is absolutely
demanded of a good professor of theology, and as far as possible of
a good student in theology. This also means that a good theological
library has to contain the best works and collections, not only of its
own country, but of every country where the theological work of
reflection and study is carried on. Every year this becomes more
difficult. Up to the First World War, one could be content with the
theological publications and reviews which were published in German
and French, the English language being rather poor in Catholic
studies. But nowadays there are very good collections of the biblical
and scholastic sources, and real theological work in England and in
both Americas, and within a few decades we may expect more publications from Asia and Africa. It is impossible for one man to keep
in touch with all the good articles and books which are published
nowadays. On the other hand we should not forget the fundamental
principle that only the *Catholica*, that is the whole Church, is in
infallible possession of the truth. Every theological school, every
theologian who cuts himself off from the *Catholica*, even if merely
because he is only interested in what is said in his own country, makes
himself more vulnerable to any infection of schism and heresy. He
has left the healthy and secure communion with the whole Church.
This was very clear during the Council, where those bishops who
felt a real difficulty in understanding the meaning of what was happening were those who had kept themselves more or less isolated
from the living communion of the Church. But if this is so, a theologian's only course is to specialise and collaborate with his fellow
theologians of the same country or faculty. Theology has become a
science that cannot be practised without a real collaboration with
other theologians, each specialising in a certain part of theology as a
whole.

There is a final reason for demanding a large and well-equipped
library: the ecumenical dimension in the Churches, which is really
the call of God in our times. We need to have at our disposal at least

the fundamental works of Anglican, Lutheran and Presbyterian theology. If it is true that these Churches have kept some part of the Catholic truth through the guidance of the Holy Spirit, wherever we wish to enter into a real dialogue with them we have to listen to what they have to say. Their objections to our Roman Catholic theology are not obstacles we have to break down with apologetical arguments, but real christian objections which force us to reflect and consider whether we have not limited or obscured the fullness of the christian message through our all too human and biased approach.

If all this is true, as I believe it to be, then any theological faculty badly needs a good library to work with. It comes before everything else, before good buildings and spacious classrooms, before any other aspect of organisation and arrangement of the matters of study. I have visited many faculties and ecclesiastical seminaries all over the world, and very often been confronted with the dangers of a poor library. Theology becomes stagnant and ceases to be real thought: in Newman's words, there is 'no exercise of the intellect. No, the system goes on by the tradition of the intellect of former times.'[1] As soon as all that is expected of the students, and probably of the professors as well, is to repeat what is written in a classical handbook, then theology, as a living form of witness to faith, is dead!

This realisation of the importance of a large library and the necessity of extensive bibliographical equipment is one of the characteristics of the University of Louvain, and of the various religious houses in and about the town that are influenced by the same climate of ideas. The Louvain Library was completely destroyed by fire, twice in a lifetime, at the beginning of each World War; but within a few years it was reconstructed regardless of cost. A good library is as vital for a faculty of theology as are clinics and laboratories for a faculty of medicine.

Louvain has always distrusted pure speculative theology, and has applied itself to the positive study of the bible, the Fathers and the medieval scholastics. This explains its attitude in matters of theological study. How was this made possible? The University of Louvain is a free university and stays under the direct jurisdiction of the Belgian hierarchy. This seems more satisfactory than being under a single local bishop. It was typical of the universities of the Middle

[1] Wilfrid Ward, *The Life of John Henry Cardinal Newman*, London, 1913, I, 588.

Ages that the popes frequently detached the university from the authority of the local bishop to commit it to the charge of one or more bishops, who were not implicated in the local and all too parochial problems of a particular town or diocese, or to a personal representative of the Holy See, who was then, as in Bologna, called the Chancellor. Where the local bishop might be misled by a too narrow-minded preoccupation with local problems, there is less danger where a body of bishops, responsible for the religious well-being of a whole people, allows for the possibility of correcting the limitations of one through the complementary qualities of the others. This principle was considered from different sides during the Council, whenever the question arose of introducing episcopal conferences into the government of the Church.

Though the university of Louvain stays under the immediate jurisdiction of the Belgian bishops, its academic degrees are acknowledged by the state, and have the same value as the diplomas of the state universities of Ghent and Liège. The faculty of theology is, however, purely ecclesiastical, because the Belgian government does not directly acknowledge as such any licentiate or doctorate in theology. Therefore this faculty is also subject to the jurisdiction of the Roman Congregation for Seminaries and Studies. It is an ecclesiastical faculty. At the same time the faculty of theology has kept a certain independence and autonomy in regard to the regulations of the Roman Curia, based on its ancient tradition.

The Belgian bishops not only tolerate, but are fully ready to defend the traditions of the university and its academic autonomy, and to permit considerable freedom of thought and discussion. The present situation of Catholicism in Belgium, and especially the excellent training of the clerics in the various diocesan seminaries, each of which publishes a theological review, known even outside Belgium, would not have been brought about without the deeper influence of the university and its faculty of theology. Most of the seminary professors were trained at the university, and many professors in the university started their teaching in the seminary.

This was made possible through the substantial financial support of the laity, but also through the important aid given by various public authorities and institutes—including the state—in Belgium and abroad; and the symbol of this national and international effort is the library, twice destroyed but now fully restored. Louvain is the sole university of the Roman Catholic Church to remain after the Reformation and the French Revolution out of the many founded on the continent during the Middle Ages.

Its old traditions, its intellectual independence, its real autonomy, its numerous institutes for research and specialised studies have prevented it from becoming a closed ghetto, which too many Roman Catholic institutes for higher learning have turned into during the post-tridentine period. There are a few Anglican and Orthodox students attending the lectures, and professors of various denominations are invited to speak to the students in the faculty of theology.

The faculty is not however open for laymen. It would be difficult for them because of the old Erasmian tradition which obliges the students to know Hebrew, Greek, and Latin.[1] We shall see how the university tried to solve this problem in speaking later on of the special institutes for laymen.

The question arises whether a purely Catholic, that is denominational, university is fully adapted to our modern mixed society; whether there is not a certain danger of inbreeding and bigotry. I do not think that this is so with the professors, who collaborate on the scholarly level with other universities, without any feeling of inferiority. There is of course a serious danger for the students. Though they are too numerous to feel enclosed and preserved, they sometimes miss the necessary and strengthening confrontation with different ways of life and opposing creeds. Also there are too many priests and nuns in the streets and in the lecture-rooms; and this very easily provokes an anticlerical reaction. Although the lay professors have the same rights as the priests and canons, and participate in the direction of the university, it is possible that if the laity were allowed a greater part in the conduct of affairs it would improve the situation. But one cannot say that Louvain has become a ghetto university; on the contrary. The only real drawback I met was that, because Catholicism is the normal climate of the university, it is too easy for students to suffer from religious conformism, beginning as most do with the disadvantage of living in a country where the Catholic way of life is simply accepted as obvious. A purely traditional religion becomes very superficial, and I am aware that too many students have no more than this superficial coating of religion. Recently a

[1] This year, for the first time, however, a woman has taken her degree in Canon Law.

serious effort has been made to foster a deeper spirituality in a town where clerics, convents and religion might become mere matters of course. But this is not a problem peculiar to Louvain, it is a problem for the whole country, where too many priests and laymen continue to live under the illusion of being in a purely Catholic country. This might explain the real paradox of Catholic Belgium, that it is simultaneously very progressive, open-minded and active at the level of theological thought, and very conservative, old-fashioned and narrow so far as the life and practice of the Church are concerned.

This progressive attitude in theological thought would have been impossible without the collaboration of the state, and the laymen and bishops who built and developed this university with great generosity, and with real understanding of the fundamental importance of academic freedom for any scientific progress, most of all in matters of theology. It is true that in Roman Catholicism theology is also taught in the name of the hierarchy, the supreme judge in matters of faith, and therefore a certain control is inevitable. But where this authority becomes too strict, normally because of over-anxiety, there is no opportunity for real discussion and thought. The human intellect does not work as a separate entity, in a closed space, but in and through the living commitment of genuine dialogue. Without dialogue, and therefore without a fair chance for discussion, there is no way left to bring together different points of view. Any progress of thought is killed before it starts.

We shall have to remember this principle as we go on to consider the third and fourth forms of ecclesiastical teaching—those concerned with the theological training of the clergy, though this touches our subject only indirectly. Since the beginning of monasticism in western Europe the religious orders have always possessed their own houses for study, either in the abbeys themselves, or, with more recent orders, in training colleges.

A few of them were recognised as pontifical faculties by the Congregation for Seminaries and Studies, and possess the right of giving academic degrees, whose value, so far, has been purely ecclesiastical: they merely enable the new doctor of theology to teach in any seminary within the Church. In many countries, however, such degrees are considered equal to the degrees of a public university, and in Holland they were quite recently acknowledged by law. To obtain the full rights of a faculty such colleges have to possess a properly

D

equipped library, and an ample body of professors who can lay claim to a sufficient amount of serious publication, especially in the philosophical and theological reviews they publish. During the last two pontificates the Roman Congregation has been more restrictive in granting this academic status than before, which is a good thing.

These faculties are, with certain limits, related to the various Institutes for higher teaching in Rome, especially to the four Pontifical Universities of Rome, the Gregorian, the Lateran, the Propaganda Fide, and quite recently the Angelicum of the Dominican order. They often interchange their professors. Students who have started in one of them can proceed to Rome to complete their studies without further examination. They also mutually recognise each other's degrees.

The Council of Trent, however, definitely favoured the erection of diocesan seminaries in which the secular clergy were to be prepared for their ministry. According to canon law they must have a roughly common curriculum of studies: two years of philosophy and four years of theology, to which quite recently was added a fifth year of pastoral and practical training for the ministry.

Such philosophical and theological colleges and seminaries are very different in theological standing and authority, for various reasons of which I only wish to analyse a few. The solid religious training of future priests is, of course, of vital importance for the whole Church. We have not yet learned what the Council is to decide on this important matter, but nowadays there is a growing feeling of dissatisfaction, a general belief that the whole conception of such religious training has to be seriously reconsidered and reformed. This opinion is very common amongst the more intellectual laity, who disapprove of the training which their priests received before their ordination.

In many countries laymen, and priests too for that matter, complain that seminaries are too sharply cut off from the realities of this world. They have developed into religious hot-houses where young clerics get acquainted with a lifeless theology and initiated in an artificial spirituality, leaving them at the end of their studies quite unprepared for the responsibilities of their ministry in this world. It is not an easy problem to solve. There is no doubt a real need for silence, prayer, recollection and concentration for seminarians, as yet without much experience, who will have to take on much greater responsibility than in former times. The urgent need for a well-trained clergy is greater than ever.

But such problems lie outside the limits of this symposium. Normally no layman is accepted in these houses of study, which are specifically organised to prepare clerics for their vocation. I can only repeat what I have said before. There is no real theology without a good library, without professors who are prepared to think for themselves and not simply to read from a handbook, without students who try to understand what they are taught, and therefore are freely allowed to discuss the subjects of their studies and to work personally on the questions that confront them.

One of the dangers of these religious houses of study is that they quite frequently get superiors who were appointed because of either their administrative capacity or their personal piety. Such characteristics are not of course to be despised in themselves, but the kind of man who has them often seems to be predisposed to distrust any form of serious study at all. He is much more preoccupied with order and discipline, and above all with safety and security, so that he gets very suspicious of any personal initiative, either amongst the professors or the students. 'To be at ease, is to be unsafe,' said Newman. Within certain limits one could say of theology: To be safe is to be dead! This is not a matter of disturbing young people as yet unable to form a balanced and adult judgment, and very prone to fall for anything new whatever it may be, but there is one kind of security in theology which means the end of any serious personal religious thought. I have met young priests in Germany whose only decision at the end of their studies was never more to open any book of theology. We all agree, I am sure, that this is not the proper end of a theological training.

But this attitude is not only to be found in religious houses of study. It is one of the most tragic problems the Roman Catholic Church is confronted with. From the time of the Reformation until now, she has had to concentrate so much on defending herself against the growing antagonism of liberals, marxists and communists, that the attitude of self-defence has become almost second nature. She grew into a religious ghetto, and built high and massive walls about herself for the protection of the faithful. Typical of this attitude is the title of Cardinal Ottaviani's book on the Church: *Il Baluardo*, The Bulwark. The walls of a fortress do not make very good pulpits; they are only good for shooting and fighting from.

Walls are generally less a symbol of strength than of anxiety, and anxiety was never productive, certainly not of thought and action. Anxiety in matters of theology means the end of any genuine theology. The fashionable word in America nowadays is 'relax'. I even heard a woman shout to her dog in the Bronx Zoo: 'Bobby, relax!' I was told that an Anglican paper headed its review of our group's previous publication *Problems of Authority*, with the splendid words: 'Roman Catholics relax!'[1] If ever there were a need for relaxing, it is now. The greatest gift of providence for our times was to give us the so-called 'Interim Pope', who calmly affirmed at the beginning of the Council: 'We feel we must disagree with those prophets of gloom, who are always forecasting disaster, as though the end of the world was at hand. . . .' And further down in his opening address Pope John repeats his confidence in man, even outside the Church:

> They (that is the men of our age) are ever more deeply convinced of the paramount dignity of the human person and of his perfectioning, as well as the duties that that implies. Even more important, experience has taught men that violence inflicted on others, the might of arms and political domination, are of no help at all in finding a happy solution to the grave problems which afflict them. That being so, the Catholic Church, raising the torch of religious truth by means of this Ecumenical Council, desires to show herself to be the loving mother of all, benign, patient, full of mercy and goodness towards the children separated from her. To the human race, oppressed by so many difficulties, she says, like Peter of old to the poor man who begged alms from him: 'Silver and gold are not mine to give, I give thee what I can. In the name of Jesus Christ of Nazareth, rise up and walk' (Acts 3: 6).[2]

It is an indication of the changing climate within the Church that when Pius IX announced the opening of the first Vatican Council, he wrote about 'the need for the Church to cope with the evils of the time'. The smiling Pope whom God gave his Church in our time spoke by contrast of the Church's obligation to adapt herself to the real situation of the age, with great confidence in the ways of God's providence and the goodwill of mankind, within and outside the Church. If we look for the chief result of this Council, which so far has formulated only the liturgical decree, there is no doubt what it is: the Church has rediscovered what it means to share in the freedom of the children of God. There is a new wind of freedom, joy

---

[1] *The Guardian*, 7 March 1962. [Ed.]
[2] *The Tablet*, 20 October 1962, pp. 998 and 999.

and confidence blowing within the Church. The Church is indeed relaxing, and this is God's doing; yet for people still retaining the former mentality whom I met in Rome during the last months of 1962, this Council is still 'sheer madness' and 'greatly endangers the Church'.

It is in this new climate that we have to discuss the last institutional form for the teaching of theology, which is developing rapidly across the continent in answer to the growing need of the laity to be instructed in their religion. The times when laymen and women left the religious thinking to their bishops and priests are happily over. No Roman Monsignor would dare any more to write as did Mgr Talbot in the time of Newman that the province of the laity is 'to hunt, to shoot, to entertain!' With his uncanny gift for prophecy, Newman saw what would arise in our times from this passive and immature attitude, from this *fides implicita* in the word of the Church: 'in the educated classes (it) will terminate in indifference, and in the poorer in superstition'.[1] We have only to look at Italian Catholicism to see how right Newman was, and how dangerous this lack of adult religious knowledge and responsibility is for the Church. In many countries of the continent the laity wants an adult knowledge of their religion, and the responsibility which goes with it. This is the origin of a multitude of institutes, schools, evening classes, and series of lectures, which are now being organised all over western and central Europe for the religious needs of the laity, together with parallel courses for religious who are not prepared for the priesthood, the brothers and most of all the nuns, especially those who are teaching religion.

It is impossible for me to describe all the forms this movement for adult religious knowledge has brought into being. Since it originated quite recently, every country, every diocese or town tries to solve the problem according to the immediate needs and opportunities they are discovering. I would like to outline a few practical solutions, which are more suggestive than others, and probably have a certain analogy with what you are planning in this country. The problem is complex. Up to now I have only mentioned the need for adult instruction in their religion for people inside the Church. But if the Church is not to be a bulwark, but rather the light on the hilltop, her

[1] J. H. Newman, *On Consulting the Faithful in Matters of Doctrine*, edited by John Coulson, London, 1961, p. 106.

witness to the truth must be to everybody. The very nature of the Church is to be missionary, or which is the better word, apostolic, and that in a society which no longer accepts the Church as the obvious depository of truth and authority. Too often we think that the Church's only mission is to keep what is left, and not first of all to gain what was lost or never belonged to her.

It is one of the fundamental themes of the revolution which is happening on the continent that we live in a mixed society, that in this world we have unavoidably to live in a diaspora situation, as was normal in the first four centuries of the Church. Another way of putting this same idea is that the Constantinian times, when the Church was accepted as the supreme authority in a feudally organised society, are over. We are now living in a new society where there is not only a clear separation between Church and state, but where the Church as such has less and less juridically and institutionally founded authority. Her only authority is the sincerity of her witness, the inner truth of her word, what Pope John called in his opening address to the Council, 'the radiating light of the truth'.[1] That is her only weapon, the only one that Christ himself has used.

The first type of institution for teaching religion that I want to mention was started by Romano Guardini in the pre-war university of Berlin, a city where Catholics constitute only a small minority of 12 per cent, a university where there is no faculty of theology at all, and no great sympathy for Catholic thought. This course was finally abolished by the Nazis. Romano started again immediately after the war, but now in Munich, a largely Catholic city, with a very large student population of mixed faith and sympathies. The idea has now extended to most German universities and forms an integral part of the normal academic framework. It has been given the title of *Christliche Weltanschauung*, and includes the historical, psychological, philosophical and theological aspects of the Christian faith. This course is open to the students of all faculties. I am told that something similar was founded at the university of Geneva and entrusted to a Roman Catholic priest, l'abbé Chavaz. The university of Innsbruck also has a chair of christian philosophy, entrusted to Prof. Marlet, a Dutch philosopher and specialist in Calvinistic philosophy; and lectures are open to all the students of the university, of whom only a majority are Catholic. The same is found in Louvain, although

[1] *The Tablet*, loc. cit., pp. 999–1000.

the idea has been modified because the university is normally attended only by Roman Catholic students. There every faculty has its own professor of religion and morals, and the courses are compulsory—this is not such a good idea. The advantage of the course in the other universities is that it is free, and therefore it must either be very good, or it is not worthwhile attending. If the professor cannot get beyond formal textbook theology, and remains indifferent to the real questions of our times, he will have a chair but no students. Therefore the academic authorities, in collaboration with the bishops, can only appoint the very best. When Jean Guitton was invited from Montpellier to the Sorbonne he was given a similar position, although, so far as I know, no special new chair was created. In France the very strong anti-clerical bias of the Ministry of Education, which is the top academic authority, makes the German solution almost impossible. It has only been found possible at the university of Strasbourg in Alsace-Lorraine, where the French Government, after the return of those Provinces to France, had to respect the agreement concluded between Bismarck and Leo XIII in matters of education. Therefore there are only two faculties of theology in French state-controlled educational establishments, both in Strasbourg, one Roman Catholic and the other Protestant. The French have to look for other solutions, which they achieve by Catholic Institutes in which laymen are accepted, and through private lectures and conferences, given in para-university student organisations.

This brings us to a second type for the higher teaching of religion, not this time bound in any way to an existing university. I shall only consider those institutions specifically intended for non-Catholics, or at least where Catholics are in a minority. After the war the Willibrord organisation in Holland, and many other smaller groups started what they call the 'Open Door' movement, in which Catholic philosophy and theology were taught as part of a very intense ecumenical dialogue with the Protestant Churches of Holland on the one hand, and with the so-called 'humanist' movement on the other. This latter is very active in Holland, and is seeking to obtain from the government all the institutional advantages possessed by the Churches. A similar outlook is of course to be found in France, especially, as I have indicated, in the state universities, and particularly among the student organisations.

In Holland two religious societies for women, the 'Women of

Bethany' and the 'Women of the Grail', both founded by a well-known Jesuit, Fr Van Ginniken, have both specialised in similar work, and are now active in different parts of the world. These women receive a fairly rigorous religious and theological training. Something similar can be found in those parts of Germany where the Catholics are in a minority. Many parishes have one or more *Seelsorge-helferinnen*, women who are responsible for parochial work amongst women and children of the parish. They could be called a kind of woman curate, though without sacramental ordination, and they receive a substantial theological training of three to four years in a special college.

As I have previously emphasised, the teaching of theology to lay-men is necessarily linked with the problem of preparing well-trained men and women to be entrusted with the teaching of religion. The two aspects of the problem cannot be separated. They are linked together socially and economically, since only those who can afford to study theology for any length of time will later be able to make a living from it. But in the nature of things there is bound to be mutual development, for now that the task is too heavy for clerics to cope with, this part of their job will more and more be taken over by trained lay people, who in turn will produce a better informed adult community, educated properly from childhood.

This enables us to understand the development of a third type of institutional training for laymen, which is now developing at the university of Louvain in what is called the 'Higher Institute for Religious Knowledge'. It was founded during the war in 1942 and at first intended to be a means of giving a broader and deeper religious instruction for lay students at the university itself. This intention, along lines normal for the development of the laity on the continent, was however modified by force of circumstances. In 1956 the Belgian bishops promoted a new development, asking for a special training programme for nuns and brothers who were to teach religion in the schools. In 1958, after the bitter fight for the free Catholic schools was over, with the new school law and the new agreement between the Government, the three leading political parties of Parliament, and the Church, the programme was adapted for training lay people who wished to become teachers of religion in the state or private primary and secondary schools, according to the provisions of the law. In 1959 a full university licentiate degree was created, with a full-time programme of studies over four years. These lectures can also be followed voluntarily by students, mostly in fact religious brothers or nuns, who want to perfect their religious knowledge. The full-time licentiate is in practice only followed by persons who have decided to become teachers of religion. The Institute now has its own building, secretariate, and—most essential of all—a good library of about 2,000 books with many reviews, and rooms for seminars. Quite recently a special 'Centre for Catechetical Research' was added, with a two-year supplementary programme, open to anyone holding a licentiate in theology (these will be priests) and to anyone from the Institute (including therefore laymen).

This development was determined by the special situation in Belgium, the agreement between the government and the Church, and the urgent need for capable graduate teachers of religion for the fast-growing number of primary and secondary schools. This Institute has practically developed into a second faculty of theology, and I think it quite possible that the same circumstances will lead to the creation of a special doctorate in theology for laymen and religious who are not priests. There are some substantial differences in method and aim between an institute and a university. There is no need for the strict scholarship of the university tradition. At the institute students need neither Hebrew nor Greek, and most of them have only a very elementary acquaintance with Latin. This lack of linguistic knowledge makes it impossible to go in for exhaustive exegetical, patristic and scholastic historical studies. The general approach is more pastoral and catechetical, although they require adequate knowledge of the Old and the New Testaments and the doctrines of the Councils. They are taught by professors of the faculty of theology and many others specially appointed in this capacity.

There are on the continent many further ways of teaching theology to laymen, but these are outside the purpose of this symposium, which is to investigate the opportunities presented by the framework of an existing university.

I should now like to draw a few conclusions, the first of which is self-evident: *there is no absolute standard Roman Catholic solution*, although inside the Roman Catholic Church there is a tendency to affirm the contrary. This can only be done by ignoring the facts of history, and what is worse the facts outside one's own country. This typical piece of 'parochial' blindness, assumes that one's own life and tradition are the best, and therefore *the* standard Roman Catholic solution; whereas the ideal solution is by no means an abstract one, based on so-called eternal principles, but is instead the one most adapted to the real situation of a particular country. The 'eternal' principles involved in our solution are very few and, for that matter, quite flexible.

The academic institutions we have discussed in the course of this paper are different in almost every country, because they remain necessarily related to the historical, cultural, psychological and religious situation of that particular country and nation. One of the most serious objections to that academic system which is imposed upon all ecclesiastical faculties all over the world by the Congregation for Seminaries and Studies is its uniformity, inflexibility, and curial centralisation. The whole system is firmly founded on the Italian situation and mentality, which is, so far as clerics are concerned, a very particular one.

If this is true, although you may look for suggestion and inspiration on the continent, you have ultimately to find your own English solution. Yet this living contact with the other parts of the Church is so important that I am indeed concerned about a certain lack of communication with other parts of the Church, which I have discovered amongst English-speaking Catholics, either in my various visits to these countries, or during the first Session of the Council. You will not mind my being outspoken, because you know I am speaking as a friend, and as a man who is convinced of the importance of the English-speaking part of the Church at this time in its history. I was deeply sorry to see how in Rome during the first Session of the Council the English-speaking peoples had by no means that influence they possess in other fields, even in matters of religion outside the Catholic Church, as at the World Council of Churches. This 'religious isolationism' seems especially to distinguish Catholics from the other religious bodies of the English-speaking world. One could say that on the whole—there were of course splendid exceptions—the English-speaking part of the Church, either from this country, or from America or the countries of the Commonwealth, was the least prepared for the Council, and the slowest to enter into the movement of thought which revealed itself during the last discussions there. As I have already pointed out, this is a very dangerous attitude, because it endangers our living communion with the whole Church, and at the same time our sense of Catholicity.

But that is your problem. In planning this Symposium you were seeking how to provide the laity of this country with a genuine opportunity for getting an adult knowledge of their religion; and I will restrict myself to those aspects of religious maturity which are related to knowledge and education in religion.

A childish knowledge as such is always characterised by the fact that it considers only extremes, and divides up reality very sharply into black and white, evil and good. A child is incapable of understanding, even of accepting the many and inevitable shades in human life, where goodness and sin grow together in the very complex mixture of our common humanity. At the same time and for the same reasons a child feels unable to distinguish between what is central in any human value-system, as for instance in a given religion, and what is more peripheral, or purely accidental, or even futile.

This distinction is so extremely important for the life of the Church at this moment of her history that Pope John himself particularly insisted upon it. It was one of his most fruitful ideas. Three times, first at the opening of the Council, then at the conclusion of the first Session on 6 December 1962, and just before Christmas in his talk to the cardinals of the Curia, he repeated the same sentences, with no fear of being considered repetitive, because it seems so difficult for many bishops and theologians to understand his point of view:

> The salient point of this Council is not, therefore, a discussion of one article or another of the fundamental doctrine of the Church, which has repeatedly been taught by the Fathers and the ancient and modern theologians, and which is presumed to be well known and familiar to all.
> For this a Council was not necessary. But from the renewed, serene and tranquil adhesion to all teaching of the Church in its entirety and preciseness, as it still shines forth in the acts of the Council of Trent and the First Vatican Council, the Christian, Catholic and apostolic spirit of the whole world expects a step forward towards a doctrinal penetration and a formation of consciences, in faithful and perfect conformity to the authentic doctrine, which however should be studied and expounded through the methods of research and through the literary forms of modern thought. One thing is the substance of the ancient doctrine of the *depositum fidei*, and another is the way in which it is presented: and it is this that must be taken into great consideration, with patience if

necessary, everything being measured in the forms and proportions of a *magisterium* which is prevalently pastoral in character.[1]

Now our need is to learn to distinguish between the substance of our faith and its different formulations as they are found in the Church. This knowledge, which is precisely an adult one, will enable us to make those pastoral adaptations in the life of the Church which will suit our modern situation and problems. If it is hard for the bishops and their theologians and canonists to enter fully into the proper object of the Council, which is the real adaptation of the Church to the needs of the times, unless they have this mature insight into the substance of the faith contrasted with the different expressions of it; we must see that it is equally hard for the Church as a whole to accept and to understand fully and freely the decisions of the Council, until they too share this maturity. The so-called 'opposition' in the Council was not so much prompted by extreme conservatism as by anxiety about their people from bishops who were persuaded that their flock would be disturbed by the reform of the Church. That Evelyn Waugh wrote the article he did in *The Spectator* of 26 November 1962 (*The Same Again, Please*) was because he was unable to understand the real motives of the Council in working on the reform of the liturgy, unable to understand the difference between the institution of Christ and the various liturgical expressions and embodiments which this sacramental 'substance' happened to receive in the Church during the course of her history. In such a situation the most 'comfortable' answer is not to change at all—but this is the negation of all reform.

There is no adult knowledge of religion when everything is put on the same level: in the bible, the central truth of original sin and the apple of Eve; the fundamental fact of Incarnation and the story of the three Magi; in matters of faith and dogma, the fundamental doctrine of grace as a redeeming act of love of God through Christ in the Holy Spirit, and the many theological definitions of various kinds of actual grace; in Church life, the vital reality of the eucharist and the laws about the eucharistic fast; the primacy of the Pope as instituted by Christ and the different juridical structures in which this primacy has found its concrete and historically adapted expression, which it will continue to find until the end of time. The primacy and the episcopacy are one, but the concrete canonical forms

[1] *The Tablet*, loc. cit., p. 999.

in which this essential structure of the Church can be expressed are many and various.

If you are looking for a real emancipation of the English Catholic laity at the level of religious knowledge, you have, it seems to me, to found the whole structure of your new educational system on this conviction.

You must avoid enclosing yourselves and the doctrine you present to your students in any particular system, even in that of Thomism.[1] Thomas never intended to preach a new gospel, but to give an interpretation of the gospel in terms that could be understood in his own day. Therefore he was at one time condemned in Paris and in Oxford, and suspected by his own Order. If he were alive today he would never think of working on Aristotle, but on Sartre, Heidegger, Kierkegaard, Karl Barth, and Wittgenstein.

Therefore I think that most of the classical textbooks of theology existing in the English language, and in other languages too, are dangerous, and inadvisable for your purpose, because they are inclined to expound and defend only one system of thought; and what is even more dangerous, they do so in that kind of popularised simplification which is still thought necessary for educational purposes, though as a matter of fact it only encourages intellectual laziness. A priest or a layman who has only learned a few simplified formulas by heart, and never thought personally about them, is a real danger to the Church.

As I have suggested, religious teaching ought to remain in living contact with the whole Church. This means that your teaching should first of all be *biblical*, in communion with the witness of the founding Church and at the same time attentive to the word of God, which has been kept by that initial and privileged witness of the apostolic Church through the special inspiration of the Holy Spirit. The bible, as the word of God to us and the Church, is the basis of our faith, and in this sense the basic rule—the *norma normans*—of the teaching of the Church. The New Testament has another advantage. It gives us the inspired expression, fresh and spontaneous, of the Church's primary experience before it became enclosed in theological systems and, what is worse, before it was made comfortable and harmless by pious commonplaces and platitudes. The bible is not comfortable but challenging.

[1] 'Three Ways of Dogmatic Thought', loc. cit.

Secondly, your teaching should be historical. There is no better way of showing the real difference between the substance of our faith and the various formulations it has found in the course of history, than a study of the development of dogma, of an ecclesiastical institution, of a sacrament, of some part of canon law. One can still meet theologians or canonists who contend that the formulations of former times were 'primitive and insufficient' when we compare them with our 'perfect' solutions, but this seems a special kind of historical short-sightedness. C. S. Lewis wrote in his inaugural lecture at Cambridge, *De Destructione Temporum*: 'The unhistorical are usually, without knowing it, enslaved to a very recent past!'[1]

Thirdly, your teaching should be Catholic, keeping in contact or, better, in communion of faith with the whole living Church; and I have, therefore, insisted upon the necessity, at least for the professors, of a reading knowledge of the most important modern languages. The theologians you need for teaching your laymen have to be able to read the most influential theological thinkers of our time, if possible in the original languages. There is no English, no French, no German theology, but one Roman Catholic theology in which we might find, what is quite normal and sound, an English, a German or a French emphasis, a particular orientation and way of looking at things. A closed theological system, I believe, possesses the seeds of schism and heresy, especially when the Church is in full development and evolution.

Fourthly, your teaching should be ecumenical. This again is only possible when one can distinguish between the substance of the faith and its various theological formulations. Every ecumenist will vouch for this. Its lack raised one of the most obvious problems during the first Session of the Council. Those bishops and theologians who had no deep theological training, and had never done more than read potted textbooks of classical theology, were unable to enter the ecumenical dialogue to which Pope John invited them. There were two reasons for this. If a man unconsciously equates the doctrine he learned from a single textbook of theology with the thoughts of God himself and the divine reality, he remains blind to its theological limitations. At the same time, whenever the ecumenical dialogue is taken up, he feels extremely uncomfortable and unsafe, because he is

[1] *They Asked for a Paper*, London, 1962, p. 23.

unable to decide what he has at all costs to keep as coming from God, and entrusted to the Church and what he can adapt and explain otherwise, as coming from man's speculation. How can we seriously and sincerely enter into any ecumenical dialogue, so long as we are blind and deaf to the real religious concerns of our ecumenical partners, and are clothing our own human views and opinions with the absolute majesty of God himself?

Fifthly, your teaching should prepare laymen for life in this world at this time of history, specifically for a pluralist society. We are placed again by divine providence in almost the same situation as our fathers were during the first five centuries of the Church. We are in fact living in a world where different creeds, different systems of thought and life are freely defended and promoted. Happily the Church is no longer capable of using the coercion of the state to enforce her own views on human life and destiny. As Pope John told the Council, this is a blessing of divine providence:

> We feel we must disagree with those prophets of gloom, who are always forecasting disaster, as though the end of the world was at hand.
> In the present order of things, divine Providence is leading us to a new order of human relations, which, by men's own efforts and even beyond their very expectations, is directed towards the fulfilment of God's superior and inscrutable desires, and everything, even human differences, leads to the greater good of the Church. It is easy to discern this reality, if we consider with attention the world of today, so busied with politics and controversies in the economic order as not to find time to attend to solicitudes of the spiritual realm, with which the Church's *magisterium* is concerned. Such a way of acting is certainly not right, and must justly be disapproved. It cannot be denied, however, that these new conditions of modern life have at least this advantage, that they have eliminated these innumerable obstacles by which at one time the sons of this world impeded the free action of the Church. In fact, it suffices to leaf even cursorily through the pages of ecclesiastical history to note clearly how the Ecumenical Councils themselves, while constituting a series of true glories for the Catholic Church, were often celebrated to the accompaniment of most serious difficulties and sufferings, because of the undue interference of civil authorities. The princes of this world, indeed, sometimes in all sincerity, intended thus to protect the Church, but more frequently this occurred not within spiritual damage and danger, since their interest therein was guided by the views of a selfish and perilous policy. . . . Nevertheless, we see today, not without great hopes and to our immense consolation, that the Church, finally freed from so many obstacles of a profane nature, such as fettered her in the past, can, from

this Vatican Basilica, as if from a second apostolic cenacle, and through your mediation, raise her voice with majesty and greatness.[1]

Circumstances are more and more restoring the Church to her original and primitive mission of witnessing to her own veracity by the convincing force of the truth itself, and not by an extraneous use of authority. For a person to complain of the ending of the Constantinian epoch is to lead one to suspect that he suffers from an unconscious, and therefore all the more dangerous, form of pelagianism, confiding more in the power of the state than in the virtue of God's grace and God's own truth.

But if the Church wants to remain faithful to the mission her Lord has given her, she must no longer enclose herself in a spiritual ghetto, in a clerical fortress, but must go out into the world and speak the language all men understand. Therefore she must first of all have confidence both in the illuminating power of her own truth and of the Holy Spirit working in her and in the preaching of the word of God, and also in the real goodwill and sincerity of so many people living outside her fold. She has to learn again the language of the time, and to share in the real worries and problems of the people, if she does not want to be rejected as foreign, antiquated, inhuman and insincere.

These are not simple solutions. We have to disengage ourselves from many stereotyped opinions and ways of life, and find the spiritual foundation for new attitudes in the ancient traditions of faith.

This work asks for a strenuous effort on a double level. There is first of all the irreplaceable scientific work of the professional theologian. By means of a meticulous and severely scientific study of the bible, of the traditions of the Fathers and later theologians, of the Councils and the Liturgy of the Church, in their own original language, he has to discover this very substance of our faith Pope John was referring to. It is also his duty to become acquainted with the methods of modern philosophy in order to ascertain what is the fitting and unfalsified expression of this substance for the people of our time.

Yours is another task. You are not aiming primarily at this kind of scholarly knowledge for laymen, most of whom do not possess the necessary scientific and linguistic training which would enable them to profit from such a technical teaching. What you want are theo-

[1] *The Tablet*, loc. cit., p. 998.

logically literate laymen, that is, laymen who have an adult and mature knowledge of their faith and religion.

They must learn to distinguish between the substance of belief or religious life and old or new expressions in terms of doctrine and of church-life. At the same time they must discover what is central in faith and religious practice, and what can always be reformed, or adapted to different needs and situations. They need most of all to know how they can think and speak about their faith in a personal and responsible way, as adults, and no longer as children. This will enable them to find those concrete answers to the questions of our time, in so far as they are, more than the professional theologian, involved in and familiar with such problems. In other words, as laymen in the Church they possess a personal, responsible, inalienable mission to witness to the truth of God in and for this world.

Although theirs is a 'practical' mission, laymen must not suppose that the study of theology is inevitably one of abstruse and alien problems. It would be completely wrong to leave the study of such fundamental dogmas of our religion, as the Holy Trinity, the Incarnation, the mysteries of Grace to the 'speculations' of professional theologians, and to reserve for laymen only the so-called 'practical' questions of social and political life. It is impossible to be a good citizen, a responsible person, and to remain a good christian, if we are not living from these central truths of our faith. It is a common error to think that the mysteries of our faith, such as that of the Holy Trinity, were revealed to keep learned theologians busy: they are the very mysteries of life, and were revealed for the salvation of all men, learned and unlearned. It would be a very dangerous solution to leave this substance of our faith to the theologians, and to keep the 'problems of life' for the laymen.

Both must collaborate in a constant dialogue, each according to his vocation and talents, and experience and knowledge.

You need as teachers, therefore, theologians who can listen to other people, and, conscious of their own 'technical' and clerical limitations, are convinced of the unique mission of the laity as full and active members of the Church. The danger is not a theology which is too scholarly, at least as long as it remains open and modern, but one which, by refusing to listen to the witness of the laity, becomes too clerical. This clerical theology cannot be offset merely by complaints and criticisms, but only by a vigorous and strong theological education of the laity. We need, not children, but adults who know what they are talking about, have a personal and well-grounded knowledge of their faith, and are able to judge for themselves according to the freedom of the children of God.

As we have seen before, no theology can be achieved in solitude and estrangement. This is the time not only for the professional theologian, but also for the theologically literate layman. True theology grows from the living dialogue inside the Church by the light of the Holy Ghost, who was given to theologians and laymen alike, but to each according to his vocation and ability. Theology is the fruit of our communion in faith.

This is the opportunity which confronts you at this moment of history. But if the second Vatican Council has any meaning at all, and if it is to have any fruit, there is only one way forward. We have been cornered by God Himself in this very difficult, yet splendid situation, and it is the call of God for our times that we should find the way out. During this Symposium you will be collaborating with Christians inside and outside the Roman Catholic tradition, in obedience to this call of God—yours is a uniquely ecumenical opportunity.

III

THEOLOGY—
its nature and practice

6. Theology and its Present Task

Charles Davis

The creative centre

As I have conceived it, my purpose here is not to give an abstract account of the nature of theology but to try to see what we want theology to *do* and, consequently, what we want it to *be* in the present concrete situation. I am going to begin with a long quotation from Mr John Wain's book: *Sprightly Running*. It may seem quite irrelevant, but I think that it does in fact help us to grasp the present problem of theology in a vivid way.

Mr Wain understands his role as an imaginative writer thus:

'To write well' means far more than choosing the apt word or the telling arrangement of syllables, though it means these things as well; it is a matter of feeling and living at the required depth, fending off the continual temptation to be glib and shallow, to appeal to the easily aroused response, to be evasive and shirk the hard issues. It is a matter of training oneself to live with reality, and, as our greatest living poet has warned us: 'Human kind cannot bear very much reality'. But, if one is to write well, one *must* bear it: increasing the dose, perhaps, until one can absorb it in quantities that would unhinge the ordinary person. This is a large claim; if what I am saying is true, the artist is better (stronger, braver, more perceptive) than the ordinary person. I shrink from my own meaning, for who can really enjoy making such a claim, with the responsibility it involves? But the claim must be made, and the responsibility shouldered, even if I myself never succeed in writing one good book.

For if the responsibility is great, and the risk of ignominious failure greater still, the reward is in proportion. An author, if he is big enough, can do so much for his fellow-men. He can put words into their mouths and reasons into their heads; he can fill their sleep with dreams so potent that when they awake they will go on living them. I have said that people live according to their mental pictures, and much of this book has been an attempt to show how that principle worked in my own case. And where do the mental pictures come from? There is no one simple answer, but I believe that the most powerful and widespread mental pictures, those which dominate the thought and action of a whole epoch, can usually be traced to the work of a few men, the supreme artists, the imaginative creators of their time. It does not matter that the majority get those pictures at second hand, or at tenth or fiftieth hand; they come from the centre, and are merely more blurred and simplified as they move outwards. There, at that centre, are the artists who really form the consciousness of their time; they respond deeply, intuitively, to what is happening, what has happened and what will happen and their response is expressed in metaphor and symbol, in image and fable. To be one of that band, to inhabit that creative centre, is the ambition of every author who has still not sold out.[1]

I have not quoted that passage in order to discuss the function of imaginative writing. Personally, I find Mr Wain's statement admirable. Because what he says is so true, I am convinced that theology, through some theologians at least, must be in touch with the artistic achievement of its age if it is to live and have an impact on contemporaries and posterity. I should quarrel with Mr Wain only if he attempted to reserve the creative centre for the artists and exclude the thinkers from it, namely the scientists, the philosophers and the theologians. But, whatever his own views, we may extend the application of the passage for our present purpose. Understood thus widely it brings three important facts home to us: first, that there is a creative centre in every culture; second, that it is only from within that centre that men can be really influenced; third, that to work within that centre makes peculiar demands. Each of these facts has a bearing on theology and its task.

There is a creative centre in every culture. It consists of those artists and thinkers who do not shirk reality but are prepared to face it. And reality for them is a present thing; they are not content with past descriptions or received ideas. They grapple with reality itself in its disturbing greatness and unexpected newness, in its unsolved problems and unexplored mystery. And they react to it creatively. They allow questions to arise that give them no rest, and they are not afraid of a commitment that can come near to making life unendurable for them.[2]

[1] *Sprightly Running: Part of an Autobiography* (London, 1962), pp. 263–4.
[2] A thinker, then, is working within the creative centre if he is reacting to present reality creatively. There is no need for him to identify the centre of the culture in which he lives. To identify the creative centre, by which I mean to delineate and describe it and if necessary to distinguish various centres according to different cultural manifestations, demands that we stand at least mentally

Such should be the position of the theologian. The christian thing he studies is a present reality, even though it joins him to the past as well. Faith is not the acceptance of what has long since ceased to be, but surrender to the divine reality here and now acting upon us. And theology arises from faith; creative theology from present faith not past faith.

I want to stress that the theologian confronts present reality, but in doing so I have no wish to minimise his constant concern with the past. The intertwining of past and present in the object of theology is due to the structure of christian revelation.

The self-disclosure of God in Christ remains always the same in itself, but it is inserted into history and comes to us as made present in the life of the Church. Revelation is an enduring reality immanent in Christ's Church. The unbroken continuity of the Church means that its present existence always incorporates the past, so that the theologian may rightly appeal to the past in tackling present problems. The riches of the Church's past are never destroyed or lost completely, but they often go unregarded. Part of theology's task is to draw attention to them. Nevertheless, despite the constant appeal to the past, the theologian is engaged in present problems. His task differs with each generation. His work is historically conditioned because the reality he studies is historically conditioned and he must begin from its present embodiment. Any creative theology arises out of the actual life of the Church. The real theological questions are always contemporary and, moreover, they can be effectively handled only by someone who is sensitive to the present action of the Spirit in the Church.

None of this is to say that dogmatic and theological truth are only relative or to deny that the mind can reach timeless, objective truth. But unless its questions are living, real questions, theology is dead. And each age has its own questions. Even when they seem to correspond to the questions of an earlier age, they are never quite the

outside it so as to make it an object of observation and study. This is the task of the historian or student of culture. It is a secondary activity. What is here asked of artists and thinkers is that they face the reality in which they live and react creatively to it; in other words, that they do not just reproduce second-hand thought or ideas. Posterity will pass judgment on what is creative and what is not. The thinker at the creative centre of his time may be unrecognized by his contemporaries.

same. They are coloured by a different context, and it is within such differing contexts that each age finds revelation for itself. So the answers, too, given by a living contemporary theology are never quite the same as before. They are in continuity with the past, since the reality studied remains essentially the same from age to age. But even where theology is simply trying to recapture an understanding that has been lost, even when the process of thought seems to be but a return to the past, the regained understanding is never exactly the same as the original. It differs in the way our insights are ordered and in the reflexive grasp of details never directly considered before. Thus, we are at present trying to regain the earlier understanding of the liturgy. When we have done so, this understanding will have been modified in the process of recovery, because we, not our ancestors, have been asking the questions. And then some questions are quite new. We cannot today confront the mystery of the Church without asking many new questions about the divisions among christians and about what is happening in divided Christendom under the action of the Holy Spirit.

In brief, the theologian must be prepared to confront the self-disclosure of God in Christ as a present reality. It is a transcendent reality and man's understanding always falls short of it. The understanding reached in the past never exactly fits present needs. The theologian, then, must not be satisfied with repeating past formulations, however valuable the insights they express. He must respond creatively to revelation itself, which is reality as well as words, not shirking questions that disturb his received ideas nor afraid of a commitment that will make his life uncomfortable. He can do this only by finding revelation as immanent in the actual life of the Church.

But this statement is still incomplete. What has been said so far would put the theologian at the creative centre of the Church, having a place in the Church similar to that of an artist in the world of his day. But it has not yet been shown that the theologian is or should be at the creative centre of the culture in which he lives. However, it is not difficult to see that this must be so. If the Church is not present at the creative centre of each age and culture, it is moribund and failing in its mission. I do not say that it must become so bound up with each culture as to make it distinctively Catholic on the medieval pattern—collaboration not dominance would seem to be the truer role of the Church. But it must be there at the centre, acting on the other elements present and reacting creatively to them.

At every point in its history the Church consists of men living at a particular time. Unless the questions that its members are asking as men of their time are raised within the Church and are grappled with in the light of revelation, the Church is dead and not bringing the Gospel to men as they are. Unless there are within the Church at least some of those who are at the creative centre of the culture of the time, sensitive to present reality and reacting creatively to it, the Church is not thinking creatively and is out of touch with the men it has been sent to save. And unless the theologian is at that creative centre, he is not asking new questions but repeating the past, he is not thinking personally but echoing the thought of others. Theology is done necessarily by men stamped with a specific culture and found in a particular situation. If a theologian thinks personally, he will react to revelation according to his own culture and from within his own situation. Theology is either at the creative centre of contemporary culture or it is stagnant. The more sensitive the theologian is to the reality that surrounds him, the more creative he will be as a theologian.[1]

Nor must it be forgotten that theology from its own viewpoint studies the whole of created reality. A new understanding of created reality, especially of man, has its repercussions on theology. Theology today is not asked about the creation of man *tout court* but about the creation of man who came into the world by evolution. The concern of modern theology cannot be with the place of Christ in the world as conceived by the ancients but in the vast universe as revealed by science. Again, philology and the historical sciences affect the interpretation of the bible; psychological and social sciences have their bearing on moral questions. Philosophy raises questions that are a challenge to existing theology. Imaginative literature presents man in his changing situation, and it is man in the concrete who is the object of salvation.

In short, the christian message tells us of a salvation for man and the universe, and it comes to us as a revelation inserted into our

[1] An excellent example of a piece of creative theological thinking provoked by a particular historical situation and cultural context is Fr Karl Rahner's *Zur Theologie des Todes* (*Quaestiones Disputatae*, 2, Herder, Freiburg, 1958). It has appeared in a poor translation as *On the Theology of Death* (Herder, Freiburg—Nelson, Edinburgh, 1961).

history. Significant advances in human knowledge of man and the universe raise new questions for the theologian who studies that message. To ignore them is to fail in one's task as a theologian. To accept them means placing oneself at the creative centre of contemporary culture.

The second point I have drawn from Mr Wain, namely that it is only from within the creative centre that men can be really influenced, will, I think, be disputed by no one. Time is needed before their influence becomes effective, but what the thinkers and artists are saying and doing today will dominate the lives of ordinary people tomorrow. This can be verified by studying the history of modern culture. If the Church with her theology remains on the periphery of a culture, then she will have no deep or lasting influence on the men it embraces. The truth of this is sadly illustrated by the history of the missions. And is not the shallowness of so much christian life and witness today due to the fact that the Church has remained outside the world in which men must live? The christian religion is confined to an isolated corner of many individual lives because that is the present position of the Church in the modern world.

The third point, that to work within that centre makes peculiar demands, could occasion an interesting essay on the personal qualities required in a theologian. The temptation must be resisted here. However, the observation is in place that a theologian can 'sell out' as well as an artist. It is possible for him to refuse to live at the required depth; he can become glib and shallow, appeal to the easily aroused response and shirk the hard issues. And he can do so for the sake of an approval or honour in the Church that corresponds to the superficial success for which the artist 'sells out'. It is a difficult vocation continually to raise awkward questions and refuse glib answers, to disturb settled opinions and upset complacency; but that is the vocation of the theologian. He cannot expect an easy life, any more than other creative thinkers or artists can, but he does need more sympathy and encouragement within the Church than he receives at present. The touchy, suspicious fear of new ideas creates a tension in which it is difficult to work. Much of the policy of protecting the faith of people by the exclusion of disturbing ideas is in fact a policy of jettisoning the faith of the next generation in an ill-directed attempt to salvage the faith of this.

There is, however, another side to the matter. The theologian must

be intellectually modest and of genuine humility, otherwise, his work
will not be a building-up of the Body of Christ but a subtle form of
destruction rightly resisted. The vocation of the theologian is a vocation within the believing Church, not over it. Professor Mascall put
the point recently in these words:

> And even when he is convinced in all conscience that he has been
> granted, as he may well have been, some new insight, profound in its
> significance and revolutionary in its implications, he is under a solemn
> moral obligation not to demand that the whole fabric of christian faith
> and life shall be immediately fashioned in accordance with it, while
> there is, of course, an equally solemn obligation upon the guardians of
> the tradition to see that his views receive sympathetic and thorough
> consideration. For—may I repeat this?—he may very well turn out to be
> wrong, and the temporal and eternal consequences for other human
> beings may turn out to be catastrophic. He may, of course, be right, but
> he is hardly the best person to pass judgment about that.[1]

Were we to pursue the examination of the various qualities required in a theologian, we should find that they can all be summed
up in the word 'holiness'. The demand for holiness makes the theologian uncomfortable and he prefers to dwell on the intellectual
requirements of his vocation, but without holiness he is eluding the
reality he claims to confront.

To draw, then, this first section to a conclusion: there is a creative
centre in every culture, and the place of theology is at that centre. If
it is not there, it is dead and failing to carry out its proper function.
Only from within that creative centre can men be really influenced.
Unless the Church gets within the centre by the fruitful contact of her
theologians with the men who form the consciousness of their time,
her influence will remain superficial and ephemeral. But to work
within that centre is an arduous task for a theologian. He must not
expect an easy life. The pressure of reality experienced there is difficult to bear. But he should receive some supporting sympathy, some
recognition of what he is trying to do.

What theology needs today

Is theology today what it should be? It would be possible to pass
from the preceding remarks on the role of theology to a critical
examination of theology as it is at present. Such an examination is a

[1] E. L. Mascall, *Theology and History: An Inaugural Lecture Delivered at
King's College, London, on Tuesday, October* 23rd, 1962 (London, 1962), pp. 16–17.

therapeutic necessity for Roman Catholic theology in this country; for our theology is still very isolated and very feeble. But here I can presuppose a general recognition of our defects,[1] and I want to turn immediately to some constructive suggestions for the healthy functioning of theology in the present situation. What does theology need today to enable it to carry out its function better?

I suggest first that theology needs a university *milieu*. This remark is, of course, provoked by the present lack of such a *milieu* for Roman Catholic theology in this country, but I think it useful to everyone here to consider the benefit theology should derive from its presence in a university.

Now I am not competent to discuss the present state of the English universities and judge how far they realise the proper idea of a university. I am aware of criticisms of them, such as that there is insufficient contact amongst the various faculties. But in so far as a university is still a junction where various disciplines meet, a place of convergence for the branches of human knowledge, theology needs the stimulus of being present there. No doubt other, usually less permanent situations, can arise that provide a comparable stimulus, but in our culture the university is the place where the various sciences exist in a common environment, with the possibility of many kinds of contact among those engaged in different lines of inquiry.

Notice that my plea is that theology needs the university, not that the university needs theology. As a matter of fact the second statement is also true, but its theoretical basis is more familiar and its practical development would come better from someone engaged in university life.[2] It is enough to remark that theology can never be successfully expelled from the concert of the sciences. When it is excluded the other sciences try to play its part as well as their own— with results that vary from the clumsy to the ludicrous. Where good theology is excluded, bad theology flourishes. Men will raise theological issues; theology might as well be there to tackle them.

But I am more concerned with the fact that theology itself needs the university. It needs the university so that it will ask the right questions, the questions that keep it at the growing points of human knowledge and within the consciousness of contemporary man.

---

[1] These are described in my article written in connection with this paper, 'Theology in seminary confinement', *Downside Review*, 81 (1963), pp. 307–16.

[2] For the case as stated by Newman *v. supra*, pp. 49–53.

The influence of the other sciences on theology is not primarily the incorporation of their results as into one body of knowledge—as if the ideal theologian would be some kind of monstrous polymath. It lies chiefly in the interaction of theology and other independent lines of inquiry, which coming together spark off a process of original thought. Only the theologian himself may see the theological relevance of what others are doing. It is not just a matter of non-theologians asking him questions, valuable as this is, but of questions arising in his own mind as he becomes aware of what is happening in the other sciences. For this it is not necessary for him to be a specialist in several sciences. His task is a theological one—he has his own sources and methods—but he must ask real questions, questions that come from the meeting of the contemporary mind with the revealed message. The confrontation can happen in his own mind, provided he does not live in isolation but in an environment alive with an awareness of what is going on in the various parts of human knowledge. Original thought is usually due to the unexpected coming together in someone's mind of two apparently unconnected lines of inquiry. Unless that kind of interaction takes place between theology and contemporary thought, our theology will always be the theology of a past culture never the theology appropriate to this.

Theology, then, to overcome its isolation needs a university environment. And it is plain that I do not mean the setting up of a faculty of theology in some remote situation, existing in its own special environment, allowing facilities for higher study but no real, spontaneous contacts with other disciplines.

The second requirement for a healthy theology today is its study by lay people. Again my standpoint is unusual. I am not arguing that lay people need theology. As a matter of fact they do. And they want it as well as need it. Admittedly, in this connection the word 'theology' is often used loosely for any knowledge of the faith that is more than elementary. The border-line between methodical, scientific knowledge of a subject and general, unscientific knowledge is always indistinct, so that it is difficult to draw the line between theology proper, which is a scientific knowledge of revealed truth, and what is simply a good, general knowledge of the faith. All the same, many lay people today are seeking, not just higher catechetical instruction, but a genuinely theological understanding of their faith. Highly developed intellectually, they are led to theology by their efforts to bring their faith to bear on their whole life. But, apart from the need they feel, many lay people just want to study theology; they are as interested in it as priests—much more interested than many priests.

So, lay people do need and want theology. But that is not my point. I am maintaining that theology needs lay people.

Theology is man scrutinising the revealed Word of God, doing this methodically, systematically, with all the resources of human knowledge, but resting upon and guided by faith, which alone gives him that revealed Word. Theology varies, then, according to the man who is reflecting on God's Word and according to the resources he brings. I cannot see it as anything but an impoverishment for theology that it should always be studied with the preoccupations and mentality of a priest and never with the preoccupations and mentality of a layman. For theology does not deal with impersonal truths. The truth it studies tells us of our destiny, which means our personal relation with God. And since God giving himself to man in a personal communion is its object, theology is reflection on transcendent truth which we can never fully grasp and of which our partial grasp depends on a personal surrender to it. Such reflection is bound to be affected by the spiritual calling and situation of the student.

Lay people are becoming conscious of their distinctive place within the Church, of its dignity and special tasks. It is to be expected that this growing consciousness will include an awareness of the special contribution they have to make to theology. Such a contribution is needed. The most distinctively lay task is the *consecratio mundi*, the insertion of the christian leaven into all the institutions and activities of this world. Is not part of this task the insertion of theology into the creative centre of the culture in which they live? And can this insertion be fully achieved without the co-operation of lay theologians?

I am not advocating the creation of a lay theology in competitive relation to a clerical theology. Theology is one; its truth is one; its methods and sources are the same for all. But it would be enriched and made more balanced by being pursued by the lay as well as the clerical element in the Church. To want to keep theology exclusively for priests and clerics is to wish to hold the laity in a state of immaturity in the Church. The highest religious culture ought to be available to those who are capable of it and want it.

Here I must mark my disagreement with Fr Congar. In his book on the theology of the lay state he has some pages on the layman and theology. He outlines the part lay people have played in the past and the part they still have in the East. He stresses the important contribution laymen have to make to christian thought, above all in matters that lie at the junction of faith and the problems of this world. But when all this is said, Fr Congar still thinks that theology is preeminently a matter for priests, a peculiarly priestly learning. Lay people will never do theology like priests; they have not the same pastoral awareness nor the same union with tradition; priests celebrating the mysteries have living contact with the realities of tradition to a greater degree.[1]

I find this attitude surprising. It seems to suppose that the priesthood gives a person an access to the realities of the christian faith and life which is closed to lay people. That is untrue. The priesthood is a special function within the community but it does not give privileged access to the christian realities. The priest, for example, at Mass has a unique function to perform involving special powers, but his communion with the reality of Christ's sacrifice is proportionate to his holiness, and he has no more access to the mystery than the humblest layman in the Church. The priest has special functions in regard to tradition and the sacraments, but his living contact with these sacred realities, as distinct from a mere handling of them, depends upon his faith and love. And laymen may well have a closer union with them.

Now it is true that priests need theology in a way that lay people do not. Their calling is more closely bound up with it. It is also true that the Church desires and tries to secure, with varying degrees of

[1] See *Jalons pour une théologie du laïcat* (Paris, 1953), pp. 428–32, esp. pp. 430–1 published in translation as *Lay People in the Church* (Newman Press, Md., 1957; London, Geoffrey Chapman, 1959), pp. 296–7:

'We must, however, here make a point and perhaps register a limitation. The laity, giving utterance to the questings and strivings of the world, can bring a wealth to the Church that it is their mission to dedicate to God. But they never handle theology like priests, they have never quite the same contact with the Church's tradition. It is not simply that the priest, conscious of the pastoral effects and consequences of his words and works, takes nicer account of all the factors and tries to balance them: having the priestly charisms, celebrating the mysteries, he has to a greater degree living contact with the realities of tradition. Theology properly so called is pre-eminently a clerical, priestly, learning. Extensive lay activity in matters of religious thought is very desirable; but, rather than in the domain of theological science, it should be exerted in the immense field that lies between the Church's dogmatic tradition and man's most actual problems.'

success, that her priests should be outstanding in holiness; so, we can say that the spiritual formation requisite for a fruitful study of theology ought to be found more generally among the clergy than the laity. The clergy are picked out and receive a special spiritual training. But none of this alters the fact that lay people are frequently much holier than the clergy, and that an intellectual layman may secure a spiritual formation for himself that adequately prepares him for theological study. And other things being equal—granted that they often are not—I do not myself see that the priesthood as such gives a man an advantage in theology over the layman.

Fr Congar is right in saying that theology done by laymen is subject to special dangers. Their openness to the world if not properly controlled could upset the equilibrium of their theology, and moreover they have not the same pastoral concern as priests. But theology pursued by priests is also subject to its dangers. In theology a collaboration between clergy and laity is called for. I agree that the clergy have a contribution they alone can make. But the laity too have their contribution to give, and I do not see why they should be warned off theology properly so-called. The task given to them by Fr Congar of bringing the faith to bear on the problems of this world needs theology in the full sense for its accomplishment.

In brief, the priesthood does not give any monopoly of theology. The charisms proper to the priest have their value for his theology, but so too have the charisms proper to the lay state. Theology suffers today from the lack of a mature lay contribution, which is particularly called for in the present circumstances.

The third need of theology today is an ecumenical structure and direction; it must be an ecumenical theology. The name 'ecumenical theology' may refer to a special part of theology, treating of the particular problems that arise out of the ecumenical movement, problems such as the doctrinal basis of that movement, the theologies active in the World Council of Churches, and so on. I take it here to mean a dimension that must be given to the whole of theology. All theology must be carried on in a dialogue with other christians. That indeed, I maintain, is the only way that theology can be in accord with the present life of the Church.

The ecumenical movement is not just one of many movements in the Church today, a movement of limited interest, affecting but a small number of specially qualified people. It is the great work of the

Holy Spirit at the present time, the main direction in which the Church is moving under his action. The other movements of renewal, such as the biblical and liturgical movements, are now seen as leading up to the work for reunion; they prepared the way for it. Renewal with a view to reunion—that is the pattern of the Church's life at present, as it is the pattern of the Second Vatican Council. The ecumenical movement is not just an affair for experts, it is a new dimension in the christian life, which every member of the Church is being called upon to accept. The life of the Church has taken a new direction, and the unity of christians is the magnetic pole towards which every activity in the Church is turned. The renewal of the Church in general and the christian maturity of individuals, for both of which we are striving, will be achieved only by turning in that direction, since that is the way the Holy Spirit is moving us.

Theology cannot remain outside this general pattern. Everyone recognises the indispensable part it has in direct ecumenical activity, but, apart from this, theology needs the ecumenical dialogue to achieve its own internal balance and maturity. This observation calls for some further explanation. I shall, of course, be speaking from the standpoint of the Roman Catholic faith.

It is our belief that the essential visible unity of the Church of Christ was not lost in the break-up of Christendom and that this unity is found in the Roman Catholic Church, so that the visible community of that Church is in unbroken continuity with the visible community founded by Christ. At the same time it is now admitted without difficulty that the Church has been wounded, her unity marred, her life damaged, her mission impeded by the disunity of christians. And true as it is that nothing essential has been lost to the Church, so that in theory Christianity would survive intact in the Roman Catholic Church alone, that is not the complete truth of the matter. It is not enough to consider the situation of divided Christendom in the abstract. God had a purpose in allowing these divisions, and we must try to discern that purpose by humble reflection on the realities of the concrete situation. Although the divisions are due to our sins, they still have their place in God's plan, and we must co-operate with his purpose. In particular, we must not carry on as if the momentous break-up of Christendom, with all that it has implied, is of no more significance to the life of the Church than the apostasy of the man next door.

E

If we reflect in this way on the historical reality of our divisions, then we shall see that in God's plan the other christian communions have played their part in keeping a clear christian witness in Christendom to certain important truths, which were not denied but which were obscured on our side, and that in God's plan it is only by working for reunion and eventually achieving it that the Church will reach that greater possession of christian life and more effective christian witness for which we are yearning and striving.

What has been said of the Church in general can be said of theology in particular. It has been wounded and damaged by the break-up of Christendom; it has not been able to avoid a narrowness and one-sidedness. It is now striving for a new balance and wholeness, but this will be reached only by working in the context of the ecumenical movement. For example, I do not think it possible for theology to achieve a properly balanced and adequately worked-out understanding of the eucharist except through the ecumenical dialogue with other christians. And that is in fact how such an understanding is being gradually achieved. I repeat that it is not enough here to argue in the abstract from the essential, intact wholeness of the Church's teaching; account must be taken of the historical situation, with its inevitable limitations, in which the Church finds itself, and of the way the Holy Spirit helps us in fact to meet the exigencies of that situation.

Theology, then, must become ecumenical in its structure and direction if it is to develop healthily and fulfil its function in the Church. Such an ecumenical dimension is not given to theology by reading books, there must be a living confrontation with the theologians of other christian communions and the establishment of personal, oral dialogue with them. It lies outside my present purpose to analyse the conditions and methods of such a dialogue. I would just like to note that, though respect and benevolence are essential, they are not enough. There must be a real acceptance of one another as christians and, at the same time, the intellectual depth and flexibility necessary to combine an unswerving loyalty to one's confessional convictions about the truth of Christ with the ability to accept and raise genuine questions about christian truths. Needless to say, we must all be prepared to receive as well as give in the ecumenical dialogue.

I come now to the final quality I see theology as needing today: an existential character. Perhaps I had better first explain what I mean by this vogue word that has not gained in clarity by its popularity. By 'existential' I mean what concerns or involves human existence in the concrete. I call a truth 'existential' when I cannot assent to it as a mere spectator or disinterested thinker but only by committing my whole existence. When I ask for theology to be more 'existential', I am pleading for a greater awareness that it is about a message of salvation that affects man in his total existence and that, consequently, can only be studied with commitment.

The existential character of theology must be reflected in what is studied and in the way in which it is studied.

Theology studies the self-disclosure of God in Christ. This revelation is embodied in history and moreover affects every part of man's existence. Theology, therefore, must take account not only of the nature of man considered in the abstract but of human life in its concrete and historical realisation. There has been an advance in our knowledge of man in his personal, concrete existence, which is relevant to theology. For example, it is not enough for the theologian to present an abstract analysis of faith; he must examine theologically the vicissitudes of faith in the concrete. In general, theological reflection is required on the personal, temporal and historical aspects of human existence. This needs a widening of theological method, for theology as a rule is still too limited in the modes of reflection it employs.[1]

Theology is existential in the second sense that it demands to be studied from within the life of the Church with the commitment that involves. Only to its great detriment can theology become an academic subject remote from the actual life of the contemporary Church. Great thought is rarely produced by people insensitive to the human concern of their time. I am vigorously opposed to any attempts to reduce the scientific character of theology and the austere rigour of its thought by shallow appeals to make it more vital, more apostolic. But theology cannot be studied in an aloof indifference to the life and work of the Church. The theology of t he patristic age was intimately connected with the life of the Church, and St Thomas, as Fr Chenu has shown, was a man of his time, sensitive to all the christian and human stirrings of the thirteenth century. The theologian must bring to his theology an evangelical and human concern

---

[1] For a further discussion see Peter Fransen, 'Three Ways of Dogmatic Thought', *The Heythrop Journal*, 4 (1963), pp. 3–24, esp. pp. 16–19.

that makes exacting personal demands on himself. A call to work within the creative centre means living at the required depth.

The nature of the theological task

So far I have taken for granted the existence of theology as a meaningful activity. It is now time to ask what theology is trying to do; in other words, what is the nature of its task.

Theology is the methodical and systematic understanding of the Triune God's self-disclosure in Christ. The phrase 'in Christ' is here taken as embracing the whole revelatory process that is centred in Christ and his work. The definition also takes for granted that the self-disclosure of God is an act of self-giving by which God calls us to share his life, not the imparting to us of mere theoretical knowledge about himself.

What, then, is the object studied by theology? By 'object', I mean what lies before the mind for its understanding. It is not a set of propositions; it is not even a set of truths; it is the reality of God in so far as this is revealed to us. Would that theologians had always remembered this! Theology does not stop at words, even if inspired, nor at concepts and propositions, even when they form a solemn definition; it is an effort to understand the reality to which the words, concepts and propositions point. But such indicators are needed, because the reality of God, when the object of theological understanding, is not immediately present to the mind; it is brought before it through an historical revelation that uses events, symbols and words. Only faith can seize upon the reality of God when presented in this way. Theology is derived from faith and remains dependent upon it. Hence the understanding it achieves is never more than the imperfect understanding of a mystery and presupposes the act of faith by which alone the mind can lay hold of the mystery. The great value of an understanding so imperfect comes from its object.

Theology, then, seeks to understand God as revealed to us. It does this under the guidance of faith by the workings and resources of the human mind. There is a higher kind of understanding that comes simply by the deepening of faith and love; as the christian advances in holiness, he increasingly discerns the truth by a higher wisdom. Such a wisdom should not be absent from the theologian; it can aid his work. But theology as such puts the human resources of the mind to work for the understanding of God's revelation. This revelation has been made to the human mind with the use of human means, such as thought and language. Once the mind has accepted God's revelation by faith, it can seek to understand it more fully by the processes of human reflection.

The chief aim of theology is understanding. The theologian is not primarily concerned with certitude but with the effort to understand. Theology is the work of developing understanding within the certitude of faith; it is engaged in elucidating the christian faith from within. We do not go to theologians for our faith—the certitudes of our faith do not depend upon theology. Theology is there to give us a greater understanding of what we already believe.

Naturally, the theologian will test the truth of the insights he gains and pass judgment upon them as he gradually progresses in his understanding of revelation. But in what concerns their certitude, the wise theologian will remain very conscious of his limitations. He is dealing with matters of faith, and so he will recognise that the results of theological reflection can be finally judged only by their assimilation into the corporate faith of the Church under the authority of the *magisterium*. I am not thinking merely of new definitions by Pope or Council, but of the ordinary processes by which a new understanding of some doctrine comes to be accepted in the Church. Theology remains subordinate to the corporate faith and teaching authority of the Church and cannot put itself above these—it is there to serve them. The theologian will publish and urge his findings, but he will be modest about their certitude and cautious about the value of his arguments until such time as his findings may be ratified by the believing community. Meanwhile the theologian continues the work that is particularly his own, namely seeking to understand. There are times when the Church urgently needs an advance in understanding for its continued existence and mission, but it is not for the theologian to remodel the faith of the Church. Rather, his suggestions have to be judged by the Church.

Does this perhaps enable us to see how the theologian can combine intellectual audacity and intellectual modesty? The combination, which is urged upon him, seems impossible. But it becomes feasible if the audacity is referred to the work of understanding and the modesty to the claim of certitude. The theologian must be bold in his quest for understanding, all the time pursuing new lines of thought;

but he remains modest about the certitude of his conclusions and theories, leaving them to make their way, perhaps slowly, perhaps with much alteration, within the corporate faith of the Church.[1]

Theology as the activity of understanding God's self-disclosure in Christ with the resources of human reason and the consequent moulding of our grasp of revelation into an organised body of knowledge is essentially one. There is only one science of theology, and the divisions introduced into theology for systematic and pedagogical reasons, necessary as they are, must not cause its essential unity to be forgotten.

This one theology can be called dogmatic theology, a name introduced in the seventeenth century, if this is understood in its widest meaning. Dogmatic theology in this sense is reflection upon the whole of revelation; it is not limited to the study of dogmas or truths already expressly taught by the Church as revealed. The name 'doctrinal theology' would perhaps be better English; for the word 'dogmatics' has not achieved full acceptance into the English language.

But dogmatic or doctrinal theology is usually distinguished from both moral theology and biblical theology.

No clear or significant distinction can be made between dogmatic and moral theology. The self-disclosure of God studied in dogmatic theology is the source of man's christian activity and this christian activity is itself an aspect of God's self-giving. Moral theology, then, when a genuine theology, is but part of dogmatic theology taken as a whole, and what is said about sources and methods applies equally to it. The distinction between dogmatic and moral theology is just a convenient, practical division of subject-matter, of superficial import, so that it is difficult to decide with some points whether to treat them in one or the other, and the decision is generally made for *ad hoc* practical reasons. The question how far moral theology has lived up to its calling as a part of theology is not for me to answer.

I must add that the distinction between dogmatic and moral theology is not a distinction between the theoretical or speculative and the practical. This latter distinction is inapplicable here for these reasons: christian doctrine is a message of salvation and therefore of

[1] These remarks were drafted before I read Professor Mascall's lecture, *Theology and History*, previously quoted. Although our immediate concerns are different, there is an interesting convergence of conclusions.

vital practical import; the christian life depends upon faith and is fostered by contemplation; the ultimate end of man is the contemplation of God in the beatific vision. Doctrine and life are inseparable in the christian thing, and in theology. As St Thomas pointed out, theology as a science transcends the distinction between speculative and practical knowledge.[1]

The distinction between dogmatic and biblical theology has more meaning; indeed, it is necessary and important, provided the unity of theology is never disregarded.

All theology is biblical in the sense of being centred on the bible and acknowledging the unique function of the bible as the inspired Word of God. But the special character and place of the bible mean that in theology, reflection precisely on the biblical expression of revelation must always form a distinct and uniquely valuable part of the theologian's task. Biblical theology is that—an effort to understand revelation precisely in its biblical form; a systematic exegesis that gathers together ideas scattered through the bible, traces biblical themes and follows the development of biblical doctrines, so as to present the thought of the bible in an ordered exposition, while keeping the same concepts and expressions as used in the bible.

Now biblical theology is fully a theology—I mean a task fully within the orbit of theology—and, consequently, it should be pursued subject to all the norms that govern theology generally. In other words, the effort to understand the biblical revelation takes place within the Church, under the positive (not just negative) guidance of her faith and subject to the authority of the *magisterium*. It is true that the biblical theologian will make use of philology and the techniques of the historical sciences—in short, of the methods of biblical criticism—and he is entitled to distinguish the limits of what, in the traditional understanding of the bible, can be established as true by such methods. To do this is merely to avoid confusion, to face and not shirk problems. But he is not entitled to present something as biblical teaching which is in apparent conflict with the present faith of the Church and say, 'Well, that's what the bible says; it's up to the theologian to solve the problem.' No, the solution of the conflict is his business as much as that of the dogmatic theologian. He must not evade the difficulty; he may find himself unable to resolve it on his own, but he must not be indifferent to it. Biblical theology, unlike

[1] cf. I, q. 1, art. 4.

some of its preliminary, auxiliary disciplines, is not a natural understanding of the bible, but an understanding based on faith and guided
by the Church. The biblicist has no more right than other theologians
to go his own way, using as an excuse the exigencies of scientific
method. Biblical theology, I suggest, must become more consciously
theological, without, however, losing its distinctive character.[1]

The distinction between biblical theology and dogmatic theology
understood in the strict sense comes not so much from sources, norms
and methods as from the fact that the biblical theologian consciously
limits the range of his questioning. This more specialised questioning
then has its effect on the comparative importance of sources and
norms and on the choice of method. But the primary distinction is
found in the range of questions.

The biblical theologian asks questions that can be answered while
remaining within the patterns of thought and the expressions of the
bible. He is of course interested in the content of the biblical revelation, not just in the manner in which it is expressed; but his concern
is with that content as yet not separated from the particular expression
it received during the time in which biblical revelation was being
given.

For the dogmatic theologian, the bible is also the primary source,
but he places no limit to the range of his questions. He brings every
resource of human knowledge to bear in an effort to understand the
content of biblical revelation. He makes this effort by a ceaseless
questioning that takes him outside the biblical formulations. When
the biblical theologian has expounded what the bible says about
Christ in the way in which it says it, the dogmatic theologian is still
asking questions about this teaching, trying to relate it to all that we
otherwise know about man and God. And in his endeavour to understand he uses concepts, structures of thought, expressions, not found
in the bible. He is led, for example, to discuss problems of nature and
person, and to reflect on the structure of Christ's consciousness. It is
biblical truth he is striving to understand, but the process of understanding involves the ever-fresh ordering of insights and the frequent
formation of new concepts. He casts biblical revelation into a mould
that is no longer directly biblical, but in so far as this new form has
value it represents a deeper understanding of the same truth.

[1] For some of the points made, see Karl Rahner, S.J., 'Exegese und Dogmatik',
Stimmen der Zeit, 168 (1960–1), pp. 241–62.

Needless to say, the process described takes place not at once nor in the mind of one man—it is a historical process within the Church. The theologian must work as a member of a corporate body extending over the centuries. Moreover, the developing understanding is not exclusively the work of theology, so that part of the theologian's task is to understand and coordinate the developments that have occurred within the consciousness of the Church. Inevitably, then, he is more concerned with the data of tradition than is his biblical confrère. Unlike the latter he deals directly with the different forms revelation has assumed in the history of doctrine.

Thus, the biblical theologian and the dogmatic theologian are concerned with the same revelation. The biblical theologian scrutinises it in the light of faith and of the tradition of the Church, as every theologian must do, but he limits his scrutiny to its biblical form and does not go beyond that. The dogmatic theologian depends upon the work of the biblical theologian and cannot do his own work without it. It is in fact part of his own total task, so that he must begin his reflection with an awareness of what has been done in biblical theology. But then he further pursues his effort of understanding and does not fear the re-ordering every truth undergoes in the process of developing understanding. He is prepared to call upon the entire data of tradition and all the resources of human knowledge in his attempts to gain a better insight into God's revelation.

If the range of questioning gives the distinction between biblical and dogmatic theology, it is plain that the distinction cannot be a hard-and-fast one. There is in fact no clear boundary between the two. The interpretation of any document is always affected by the standpoint of the interpreter, and the questions asked by the biblical theologian even within the limits which he assigns himself will be determined in part by the historical situation and his prior understanding of christian revelation. Again, what is happening in dogmatic theology as a whole will have repercussions on biblical theology. This is as it should and will be, if biblical theology remains a genuine theology.

On the other hand, the dogmatic theologian can never put his bible away, and he must allow himself to be influenced by developments in biblical theology. This is because the bible is the privileged expression of the christian revelation and can never be superseded. It is not just a document of the past, but a present reality, acting as the sacrament of God's Word within the Church. No other expression of revelation is the Word of God in the unique sense in which the bible is, as inspired. Furthermore, it gives us the deposit of faith in the original, apostolic form, which is the norm for all future developments. It is, as it were, the permanent presence of the apostolic consciousness in the midst of the present consciousness of the Church.

Designed by God for the purpose of serving as the centre and norm for all subsequent christian faith and thinking, the bible is inexhaustible. In his search for understanding, the theologian pursues one or other line of thought. He increases his understanding along a particular line of inquiry. But his thought is necessarily selective. He cannot consider all aspects at once, and there are always further aspects unconsidered as yet. So the dogmatic theologian can never leave the bible behind; he must keep coming back to it, to draw on it afresh as well as to check his insights. Although theology is reflection on the revealed reality of God, not just on a form of words even if they are biblical, the bible as inspired is both a privileged place for our encounter with God revealing himself to us and the central expression of our christian faith. For this reason every true theologian is a man of the bible, and all theology is biblical.

At the same time, the restricted range of questioning within which the biblical theologian confines himself shows how necessary it is that theology should not be limited to biblical theology in the strict sense. Biblical theology by itself is incapable of answering all the questions that modern man asks about revealed truth. It is not enough, for example, to present the christian doctrine of man in biblical terms; the theologian must grapple with all the questions that arise about the doctrine in relation to what modern knowledge says about man, his origin and nature; and that is beyond the scope of the biblical theologian as such. Pursued by itself in isolation from the rest of theology, biblical theology can become as remote as Egyptology and as irrelevant for the life of mankind of today. The renewal in theology and in the life of the Church brought about by the biblical revival can be deceptive here, if we are not careful. It has been a time of necessary *ressourcement*. But if the biblical revival hardens into an exclusive biblicism, it will peter out as an ineffectual anachronism. The biblical revival must be prolonged into a general renewal of theology. The bible, it may be remarked, has been given to start christian thinking, not to abolish it. We must not refuse to pursue our questions beyond its formulations.

Here it is worth noting that the idea is false that the division between biblical and dogmatic theology corresponds to the division between Protestant and Catholic theology. Protestant and Catholic theologies differ according to the differences between Protestant and Catholic ecclesiologies. Just as we differ, according to our respective ecclesiologies, about the norms governing christian faith, so too we differ about the norms governing theological thought. Both accept the privileged place of the bible but differ about the norms governing its interpretation; both in some way accept an interpretative role of tradition but differ about its normative value.[1] So, Protestant Biblical theology differs from Catholic biblical theology in this respect, and Protestant dogmatic theology differs from Catholic dogmatic theology in the same respect; but for both Protestants and Catholics a biblical and dogmatic theology are possible.

The false idea I have mentioned is due to the vicissitudes that have affected theology in the past. For a period the bible was unduly neglected in Catholic theology; a neglect, however, which was never justifiable on Catholic principles and which is being speedily remedied today. On the other hand, their insistence on the bible and their rejection of Catholic ecclesiology have made Protestants more subject to the danger of an exclusive biblicism. But dogmatic theology, in the sense of the unlimited questioning of revealed truth and a going beyond biblical formulation, has flourished and still flourishes in the Protestant Churches. Indeed, the first impression a Catholic may receive from Protestant theology is the immense extent to which it has been influenced by current philosophy. To understand much Protestant theology a greater knowledge is required of modern philosophy than is customary in a Catholic theologian.[2]

The distinction between biblical and dogmatic theology is basic and important. The division of dogmatic theology into various branches according to subject-matter, such as into Christology, ecclesiology, sacramental theology and so on, is far less important. Revealed truth forms such a close unity that the various branches constantly overlap and the division is often a matter of practical convenience. Again, new branches are formed, as the need arises for a more developed consideration of a particular point, as, for example,

[1] *v.* Reid, p. 138 and note.   [2] cp. Kenny, p. 224 (*infra*).

the recent formation of ecumenical theology understood as a particular part of theology studying special problems.

I do not think that dogmatic theology can be divided into positive and speculative theology, so as to make two parts of theology that can be pursued as separate though related sciences. In its effort to understand revelation theology uses both positive and speculative methods, but the two are inseparable in their working. It is true that on its positive side, theology gathers round itself various auxiliary sciences that investigate the positive data strictly according to the methods of historical criticism, but the scrutiny of the positive data becomes properly theological, is positive theology, when it is carried out by the theological mind using all its resources and criteria. Consequently, positive theology advances under the light of the speculative understanding. On the other hand, speculative theology is an attempt to understand a historical revelation; it can proceed, then, only by scrutinising the data of revelation and tradition more and more carefully. The importance of a profound study of tradition for any fruitful theological reflection can hardly be exaggerated. A great speculative theologian would be able to break out of the limited doctrinal understanding of his time by means of his immense knowledge of tradition, as Scheeben did. The two facets of the work of theology, the positive and speculative, must go together. To divide them one from the other and pursue them separately is fatally to distort both. May I remark here that it would be better to use the word 'Scholastic' exclusively in a historical sense as referring to the thought and methods of the Scholastics? To use it of speculative theology in general is misleading, since it seems to limit the theologian to the methods known and practised in the Middle Ages, and isolate him from the advances made on the positive side of theology. Theological method has developed since the Middle Ages.

On the practical level of the establishment of theology in the universities, what is important is that theology should not be reduced to a collection of its auxiliary sciences, such as patristics, history of theology, and so on, placed alongside a biblical theology conceived more as a historical science than as a true theology. There ought to be a full-blooded dogmatic or doctrinal theology, which tackles the full range of theological questioning, using both positive and speculative methods. It must, however, be no longer controversial but ecumenical in character.

The distinctive characteristics of Catholic theology

To examine adequately the distinctive characteristics of Catholic theology as Catholic would necessitate outlining the Catholic doctrine of the Church. But presupposing that doctrine and its obvious implications, such as the doctrinal authority of the *magisterium*, the position of the theologian can be very simply described in the phrase *sentire in Ecclesia*. That form of the phrase is preferable to *sentire cum Ecclesia*, which can give the impression that the Church is identical with the hierarchy.

Theology is not and cannot be an individual enterprise—it is an ecclesial activity. That it is a cooperative enterprise in the sense that all other sciences are cooperative enterprises is plain. But just as the Church is more than a social organisation, so also the social dimension of theology is deeper than that found in the other sciences. The theologian can do his work only from within the corporate faith of the Church, and the nature of his work demands a constant effort to increase his union with that corporate faith. *Sentire in Ecclesia* means that the theologian accepts fully the norms that govern the corporate faith of the Church, in particular the authoritative teaching of the *magisterium*. But more is involved than this. A theologian does not satisfy the demands of his calling by giving each decree of the *magisterium* its respective measure of authority and then going his own way. God's revelation is present to us as immanent in the corporate faith of the Church. The theologian must work in the midst of the Church, sensitive to every aspect of its faith and life. This is not a denial of the need for a discernment of spirits, but an exhortation that the theologian should not isolate himself from the general life of the Church. The manifestations of its faith, its liturgical life, its missionary work, its ecumenical concern—all these and other aspects of its life are the soil in which alone theology can be fruitful.

The present situation of a divided Christendom is inevitably reflected in theology. Since theology is an ecclesial enterprise, its state corresponds to the state of the Church. As long as the christian Churches are divided they cannot have a common theology. Theology cannot be one when the Churches are many. Catholics, then, must be separated from other Christians in their theological work, as long as they are separated from them in their Church life.

But if theology must reflect the divisions of christians, it must at the same time reflect the degree of unity they already possess. Separated christians have much in common with each other; what they have in common makes possible a theological co-operation, and the closer christians draw together the closer can become their theological co-operation, until when the unity of christians is achieved, so too will be the unity of christian theology.

The present unity in division among christians affects the different parts of theology differently. Thus, a much closer collaboration is possible in biblical theology than in most parts of dogmatic theology. Much biblical theology is common to both Protestants and Catholics; indeed, Catholics have drawn heavily on Protestant authors. Nevertheless, the inevitable difference of norm governing the whole enterprise of biblical theology must not be overlooked. Much collaboration is possible also on the positive side of theology and, again, in areas, such as Christology, where there is a large measure of agreement.

Even where, owing to our divisions, there cannot be a common theological understanding, there can be an ecumenical dialogue. Where we cannot as yet share the same theology, we can turn towards one another in an effort at understanding.

In brief, divided Churches must have divided theologies, but what they have in common allows a common theology to the same extent. Divided Churches in dialogue have theologies in dialogue.

What this should mean in terms of practical organisation at the university level is not within my competence to say. My aim has been to set down the principles that should guide practical decisions.

A last word. Theology is a noble task. But like every other task or function that arises from our christian profession it is a service within the community. It is a great privilege to have the opportunity of developing an understanding of God's Word, but it is a privilege for the service of the community of believers. Theology must serve, otherwise it becomes both sterile and harmful.

7. The Existing Practice in the British Universities

(I) SCOTLAND—THE BIBLICAL TRADITION

J. K. S. REID

Basis of Theology

The beginning is made with Holy Scripture. All christians and all christian Churches set out from this point; christian doctrine, all would agree, is essentially related to Holy Scripture as to an indispensable source. Here is a basic agreement that transcended and survived the Reformation: *Articulae Schmalcaldicae* (1537)—verbum Dei condit articulos fidei, praeterea nemo ne angelus quidem; *Concilium Tridentinum* (1546)—(evangelium) quod promissum ante per prophetas in Scripturis sanctis, Dominus noster Jesus Christus, Dei Filius, proprio ore primum promulgavit, deinde per suos apostolos, tanquam fontem omnis et salutaris veritatis et morum disciplinae, omni creaturae praedicari iussit; *Confessio Scoticana* (1560)—credimus et confitemur, ex Scripturis divinis Dei cognitionem abunde hominibus tradi. Christian doctrine reposes on Holy Scripture.

In a sense it is a pity that we cannot simply remain at this starting point. The Church itself accepts and believes the Scriptures; it continues to draw nourishment for itself from them; and it is obliged to commend them to all men by every possible apologetic and declaratory means. But the Church does not remain content simply with the Scriptures alone. Divine Service does not consist only in reading the Scriptures; christian pedagogy does not simply require that passages of Scripture be memorised; christian obedience is not fulfilled simply by conforming to the Decalogue. Above all, doctrine does not consist simply in the repetition *in extenso* or by selection of the written words of Holy Scripture. In other words, doctrine is not identical with Holy Scripture. Scripture declares that 'the Lord is my shepherd' (Ps 23:1),

133

but the theology of today puts the matter otherwise: men stand in an I–Thou relationship to God. Or again, according to St Paul, 'God was in Christ, reconciling the world unto himself' (2 Cor 5: 19), and he might be expected not immediately to recognise as implicated in what he says, the doctrine of the *communicatio idiomatum*. There is no identity between the two statements paired together; yet in each case the non-scriptural statement is not judged untrue simply because it differs in phrasing from anything contained in Holy Scripture. The relation of doctrine to Scripture, though essential in character, is more complex than mere identity.

Further, once we move beyond the simple citation of Scripture in order to discharge the doctrinal obligation, we are faced immediately by the phenomenon of difference among doctrinal statements. For example, in the case of the central doctrine of the incarnation, Cyril of Alexandria (perhaps anticipated by the heretical Apollinarius) deals with the problem of the *persona* (almost 'personality' in modern language) of Christ in terms of *anhypostasia*, declaring that the second person of the Trinity assumed human nature, that the *persona* in Jesus Christ is to be located in the Divine Son or Logos, and that strictly speaking there was no human *persona* but only an impersonal humanity. But on the other hand it was maintained that the humanity assumed cannot be said to be impersonal, though we may properly say that it possessed no independent personality; and Leontius of Byzantium and John of Damascus accordingly give a solution in terms of *enhypostasia*, that the humanity of Christ is personal in the Logos. This is only to illustrate that when a move is made beyond the terms of Scripture, it is not only difference from Scripture that occurs, but also difference amongst those who, with every intention of remaining faithful to Scripture, proceed to state christian doctrine.

But even more: the appearance of such difference is to be traced behind explicit doctrine back to the more basic level of Scripture itself. When the statement is made: God is love, it might seem that no departure is made from the testimony of Scripture itself. But this is not the case in any simple sense. The question is quite properly asked: in what sense is the English word 'love' used here? Is it to be understood in the sense of *eros* or of *agape*? Thus formulated, the question is of course readily answered: reference to the original language in which the New Testament Scriptures were written assures us that it is *agape* that is meant. But there are other questions of the same kind that are not so easily solved. In Mk 1:15, the term *metanoeo* is used; and this is translated in the Authorised Version, Douai, and the New English Bible alike by the English 'repent'. But the same Greek word is used also in Lk 13:3, 5, and here the Authorised Version and the New English Bible render again 'repent', while Douai gives 'do penance'. Those who do not adhere to the Roman Church have been accustomed to detect here a sensible and significant difference of a doctrinal kind, but this difference is embedded in Scripture itself through the medium of translation. Or again, Fr Corbishley of the Farm Street Church, London, commending the N.E.B. New Testament as a 'most useful instrument in the business of promoting unity between all christians', went on to point out that some details 'undoubtedly would have to be modified in the light of Catholic sentiment' (reported *Ecumenical Press Service*, 31 March 1961). But to modify any part of the translation to suit Roman Catholic sentiment would constitute a quite new and inadmissible factor in this enterprise of translation.

We are thus faced with the phenomenon of difference (to use a neutral and indefinite word in preference to 'deviation' or 'divergence') as we turn to the very source from which, as is allowed on all hands, christian doctrine springs. Its presence is made especially evident when translation is being done; and historically the problem of the status of translations of the bible was never solved. Besides, no one nowadays thinks that words in one language have always, or even often, exact equivalents in another language; and this means that the process of translation is not absolutely distinguishable from that of interpretation. But then too, at a deeper level, no one believes that the conceptual value of any word can be exactly defined, as the monetary value of the pound sterling is defined against the standard of gold. Certain measures have been proposed to eliminate this perplexity. I think not so much of the simple person who said: The A.V. was good enough for St Paul, and it's good enough for me. More clearly theological suggestions have been made. It is proposed that one version of the Scriptures may and must be regarded as authoritative, e.g. the Vulgate. Yet I do not know that the problem has ever been finally resolved, whether the Tridentine decree recognised the Vulgate as the absolutely authoritative version, or simply as the authoritative version among Latin translations. Again it is proposed (see *Divino Afflante Spiritu*) that it is possible to construct 'a purer

and more accurate edition of the Word of God', so that we may
finally repose upon a perfect 'original text'. But in the nature of the
case, this 'infallible Bible-X', as Brunner calls it (see *Revelation and
Reason* (1947), p. 274), can only be hypothetical. Nor does it seem to
be a more competent solution to suggest that Latin is the language
of absolute precision; or, even more fancifully, that it is Hebrew that
is the language of heaven.[1]

If, however, it is perplexing that this phenomenon of difference
should be lodged in the source of all doctrine itself, one consequent
advantage deserves notice. The considerations just urged, and others
like them, have done much to mitigate the sharpness of the difference
between those who hold a 'fundamentalist' view of the bible and
those who cannot accept the 'literal inerrancy' of Scripture. There is
still of course skirmishing, but the front between them has been
softened up. There is an increasingly extensive ground common to
those who seriously look to Holy Scripture as the source and the
norm of christian doctrine.

These rather perplexing facts are noted here, however, for a quite
specific reason. This reason is of course not to detract from the
authority of Scripture, but to reveal the character of the authority it
has. The fact is 'we have this treasure in earthen vessels' (2 Cor. 4:7).
No doubt God could have arranged the matter otherwise; but he has
not done so. The source for all christian doctrine is itself, and has an
authority, of this kind. To realise that it is in this way that God works
is of great importance, as we go on to examine the relation between
doctrine and this source. It pleases God to contrive the conservation
of the deposit of faith in this indirect and even contingent way. Of
course adequate safeguards there are—the *testimonium internum
Spiritus Sancti* against arbitrary interpretation, and against individu-
alism the membership of the body of Christ. But there is no cast-iron
guarantee protecting the authority of the source. Neither then shall
we expect, when it comes to the expression and development of this
deposit in doctrine, that there should be any such cast-iron guarantee.

If Holy Scripture is regarded as in and by itself the sole authoritative textbook of the knowledge of God, then doctrine, including
that element of difference already noted, would arise by logical de-

[1] This question is a little nearer solution with the publication of a new edition
of the Revised Standard Version acceptable to Roman Catholics. (*Editor.*)

duction. It would consist in conclusions being drawn from data or premises contained in Scripture, which, however, Scripture itself refrains from stating. Such a view may seem to be required if the Scriptures be held to have come about *Spiritu Sancto dictante* (Co. Trid. IV), or if they be held to impart 'instruction' (so Beveridge translating *Inst* 1.6.2, though Calvin himself has *doctrina*). But the true character of Holy Scripture and the nature of its determination of doctrine do not come to adequate expression in either of these statements, true enough though they are in themselves. The office of Scripture in giving rise to doctrine is not the provision of a number of fragmentary syllogisms which doctrine must simply complete. Its office is rather to witness to him who is not only *dominus et rex Scripturae* but also the *res* of what is written; and at the same time both to conserve for and to offer to the Church as it addresses itself to the doctrinal task this same Jesus Christ. The Jesus Christ who is thus conserved and presented is conveyed in his entirety: he is both the incarnate Jesus and the risen Christ. And the Church which allows itself to be addressed by Scripture is exposed to Christ both in his humanity and his divinity, both as incarnate and as risen and regnant. Holy Scripture is thus the norm for all that christians can rightly say. For in Scripture we have the uniquely original and proximate witness to him who lived and died and rose again. When this Word of God is read or preached, then he who is himself the *res* as well as the *rex* of the written Word recognises what is done, and is present, not of course as recollection and remembrance only, but as risen reality. Jesus Christ acts now 'as it is written of him', and will continue so to act until the end of time.

As Scripture is the source of all right doctrine in the sense that by its statements it presents and has presented since it was written a historical Jesus who is also a risen Christ, so doctrine is the function of these two moments. Because Scripture presents believers with a historical Jesus, anything said doctrinally by the Church must be faithful to Scripture. On the other hand, because Scripture is not less witness to a risen Christ, the Church has to exercise its doctrinal function with some difference from the bare words of Scripture, using different terms, employing different concepts, restating what the Church has always believed in a faithful dissimilarity to Scripture which can be characterised neither as deviation nor as identity. With reference to Scripture, the Church is *ecclesia audiens* and also *ecclesia obediens*, and only so can it rightly and authoritatively be *ecclesia docens*.

In determining what it *hic et nunc* ought to teach, the Church is determined primarily by these two moments. But for its guidance it has also its continuity with its own past—what can be called tradition. For the Church of today has not only to reckon with the facts of a historical life, but also with a risen Lord present to the Church of every age and generation. The Church has always had not only to be obedient but also listening, and consequently upon these activities to undertake its duty of teaching. The doctrine that then arises is not a development in any ordinary sense: not a historical inevitability as Harnack supposed, not a positive statement of the contents of the religious consciousness (cf. W. Koehler's *Dogmengeschichte*, als Geschichte des christlichen Selbstbewusstseins, with F. Buri's *Dogmatik*, als Selbstverständnis des christlichen Glaubens). But neither is it characterised at any point by infallibility; when Dr Dwyer of Leeds asks (*Breakthrough*, Winter 1962), 'how are we to be sure that the development of dogma, the insights into and unfolding of the revealed deposit are in fact in accordance with that revelation and not simply unbridled imaginings and indeed errors?', the answer is that we are not made sure by means of any external guarantee, or any built-in 'safeguard of infallibility'. On the contrary, we have to go about the matter the hard way: we must 'try the spirits' (1 Jn 4:1).[1] To survey the history of doctrine is such a process of testing. Secular

---

[1] Who may interpret Scripture?—from one point of view this is the issue that precipitated the Reformation. Whatever may be thought of H. Küng's judgment on the narrower question (op. cit. *infra*, p. 195), it is certainly not possible to say that Luther's interpretation in general was a consequence of his opposition to the Pope. Luther had begun to interpret Scripture long before he moved on to radical mistrust of the Pope. This interpretation differed from that of the hierarchy. Now undoubtedly the hierarchy has the right and the power to excommunicate in certain circumstances. Did Luther's variant interpretation of Scripture constitute such circumstances? If the function of interpreting Scripture reposes solely with the hierarchy, then the hierarchy was right to extrude Luther as soon as possible from the fellowship of the Church, if only *pro salute animarum fidelium*. But supposing that the function of interpreting Scripture is vested properly in the Church as such, that the hierarchy (or whoever is the authorized custodian of doctrine) exercises here a *diakonia* within the Church, that its office is to give public definition to what Scripture is saying to the Church, then simple divergence from what has been defined cannot alone be the standard of what is true interpretation. The shutters may not be brought down too soon to exclude the divergent witness. Otherwise the hierarchy is shut up to talking merely with itself in the company of the archaeological survivals of its own statements.

wisdom realises that it is a foolish man who has to learn from his own experience; and the Church has a right to be as wise as he. Hence what is doctrinally said must pass three tests: is it what *hic et nunc* the risen Christ (perhaps newly) requires the Church to say; is it faithful to what Holy Scripture has declared; and what has the experience of the Church to contribute for the guidance of the present day Church at this point? There is no easier or more automatic way of determining doctrine than this; it is thus that we are required *sentire in ecclesia* (see H. Küng: *The Council and Reunion*, and of course Ignatius).

As the character of the source determines the special way in which doctrine arises, so it determines also the character of the knowledge of which doctrine is the systematic statement. Here we are again back on ground that is held in common by those adhering to different forms of christian belief. This mode of knowing, Scripture calls faith (as Rom. 1:17). When this mode of knowing is spoken of as something in which men are active, Scripture refers to it as believing (as Ac. 16:31). To know by means of faith and to know in some other sense are different things. Yet both may be present when it is a public historical object which is the object known. The cross of Jesus Christ is such a public historical object. Of it, two quite different estimates are possible: for the Roman soldiers the cross was simply a distasteful duty to be discharged, and they diced away the long hours of guard duty; but St Paul saw the same cross as 'the power of God unto salvation' (Rom. 1:16). When it comes to a comparative assessment of these two typical estimates, the believer is bound to affirm that by faith St Paul has been admitted to a fuller understanding of what is there, and that faith accordingly is a truer mode of apprehension than unbelief. We cannot, however, say that this truer mode of apprehension is simply an extension of the powers of thought, reason or intelligence which belong naturally to man. It is according to Scripture both a gift of God and an act of man. Hence Scripture can both declare that 'flesh and blood hath not revealed it, but my Father which is in heaven' (Mt. 16:17); and also lay it as an injunction upon men, 'Believe on the Lord Jesus Christ' (Ac. 16:31). Jesus *kata sarka* remains simply a historical figure of some distinction. But Jesus *kata sarka* is an unreal abstraction. It is the same Jesus who also is the risen Christ; and *kata pneuma* he evokes from men that mode of apprehension which is proper to full understanding of himself. As

Hoskyns (*The Fourth Gospel*) says: Jesus Christ is 'the place where it is demanded of men that they should believe'.

Here then is the distinctive substance of doctrine. Of course, on the evidence to be found in Holy Scripture and also in the not negligible testimony of secular witness, we believe *that* Jesus lived at a certain point in space and time. But we believe also that this same Jesus is the Son of God who is at the right hand of the Father in the heavenly places and so we believe *in* Jesus Christ our Lord. The unfolding record of doctrine is pinned down at the spatio-temporal point 'under Pontius Pilate'. But doctrine has another moment in the continuing presence of the risen Lord with his people. We may put it thus: the written record brings to our *notitia* the facts concerning Jesus and leads us to *assensus* of them; but that we are brought to *fiducia* is due to the fact that this same written record is the Gospel of him who is alive for ever more. Doctrine is the function of these two correlates.

Theology in the University

By theology is here meant the systematic exposition of such doctrine as has just been spoken of. Comprehensively understood, such a systematic exposition includes an account of the epistemological basis, and also auxiliary adjuncts like Church History. That theology has a place in the university is impressively demonstrated by the fact of the continuous existence of faculties of theology in the ancient universities of England and Scotland from the time of their foundation to the present day. Further, it is evident that, the validity of its basis and presuppositions being allowed and admitted, theology has an incontestable right to a place among the various disciplines which universities exist to pursue. Hydra-headed as it is, it is represented by individual subsidiary disciplines of extraordinary antiquity among many parvenu subjects which universities have later admitted. Modern European History is considered a respectable subject—but the history of the christian Church goes back for more than 1,900 years, and the scholar who professes the subject must be in some sense and degree master of (say) another 2,000 years. Modern Languages have carved a niche for themselves in the modern university situation—but theology has been studying the languages of the original Scriptures for two or more millennia. Divinity has, for as long as the venerable subject of philosophy, and of course for much longer than any of the experimental sciences, been making affirmations about truth and the ultimate nature of things. Study in any of these fields, even if it is only of the kind that can be called 'research', is eminently worthy of academic pursuit in the university context.

If this were all that could be said, theology could be regarded as contributing an element to the whole pattern of university studies: it would be one element among many, valuable for helping to complete a total picture, but not otherwise distinctive. But theology has something more to give than this. We may put it thus. Theology contributes not so much to the comprehensiveness of the whole field of university study as to its comprehensibleness. In wide terms, the specific obligation of theology in the university is to set all that is done in the university, and indeed the whole of life, in its supernatural context. The impatience with which this statement is often greeted is justified if nothing more is said. For then the serious-minded university lecturer in Botany or the earnest schoolteacher of Maths must be pitied. How can there be a christian Botany or a theological Maths recognisably different from the ordinary secular variety? The question is so difficult to answer that many feel forced to content themselves with admitting the existence of a supernatural context and reconciling themselves to its practical irrelevance and hence its fundamental dispensability. At the best, one must then put up with compartmentalism: there is mathematical truth, and also there is (one may suppose) doctrinal truth; but between the two there is no connection either practical or theoretical.

Yet there is a better answer than this. As already said, the moments that determine doctrine are two: the historical Jesus and the risen Christ. The mode of apprehension characteristic and proper here is faith; and faith beyond *notitia* and *assensus* involves *fiducia*. Recent philosophy, both theological (as in Kierkegaard) and also secular (as in Existentialism) has given sharper point to the issue here: truth is apprehended by means of commitment (cf. the more recent involvement). If theology can firmly and effectively say this, then into the university situation, in which so many immensely absorbing and also important intellectual pursuits are carried on, it will be precipitating an element of singular significance, which helps at once to define and also to orientate other disciplines without invalidating them. To take out of its context and slightly adapt a phrase which must be regarded as significant (see Sir Walter Moberly: *The Crisis in the University*) theology must 'explore the concrete actualities below the conceptual currency'. The phrase is percipiently apt. There are constellations of concepts worked into systems which serve to express certain aspects of the concrete underlying reality. And yet the aspects thus duly recorded are neither integrated nor exhaustive. In this situation, theology has to affirm the epistemological validity and effectiveness of its own proper mode of apprehension, *fiducia* or faith. It should not allow itself to be diverted by the extraordinarily impressive accomplishments of the experimental sciences to pretend to be a science whose method and means are identical or even similar. On the other hand, it must resist the high-spirited but finally rather naïve attempt to rationalise theological judgments into 'emotive states' (A. J. Ayer). It happens here, as often, that the point which is most vulnerable and accordingly most frequently attacked is in fact the pivotal and also the most impregnable in the whole line. From here the other partially true aspects receive their definition and their orientation: they are shown to be not the only aspects; and the whole, of which they are the partial aspects, is itself finally knowable in terms of commitment or faith.

We have here a key to the understanding of certain puzzling aspects of the university situation today, though a distinction has to be made between the ancient universities, the redbrick institutions of a few years' existence, and the more elderly redbrick universities. Action has recently been taken by one of the last type to remove from its charter an impediment to the teaching of religion within its precincts. The situation to be remedied is due to historical and local factors of a complicated kind. Suffice it to say here that it is symptomatic of a fairly general condition at the beginning of the century, in which those dealing with public affairs, while they might be themselves favourably disposed to religion, knew that to touch religious matters publicly was to meddle with fire, and that even beneficent action was likely to incur at least denominational odium. It is gratifying to have proof on all hands that the inflammation has receded from this morbid condition, though some of the senior men in the universities have neither forgotten it nor ceased to be alarmed by it.

But further historical fact supplies the ground of another and even more prevalent attitude sometimes exemplified in the university towards theology. In another university of the same age group, when private benefaction made it possible to found a chair of theology, it was primarily to be concerned with the so-called history of religion; and when its field was extended there was added biblical and historical theology—a title which has its parallels elsewhere. The chief motive for giving this title to the subject is evident: so named, the subject connoted a discipline that was positivist and, if strictly interpreted, the teaching of it would have to be limited to purely factual accounts of what at different times has been offered as christian doctrine. The reason for wishing to limit what was being done in the name of theology is equally evident. A principle of importance, though not of the first importance, was invoked to justify what was being done and what intended. It was the principle of 'academic detachment'. Personal adherence to religious belief was (rightly) regarded as involving commitment, and commitment was (wrongly) thought to impart to the situation a subjective and ultimately distorting element. It was not widely enough noticed that thus to proscribe commitment was itself a radical commitment.

The pattern in the older universities is naturally different. There, faculties of theology are securely present and, even if the numbers who read theology do not increase in the same way as do the science and even the arts faculties today, the continued existence of faculties of theology is not in danger. This is not surprising, but it must not lead us to suppose that things are fundamentally unchanged. In their beginnings, the universities were in a sense a department of the Church. 'During the early Middle Ages, the Church was the sole depository of culture. . . . The thinking of Europe, whether in the schools and universities or outside them, was carried on by tonsured clerks over a field of experience which was strictly confined by the sacred texts and their ancillary literature.' A. J. Toynbee has told us that for long enough, Mathematics was chiefly studied for the purpose of determining the date of Easter. But of course times changed. For an assessment of what then happened, it is illuminating to turn to a secular historian—not because what he says is necessarily true, but because it is the kind of thing he says which, rightly or wrongly, has made the situation today what it is. H. A. L. Fisher (*A History of Europe* from which also the last quotation is taken) writes of the sixteenth century and the emergence of the 'lay mind': 'Strong and continuous as were the theological interests, they were now balanced by an exciting body of new knowledge, having no connection with theology, and the fruit of mental processes which theology was unable to turn to account. With a sharp gesture of impatience, Europe turned away from the vast literature of commentators and glosses, which the pedants of the late middle ages had inscribed.' A movement of separation took place; the newer studies floated out on a floodtide of increasing independence and theology was left insulated. In some instances this was supplemented by a movement of extrusion: theology made its own isolation more complete by denouncing certain of the newer studies and their results. Further, it was only natural that with a growing number of disciplines from which to choose, those who studied theology should constitute a diminishing proportion in the universities. But the tendency for theology to understand its task in terms only of taking in hand those who intended to take holy orders impoverished the universities, and the impoverishment has been undoubtedly accentuated where, as in the case of England, large and influential Churches adopted the policy of 'withdrawing (their ordinands) from the strongly staffed university to read their theology elsewhere' in seminaries (see F. R. Barry in *Expository Times*, November 1962).

But something takes place here which is more important than the withdrawal of one touch of colour, leaving the academic scene just so much the less gay. What is lost by such retreat on the part of theology is an element that cannot be replaced from any other source. If faith really is a valid mode of apprehension, then knowledge is not only the poorer but must be disturbed and distorted, when it is not making its contribution. No wonder then that the 'scientific mind' dominates the scene; and no wonder if it is assumed that faith is simply a matter of looking at things from a private and fallacious point of view.

It is not possible to say much here about remedying the situation. But at least two measures seem primarily necessary. There has been a tendency to seminarisation on the part of theology—partly inevitable, due to the rise and growth of other independent disciplines; partly culpable, due to a certain failure of nerve in the face of the vigour and prestige of these new studies. It is time that this tendency be reversed, since (*a*) there is need for theology to be readily available to all university students—not so much the contents of theology as its methodology as a valid mode of apprehension of truth; and (*b*) it is needful that such a discipline should be fully decloistered so that both those who read and those who profess it should be in touch with cognate disciplines—and indeed, since religion is a universal humane interest, with as many disciplines as possible whether cognate or not.

Academic disciplines have been and are being admitted to the newer and the older universities which interpret man and the human situation in terms markedly different from those admissible in the christian religion. These newer disciplines focus attention not on things but on man. For example, sociology, psychology and even education take their place alongside the other sciences. Knowledge which has long enough meant power over environment has been turned in the direction of man himself. Not enough people are aware how profoundly the development of these disciplines has already affected ordinary people's understanding of ends and means, directed into different channels, what ordinary people want or hope for, and eroded the common moral standards by which in western and christian civilisation they have hitherto lived. It is certain that theologians ought not to remain content that in one classroom or seminar a lead is being given to studies along purely anthropological lines, while, safely boxed up in their own different classrooms and seminars, only the small fraction of students studying divinity are given a chance of realising that there is another possible and academically respectable point of view. It is equally certain that not enough is being done to bridge, at the teacher level, the widening gap between the sharply divergent disciplines, or to provide at undergraduate and graduate levels the opportunity to become acquainted with the characteristic constituents of theological methodology. It is from such contact that there might be expected to arise (if a word may be borrowed) an *aggiornamento* of theology. Then without detriment to the *given* and the *givenness* of the revelation which the Church is charged to formulate and proclaim, such new expression might be given to doctrinal truths as would commend itself to those thinking men and women who are in our day so used to an entirely different mode of thought and kind of terminology (see H. Küng op. cit, on the human and the divine elements in dogma).

Either of two procedures would demonstrate decisively that the theologian has not comprehended what is at stake: that he should feel himself neither able nor called on to say anything in such conversation; and on the other hand, that he should claim to be able to say everything.

(II) OXFORD—THE ANGLICAN TRADITION

DAVID JENKINS

I wish it to be clearly understood that I speak *from* the existing
practice of one of the English universities rather than *of* that practice.
I am not sure what would justify the claim to represent the Oxford
faculty of Theology. But whatever would is certainly no possession of
mine. I must therefore disclaim any representative status. I must also
repudiate any strictly representational function. I have not taken
pains in what follows to ensure that I give an accurate historical
account of the faculty (although I hope that when I refer to history
I am not inaccurate). Nor have I taken pains to ensure a comprehensive contemporary account of the faculty and its present concerns
(although I hope that the points which I wish to raise are truly
embedded in the contemporary situation). I have thought it proper in
accordance with our concerns in this symposium to concentrate not
so much on reporting as on questioning. All of us are limited (although we may hope not entirely determined) not only by the broad
traditions in which we respectively stand, but also by the narrower
definitions of our own particular tasks and experiences within these
traditions. The great merit of the symposium method of investigating
a subject as wide and important as the one before us is that each
individual contributor can speak with uninhibited (but not un-
disciplined!) frankness from the inevitably limited position which he
occupies. He is not concerned to establish or to justify his position
but simply to make a contribution which may help to relate the whole
discussion more realistically to the actual situations in which we have
to operate, and may perhaps also help to draw attention to one or
two matters which serve to highlight particularly pressing problems
or pinpoint particularly promising opportunities. Hence I disclaim
representativeness and hope only that I may achieve some relevance.

Having made such a disclaimer I may now seem to go on partly to
contradict it. For in putting a stress on questioning as a main part of
my purpose I think I am displaying an approach which is not un-
common in the practice of theological teaching and studying at
Oxford. Indeed it might be said (although anyone who said it would

certainly be laying himself open to misunderstanding) that the atmosphere of the Oxford Theology School at present is particularly congenial to those who are sometimes inclined to more than half believe
that justification is at least as much by doubt as by faith! Certainly
the tradition of teaching which I received and to which I now attempt
to contribute does seem to me to be characterised as much by questioning as by statements. In the faculty of Theology we see ourselves
as one particular group of university teachers and researchers among
all the varieties of groups and faculties that there are. As such, our
main task is that of all the members of a university, the rigorous
pursuit of knowledge and understanding in our particular field of
study. In our case this field of study is primarily defined by a set of
data, both literary and historical, the main focus of which is the
compilation of documents which constitute the 'Holy Scriptures' of
the christian Church. (Those of the Roman allegiance, but perhaps
not those of the Reformed, may like to know that, at least for the
purposes of examination, the Scriptures are deemed to include the
Apocrypha.)

This definition of the field of study came about for one set of
reasons but it is now held to be justified by a very different set.
Originally (i.e. in 1868 and the years following, when a separate
Honour School of Theology was being founded and launched), the
School was intended by those who promoted it to meet the need for
the better theological training of the clergy of the Church of England.
This Church holds that 'Holy Scripture containeth all things necessary to salvation so that whatsoever is not read therein, nor may be
proved thereby, is not to be required of any man, that it should be
believed as an article of the Faith, or to be thought requisite or
necessary to salvation.' (Article VI—Of the Sufficiency of the holy
Scriptures for Salvation). Consequently the basic subject of the
Honours School was 'the Holy Scriptures'. The continued dominance
of the Holy Scriptures in the Honour School (which of course sets the
tone for much of the work in the faculty) can be seen from the fact
that today, of the ten papers which are compulsory in the Final
examination, eight are on the Scriptures. Other subjects could and
can be studied, and some additional subject was and still is required.
In 1870 the other subjects were listed as 'Dogmatic and Symbolic
Theology, Ecclesiastical History and Patristic Theology (by 1875, as
now, "and the Fathers"), Evidences (now "The Philosophy of

Religion"), Liturgies, and the Criticism and Archaeology of both Testaments'. With the alterations mentioned in brackets and the addition of the specific mention of 'The Hebrew of the Old Testament' the list of subjects in the statute 'Of the Honour School of Theology' stands in the 1962 Statutes as did the list in the 1870 University Calender. Then, the practice was to require of candidates 'for the highest honours' Dogmatic Theology and two further subjects in addition to 'Holy Scripture'. Other candidates could choose any one of the remaining subjects. Now, the practice is to require all candidates to take 'Holy Scriptures' and Dogmatic Theology, while any further subject is optional, although candidates for the highest honours are advised to offer one. The only subject which the university makes compulsory by statute is that of 'the Holy Scriptures'. Requirements concerning the other subjects depend on the regulations of the Board of the faculty.

It therefore remains formally true that the Holy Scriptures dominate the work of the faculty, and it is in fact the case that the majority of undergraduate teaching time and the studying time of the undergraduates themselves, is spent on the study of the bible. This is so, however wide may be the range of subjects which may be offered for examination, and however wide may be the variety of interests of individual members of the faculty or of research topics being pursued in the faculty. Nor does the fact that Oxford has had a long tradition of patristic studies (which we dare to believe still flourishes) really alter the way in which it is necessary to describe what I might call the theoretical basis of the field of studies which is the concern of the faculty of Theology. The data which fall within that field are data which can reasonably be related to the documents, which are the christian Scriptures.

This focusing on the Scriptures as the means of defining the concerns of the Oxford faculty of Theology is, I think, correct and illuminating despite, for example, the fact that the faculty lecture lists for last term and next contain about as many entries under headings other than 'Holy Scriptures' as they do under that heading, or despite the further fact that of the eight Theology Professors only three lecture directly on the Scriptures. My meaning in and my justification for maintaining this point will, I hope, become clearer in what follows, but I would reiterate that this dominance of the Scriptures came about in the first place for dogmatic reasons. However in so far as the situation is now held to be justifiable the reasons given would be very different. This is where we come back to the point about 'one particular group of university teachers' among many, and about the tradition characterised rather by questions than by statements, to which I referred in commencing the discussion. Christianity is not now taken for granted. (It was not in 1870; but it was still possible, as will appear from contemporary quotations of which I will later make use, to refer in all seriousness to 'the character of Oxford as a Church university'.) There is therefore now nothing 'sacred' about Theology, as far as the general opinion of the university is concerned. Consequently, amid the surviving evidences of the lingering effects of 'the character of Oxford as a Church university' (such as Canon Professors, admission to senior degrees by a formula which includes the name of the Trinity, and university sermons statutorily required), the teaching members of the faculty are acutely aware that the 'justification' of their subject must lie strictly in the academic sphere, in the fact that the subject matter is important historically and culturally, whatever personal view may be taken of the christian *faith*, and in the preservation and practice of a rigorous academic discipline, which allows no questions to be foreclosed by faith, and which requires them always to be open to all available facts and challenges.

In such circumstances the basis for defining the concerns of the faculty is clearly likely to be sought in data which is as 'hard' as possible, i.e. which believer and unbeliever alike will agree are indeed 'given', however much they may disagree about the significance of the givenness. At the heart of the historical phenomena which might roughly be designated 'Christianity' there lies historically the christian 'Scriptures'. Of their existence and influence there can be no doubt. These therefore are the 'texts' to which one must 'get back', just as in classical studies, which were *the* study of the University at the time when the Theology School was first formulated, it is the *texts* which form the necessary basis of everything—literary appreciation, historical study and knowledge of the philosophers. From the study of these texts all the other interests spring. And the discipline of the study is not the discipline of faithful believing, which is an intrusion of bias, alien to the purposes and approach of a now secularised university, but the discipline of facts, even if they are sometimes only literary facts ('what the texts say'—regardless, for example, of Luther

or the Council of Trent—or *a fortiori* of Cranmer!) and the discipline
of constant questioning. Opinions are all very well. So also may be
dogmas. But what is the *basis*? The discipline must be to strive
always to return to the primary authorities—as for example in the
Ancient History part of the 'Greats' course (*Literae Humaniores*),
the earliest original evidence, written and archaeological—and then
to decide what the evidence will warrant. And where it will not
warrant much, then this is the data you have arrived at.

Now many caveats may be, and may need to be, entered here—not
least, questions about the possibility of a 'presuppositionless' study
of 'pure' data, about hidden presuppositions in phrases like 'primary
authorities' and about the worthwhileness of asking questions without
a viewpoint from which to ask them. In particular, one such might
be that theologians have 'lost their nerve', and succumbed far too
much to the prevailing 'Oxford' philosophy of the analytical and
empirical type. This is a vast question. But while one would agree
that ultimately theology is and must be dealing with 'mysteries' (the
'true' or 'real' mysteries of God, His Being, His love, His redemption),
it is surely clear that theology turned in on itself breeds many
muddles and mystifications which masquerade as mysteries, and
thereby distort and obscure the true mystery. Further, the mysteries
are mysteries of revelation which are given to us to be revelatory, so
that analysis in terms of current concepts is a repeated necessity in
every age, if the mysteries are to speak to us as they spoke to our
fathers in the Faith. Hence both to free theology from accidental
accretions and to make theology speak in a lively way today, the
technique of logical analysis is of first-rate importance. In challenging
the theologian with the questions '*What* are you saying?' and '*Why*
are you saying it?' analytical philosophy is playing a very important
role, to which the theologian must seek to submit humbly and in
good faith, even if—or rather, perhaps, just because—as a christian
believer he must also maintain humbly and in good faith that true
sources of real knowledge lie beyond those commonly allowed by
many philosophers of the analytic school.

But however that may be, I am seeking in the short space at my
disposal to convey impressionistically an approach. And I must
largely leave these questions to be investigated elsewhere in the symposium, although I hope not to leave them entirely untouched in the
latter half of my paper. But it is surely clear that anyone who is

concerned with 'doing theology' today must be aware that it is in this sort of questioning, challenging, and not infrequently arid atmosphere that his faith has to live, and that it is in this sort of atmosphere that theology as an academic subject must be prepared to live, if it is to stay alive in or freshly venture into the secular universities of today. So the present atmosphere and approach of the Theology School at Oxford is no mere accident or irrelevant freak, although it has its distortions and problems.

The approach of questioning, of analysis and of basically historical study has both been forced upon and chosen by the scholars of this school as they work out their callings and their interests. The documents which constitute the bible are the basically defining data, and concerns work outwards, backwards and onwards from there. The literary criticism of the documents leads back into the communities which produce the documents or were the context of the men who wrote them. The communities have their own 'setting in life', which requires studying with the help of archaeology, comparative religion, philosophy, and history of ideas, and so on. The analytical and historical 'slant' of the approach is exemplified not unaccidentally in the titles of the two main Old Testament papers in the Finals examination—'The history and religion of Israel from . . .'. And this is extended forward into the life and thought of the christian Church. The compulsory 'Dogmatic Theology' subject turns out to be 'the *history* of christian doctrine to A.D. 461' (This has been so since circa 1904, when the close connection of the syllabus with Anglican formularies was significantly loosened. I shall refer to this later.[1]). Of the two papers involved one is given over to texts. The same impression is maintained (within the limits proper to each sphere) by all the possible additional subjects. They are examinable by a paper of general questions and a text paper; and the text papers, at any rate, are always slanted towards the historical development of the subject. The concentration is really on studying the material for theology, rather than on theology—which is 'theologising'. There is inbred in the tradition a profound distrust of theological and systematic edifices, which might turn out to be merely castles in the air with no

---

[1] For the record it should be stated that there has just come into force a modification of the syllabus, whereby there is now a *systematic* theology subject as an optional alternative to this history of doctrine; and other changes may well be afoot—should the time prove ripe!

F

sound basis in the data. The basic concern thus becomes one with history rather than religion. Indeed more than one tutor has shocked more than one earnest student by so far forgetting himself as to rebuke the wretched enthusiast for clouding and confusing his essay (even, or indeed especially, on a biblical subject) with far too much religion. The concern is with the data for holding a view or forming a faith. And the belief is that the rigorous analysis of sound learning cannot but contribute in the end to the firmer establishment of true religion.

I cannot but believe that there is very much that is healthy and necessary in such an approach, but it must be confessed that it is much mightier to the breaking down of strongholds than to the edification of the faithful; although it may perhaps be pleaded in mitigation that many of the faithful are really very difficult to edify in a really edifying way. It must also be confessed that one gets the impression that while, to the 'faithful', the theologians seem on the whole to be unfaithful underminers of the faith rather than, as they themselves believe, concerned with the ultimate strengthening of that faith by making it face the facts, to the unbelievers in the university the theologians still seem to be dogmatists (in the common pejorative sense of that term) living in a world of their own, a world to which real rigour and unbiassed open-ness are largely foreign. Thus all is certainly not well with the present position and practice.

It might not be wholly misleading to put the dilemma of the present position by saying that for believers the present performance of the faculty of Theology is not constructive enough, while for unbelievers it is not open and relevant enough. I think there may well be a connection between the two horns of this dilemma which is central to the whole question of the use and practice of theology today, and I shall therefore return to it at the end of my paper; but I think it may be useful to prepare the way for this discussion by first asking in a severely practical way what the role of a faculty of Theology in a non-church university is. Under the sort of pressures which I have been referring to above (about what 'justifies' the continuance of an academic discipline) one not infrequently hears it said by one's colleagues or says oneself that the job of a faculty of Theology is *not* to train ordinands. It is to study and promote the study of theology as an academic discipline in its own right. The training of ordinands is the job of the seminaries. It is highly desirable that as many ordinands as possible should have the benefit of the rigours of the Theology school, but we cannot adjust our syllabus to meet the specific needs of the training, even on the doctrinal and exegetical side, of the priest, pastor, or preacher. Now there is a simple practical tension here, since the vast majority of the students in the faculty are, in fact, ordinands. And there is also a historical tension for, as I have said, the Honour School of Theology and the separate faculty as such arose out of a response to the need for the training of the clergy of the Church of England. It will, I think, be not without interest in itself and also illuminating for our wider concerns if we take a look at certain controversies, which arose at two stages in the history of the Honour School, and which illustrate singularly clearly the tensions that arise when theology has to combine the attributes of an academic discipline, a discipline that is concerned with the training of priests and ministers of a church, and a discipline that is concerned with the revelation and knowledge of God.

In 1868, the Reverend John W. Burgon, M.A., Fellow of Oriel, Vicar of the St Mary-the-Virgin's, published a 'Plea for a Fifth School—A Letter to the Reverend the Vice-Chancellor of the University of Oxford'. In it he said, 'we of this place are knowingly training up a large body of young men to be clergymen, to whom we are careful to impart *no special knowledge* of the Science which, *almost in the same hour* that they leave us, they are expected publicly to profess and teach'. (En passant, he quotes from a Bishop a similar complaint—only in this case the university is Cambridge and the date is two hundred years earlier!) He is persuaded, he says, that 'an effectual remedy (is) the establishment of a Final Divinity School'. But he is aware that he will be opposed. 'And first, I anticipate that I may be charged with proposing to alter, (and so, to lower) the character of an Oxford education in the case of the clergy, by making it professional, not general. Do I then wish to see Oxford converted into a Theological Seminary?' He presumes that no one could really wish to do this, and argues that in fact the study of theology (including such authors as Eusebius, Tertullian, Augustine and Ignatius) *carries on* the classical studies and in no way *narrows* them. (We see how, as I have already hinted, the formulation of the Theology School presupposed the prior study of the Classical School.) He then comes to what, as we shall see, seems to have been the nub of the contemporary doubts about the proposed school. He feels himself

obliged to enter into a long argument concerning the alleged incompatibility of impartial and detached examining and the fact that
the subject matter is that of the christian *faith*. He urges that the
examination should be concerned to test *intellectual* qualities; and
'why should not men be constrained to master the *contents* (his
emphasis not mine) of the Holy Scripture: the *history* (my emphasis
not his) of the Patriarchal age: the provisions of the Mosaic
Law . . . ?' Throughout his argument it is very clear that his assumption is that detachment is of the essence of examinable subjects, and
we are brought face to face with one of our continuing questions. The
christian faith implies and demands commitment. How can there be
'detached' theology? But how does one draw the line between
commitment and bias, so as to satisfy the academic conscience?

But there was, of course, trouble from the other side too—from the
side of the committed and believing Church. 'But then, it will be
objected,—Will it not be a public mischief if men go forth to the
world decorated with a First Class (suppose), who yet may hold
sceptical views and preach false doctrines? Would not the character
of Oxford as a Church university be seriously imperilled if she were
thus to become the open patron and rewarder (as it were) of unsound
teaching?' But, he says, the examination would not be a measure of
Orthodoxy. 'Of course, if *unsound* views had been put forth, the man
would have been rejected: but to certify the world of his *Orthodoxy*
will never certainly be the intention of his Examiners.' (There is more
to this than meets the eye as will appear subsequently.) He apprehends
that the alarming accusation will be made against him that 'you are
recommending a scheme which, if it be adopted, may in a few years,
lead us into all the abominations of a German University'. But he
points out that if the opportunities of the present time are to be
seized and its needs met, then one must be prepared to take risks and
be bold and faithful—surely a point to consider very carefully as we
review present possibilities. He believes however that the risks may be
in any case held in check. Like us he is in favour of taking risks in
theory, providing that they are eliminated by safeguards in practice.
'I propose, as the *sine qua non* of this fifth school, that its three
Examiners shall be jointly nominated *by the Vice-Chancellor and the
Divinity Professors of the University*. This, I think, will be a sufficient
safeguard for their Orthodoxy.'

But, alas, as no less a person than Dr Pusey pointed out, the whole debate was being carried on under the shadow of 'Mr. Coleridge's Bill' (concerning the abolition of religious tests for admission to the universities) which would mean that there would be 'no security that the Proctors should be even Christians'. (The Proctors are *ex officio* concerned with the nomination of examiners). Secularisation was creeping in, even on Oxford. Therefore, Pusey argued, special arrangements for examiners were essential, for 'Theology is a subject quite apart, in that in it, the question is not one of mere knowledge of facts, or of opinions, or of philosophies, or of philosophical theories, but of a revelation of God for the salvation of men.'

But at this point a different breed of rat was smelt by Henry J. S. Smith, Savilian Professor of Geometry. He asks Pusey—'Does he still think that a 'power of rejecting a student on doctrinal grounds, apart from the question of his theological attainments' is a power essential to an examination in Theology?' He also takes up Burgon's remarks on 'unsound views' quoted above, and asks 'is this view not utterly irreconcilable with the conscientious convictions of a large majority of the educational body of the university?' The issue is very clearly posed: academic consciences and theological consciences are at variance. Pusey, however, was quite clear. 'The School was instituted to meet a want . . . the education of our future clergy,' and because there were only a few theological seminaries. There was therefore clearly a 'need to *control* the examination, so that those taking it profess the doctrines of the Church of England'. Pardonably enough, Professor Smith continued to express printed suspicions and to fear that candidates would suffer for their opinions. 'It is surely a pardonable suspicion that these persons would wish to work the school in what we should deem a narrow and exclusive spirit, discreditable to the university, and unfair to the candidates.' This provoked replies from both Pusey and Burgon, which surely from the point of view of a university today—and, indeed, largely then—properly let the cat out of the bag.

Burgon wrote: '*Opinions* will have no more influence on an examination in Divinity than on an examination in Mathematics. Science has to do with *Truth*—not with *Opinion*. Of course (to cite your own instance) if a candidate for honours in Divinity is so unreasonable as to insist on emphatically denying what Our Lord most emphatically affirms—namely that "He is the great object of Prophecy" (and Burgon cites various texts from the gospels)—or again is so foolish as to assert that the Ante-Nicene Fathers teach "the doctrine of Transubstantiation", it is probable that he will find it a hard matter to persuade any examiner in his right mind to reward him with a First Class. The former statement would be just as monstrous—the latter almost as silly—as if one of *your* candidates were to deny that the three angles of a triangle are equal to two right angles. . . . These are not matters of opinion but of fact. That the man would suffer, is likely enough; but it would not be *for his Opinions* that he would suffer. It would be *for his Ignorance.* It may be calamitous that the truths of Divinity are *not of the same kind* as the truths of Mathematics: but it is unavoidable.'

Pusey's contribution included the remark that 'such a School must be either a great blessing or a great curse. And whether it shall be a blessing or a curse depends, humanly speaking, on the examiners.' He later continues: 'Professor Smith could not, I am sure, wish that one should be admitted into a School of Christian Theology, who would patently contradict the authority of Christ. We provide schools for the benefit of our Church and people, not to gratify the caprices of individual students. All would regard it as an idiosyncrasy for a candidate to present himself in any other school while denying the first principles of the science of that school. Why should we suppose that they should be guilty of such idiosyncrasy as to the highest of all sciences, the knowledge of Almighty God?' One sees, indeed to some extent, shares, the difficulties of Pusey and Burgon. The nostalgia for 'better days' and perhaps neurotic fears of the more 'open' future—a nostalgia and a fear from which we are probably still not immune—are well shown by some words written by Burgon in 1854, after the passing by Parliament of the first of the measures which between 1854 and 1871 were to terminate the Church of England's monopoly of Oxford and Cambridge:

> Oxford, I fear, has seen her best days. Her sun has set and for ever. She never more can be what she has been—the great nursery of the Church. She will become a cage of unclean beasts at last. Of course we shall not live to see it; but *our great-grandchildren will*: and the Church (and Oxford itself) will rue the day when its liberties and its birthright were lost by a licentious vote of a *no longer Christian* House of Commons. (M. Goulburn, Life of Dean Burgon, 1892, vol. I, p. 283).

But must it not be on Henry Smith's terms that theology takes its place in any ordinary university today?

The passing of the statute setting up the Honour School was de-layed through the dispute over the question of the examiners, but the matter was settled in time for the first Class list to appear in 1870—four candidates placed neatly one in each class, and a Bishop among the examiners. But at the turn of the century the examination regu-lations were altered, not in outline but in details, so that the various subjects were not necessarily tied to Church of England formularies. For example, in the Liturgy subject, the Book of Common Prayer became optional, with the early history of the Liturgy as a possible self-contained alternative. This was also the point at which the 'Dog-matic' subject became the history of christian doctrine to A.D. 461, as it is now. But even greater and graver changes were in the air. There was a proposal to remove a clause in the statutes which required the Theology examiners to be in Priest's Orders. As one of the disputants, the Reverend W. C. Allen, Chaplain-Fellow and Sub-Rector of Exeter College, pointed out, 'The wording of the Statute seems to include priests of the Latin and Greek communions.' The intention was for Oxford to remain a Church of England university, despite misfortunes like the University Tests Act of 1870. This proposal moved Dr Walter Lock (Warden of Keble College and Dean Ireland's Professor of the Exegesis of Holy Scripture) to address a printed memorandum 'To members of the Board of the Faculty of Theology', dated 14 January 1904. The time was not yet ripe (sic!) to admit non-Anglicans to the conduct of this examination. The Honour School is 'very analogous' in its position, to the establishment of the Church of England, the Divinity Professorships and the College Chapels—all of which we still have in Oxford. He went on: 'from its very outset it has been linked with the Church of England by the provision of the statute now under discussion; by far the greater majority of the students who have offered themselves for examination in it have been and still are members of that body. . . .' There were, Dr Lock suggested, 'two logical theories of an examination in Theo-logy'. The first was 'an entirely open examination, which treats Theo-logy as being *only* a method of education in the development of human life and thought, which takes no account of denomination or of creed, which assumes no superiority of one religion or revelation over another, which resolves Theology into its human elements of history and philosophy, which allows the teaching of the school to be denominational if the teachers wish, but requires the examination to be undenominational.' (He cites the practice of the university of Manchester.) 'This is a perfectly tenable theory and a method which Christians and Churchmen need not fear to face.' But, he points out, this approach requires advanced students, and 'the subject so defined is an unreal abstraction. Theology has never been developed apart from a living society, which has assumed some Revelation as true, and which has created its theology to interpret adequately the secrets of its own religious consciousness and its own history. Nor can theology ever be profitably studied except in its bearing upon life and conduct. . . . What Tutor has not, at some time in his life, found it necessary to warn a pupil of the danger of treating theology as only a subject of examination, and to advise him that it is better not to handle it at all, if he cannot handle it in its serious bearing on his own moral and spiritual life?' He closes his discussion by suggesting that perhaps *eventually* there should be 'concurrent confessional faculties each examining in its own subjects'.

Here, surely, is our general problem put with singular clarity with regard to a particular problem which no longer obtains. The 'safeguard' of examiners in (Anglican) priest's orders, like so many other 'essential' safeguards, is a thing of the past. But have we yet really got round to asking what the position of theology as a general and open discipline—and, therefore, a university one—is, and to the problem of relating this to theology as a training for priests, that is, as a seminary discipline? Should they be different at all; and, further, have we faced the question whether theology ought to be a subject for students other than prospective priests and ministers?

With that barrage of rhetorical questions I must pass to my concluding reflections. I have cited from these past controversies not only because I am supposed to draw on Oxford experience but because in their own terms they surely represent precisely our doubts and difficulties; and it is often easier, because less immediately painful and unsettling, to face present problems when they are mirrored in the past, with which we may deal in more tolerant and cooler fashion than with the hasty rush to defend familiar and cherished positions, which present threatenings instinctively provoke.

What safeguards do we need for theology? What safeguards *must* we have? What safeguards *dare* we ask for? For what *is* theology? For us who have received, however imperfect our understanding and disobedient our response to what we do understand, something of the revelation of God which is perfected in Our Lord Jesus Christ, theology is the whole study of all that constitutes that revelation, all that prepares for that revelation, and all that follows from that revelation. For us it is indeed *sacra theologia*, sacred with the holiness of God, the Holy and Blessed Trinity. But I wonder if this entitles us to insist on *our* terms for studying theology and for its place in a university. The revelation which is our subject-matter is fulfilled in him who brought the fulfilment by 'emptying himself' and taking the form of a servant. Perhaps we are being taught by the secular and secularising pressures to which I have drawn attention, and to which I am inclined to believe the practice of theology in some circles, including Oxford ones, has yielded overmuch, that we are mistaken in supposing that theology is 'the queen of the sciences'—or rather, perhaps, that we have misinterpreted and misapplied that phrase. *We* know that it is only in the knowledge of God that all knowledge is crowned and fulfilled, indeed brought to ultimate reality. *We* know also that it is the good pleasure of God to sum up all things in Christ. Theology is therefore directly related to the highest knowledge there is or can be. But we cannot claim for theology, still less for our imperfect practice of it, a privileged position in the modern world or in the modern university. Here it has to find a place which is not based on the status of its true subject, the Almighty and Everlasting God, but on the basis of the contribution made by its practitioners to the common concerns, in so far as they are good, of the academic community and the community at large. And its standing in the academic community must depend on the efficiency, rigour and relevance of its academic practitioners. The status depends in fact not on the divine end but on the human end of the practice of theology. And might there not be perceived in this the logic of the Incarnation and the pattern of the discipleship of Jesus?

I venture to give it as my view that our present practice in the Theology faculty at Oxford is not constructive enough for believers and not open and relevant enough for unbelievers. Continuing my rash generalisations for the sake of making what I hold to be a relevant general point about theology today, I would suggest that this is because we have rightly shrunk from demanding a special position of privilege and dominance, that we know that we must thoroughly submit ourselves, our studies and our subjects to the same disciplines as everyone else. We have got our narrowly academic status more or less right; but in reacting from the dogmatism and demands of a Burgon or a Pusey we have somewhat lost our grasp upon the fact that we have a special position not of privilege but of responsibility. And that responsibility is twofold, it is a responsibility on the one hand to the Church and on the other to the university.

To seek to discharge our responsibility to the Church we have to seek, in whatever fear, trembling and tentativeness, to go beyond historical study and analytic investigation to suggestions of possible syntheses and systematisations, which may help to build up those who are seeking to make sense of Christianity under the pressures of today. But to do this with any chance of success we must be concerned not only with our particular disciplines but also with our other responsibility, that to the university at large and therefore largely to unbelievers. We have to be open to all the questions that are put to us, and we have to face all the challenges to our relevance which are directed against us. This is necessary if we are to have any success in our systematic work, for the people who desire us to be constructive are themselves people conditioned by the very world which produces the challenges directed against us. If we cannot establish our relevance in the face of these challenges we cannot be constructive for those who already give us a hearing. But we must also face these challenges, because all seekers after knowledge require also and above all the knowledge of God. Therefore we must seek to enter into dialogue with them that together, whenever it is possible, we may find ways of speaking of God.

But our approach must not be that of the 'Master-Theologian' providing the theological glue essential to any synthesis of the 'fragmented university' or the theological depth which will give 'ontological reality' to the souls lost in the relativity of all other studies. Our own subject as we practise it is likewise fragmented by modern pressures; and outside the certainty that the ultimate reality is God (unshaken, I am sure, by the perennial, inevitable and proper doubts about the adequacy of any particular set of images about him) we, too, are perplexed by many relativities. Moreover, the other studies have their autonomous disciplines and autonomous knowledge of the realities of God's creation. We enter into the dialogue, therefore, not with the form of the master but with that of the servant, in the hope that we may be used as veritable ministers of the word of God and that out of this dialogue may grow a common increase in the knowledge of God, his works and his worthiness.

But who is sufficient for these things? None the less as the challenge is there, we cannot but be convinced that the grace will be forthcoming. God never commands what he does not offer. The task in the university, and indeed in the world at large, seems threefold. Within the overall commitment, assurance and obedience of faith, *the* basis of the task is the rigorous and analytical approach to the data. This is demanded *in* the modern world and *by* the modern world, which is not an easily believing world and respects only (if at all) practical and technical efficiency and openness of investigation. We cannot make *our* terms. We must accept the terms thrust upon us—no bad terms for faith in any case. But on this basis we have to seek faithfully to construct that which will edify the faithful to faithful living and also to try to be allowed to take part in building bridges to the knowledge of God with students, researchers and thinkers in all fields of knowledge, wherever they cease to be mere self-contained technical specialisms and spill over into the conditioning and developing of human life.

But finally (because the paper must come to an end, not because the subject is exhausted) all this means that Theology must be done *with* the layman and is necessary *for* the layman. It cannot be a speciality for priests. It must be done *with* the layman, because the complexities of the discoveries and of the pressures of the modern world cannot be appreciated sufficiently by any one class, least of all a priestly class. There *is* autonomy of knowledge, and if the Church is to do theology, she must use all the qualified members of the Body, i.e. she must draw on all the resources available in the educated laity. Otherwise theology is deprived of a prime means for her life—living and effective contact with what God is doing in the world outside the Church, within which the priest is of necessity very nearly entirely confined.

Theology is also necessary *for* the layman, at least for the ever-increasing number of educated laymen. How else can he, or she, help to play his part in the Body and, indeed, to retain his faith? He is fully exposed to the questionings of the world. They are the very stuff of his life, and it is no longer a possibility for him that the dogmas of the faith should work in some mysterious formula-like fashion. They must be understood and be seen to be relevant, or they cease to be real to him, and his religion is well on the way to becoming a lie. Theology in such a home of lost causes as Oxford may still show some vestigial signs of attempting to ignore the secularisation of the world. Theology in seminars may still seek with, alas, considerably more success to do this, but the layman *is* secularised and must be a secular christian if he is to be a christian at all. And is not this the true calling of the christian, for surely the plan of redemption is to convert the world and to unite it to God in Christ, not to cause it to cease to be the world? Thus a liberated and open theology free from the sheltered indoctrination of the seminary is necessary for the layman and necessary for the communication of the Church with the world; and, if this is so, it is a necessity also for the priest. And it may well be that it is in the severe openness of a secular university that this sort of theology can be alone worked out.

One thing, I would submit, is clear. Theology will progress in her task only as she learns not to make terms but to face up to the terms laid upon her by the present state and attitude of the world. The more she takes on the form of the servant, the more will the Word of God be manifested to men.

(III) THE PLACE OF A DEPARTMENT OF THEOLOGY IN A UNIVERSITY

ALAN RICHARDSON

Theology has always been studied in the older universities of England and Scotland, and indeed the faculty of Divinity in those great institutions still formally retains its ancient primacy. It has no such status in the modern universities; and in the newer ones it is not an independent faculty but simply one department amongst several in the faculty of Arts. Despite its age-long establishment in Oxford and Cambridge, it did not there become a subject of undergraduate study until the 1870's, when the curricula of the ancient universities were beginning to assume something like their present shape; even then it was usually read as a second Honour School or Tripos rather than as the first. In either case it was assumed that the undergraduates reading Theology would already have had a sound classical education at school. Almost all those who read the Theological Honour School or Tripos were Anglican ordinands, who subsequently proceeded to theological colleges such as Cuddesdon or Wells. In due course faculties of Theology were developed elsewhere, notably at London and Manchester, where Free Churchmen might feel more at home than in the decidedly Anglican atmosphere of Oxford, Cambridge and Durham.

The development of theological study as a normal university discipline was the result of the emergence of a sense of history and of the consequent application of historical method to every field of human interest during the nineteenth century. This development of historical method was, in fact, the great intellectual revolution achieved in that century. It came to be taken for granted that it is impossible to understand what an idea or an institution is unless it is known how it had come to be what it is; to know something was to know its history. This attitude is nowadays called 'historical-minded-ness', and it has entered into every corner of the modern mind, except perhaps the recesses of extreme rationalism. It was inevitable that theology itself, like every other discipline, should come to be studied by means of the historical method. To understand a doctrine meant to be able to give an account of the various forms which it had assumed down the ages in the course of its coming to be what in fact it now is. This meant beginning with the bible, or even further back, since all the great theological themes are to be found—if not authori-tatively, then at least classically—in the bible. In the climate of opinion of the later nineteenth century it was held that by means of the historical method an objective statement of historical facts could be made, which must be true for all men, whatever their religious or political opinions. 'Scientific' history could rescue facts from the conflict of opinion. Lord Acton tells us that Ranke held that 'con-cerning the facts about Martin Luther and the figure of the man as he appears in history, there is no reason why Protestant and Catholic, conservative and liberal, should ultimately differ.' History was a science; it could tell us what the facts were, and beyond this it did not go; it left the interpretation of the facts to others.

Today this view of history is almost universally abandoned. But it must be acknowledged that it was of great importance in the intro-duction of the study of theology into the curricula of the English universities, ancient and modern. Scholars from different denomina-tions, or none, would work together as colleagues in the objective study of the facts; they taught their pupils how the books of the bible had come historically to assume the form in which we find them, how the Creeds of the Church were originally formulated, how the doctrines which they enshrined came to assume this or that form in the various epochs of history. What they did not discuss was the contemporary significance of these documents and doctrines; that was a matter of interpretation, of opinion; it was to be left until the student had arrived at the theological college of his own denomination. In the days of bitter denominational controversy and of rationalist resistance to the teaching of 'religion' in any form whatsoever, it was the only way in which theology could have been studied in the universities, especially the modern ones. In certain of the latter a strange alliance of sectarian enthusiasm and rationalist opposition defeated all attempts to introduce the study of the bible or theology; the Unitarians often managed to combine both these attitudes in their own persons. It was only last year that the restrictions upon the teaching of theological subjects in the university of Liverpool were finally removed after recourse to the Privy Council. In these circumstances it must be recognised that the old conception of 'historical theology' was a necessary instrument of introducing theological teaching into the modern universities. One of its achievements was that scholars of different denominations found common ground upon which they could work together, and in the process they learnt a new respect for and appreciation of one another's positions.

There were certain serious disadvantages in the study of theology in the universities under the form of 'historical theology'. One of them was that its historical methods were not acceptable to all forms of christian opinion in the country. There were, of course, the older type of Tractarian Anglicans, who under the leadership of Pusey and Liddon had resisted the introduction of the new theological methods (and many other innovations) into the university of Oxford; but, with the secession of Gore and his friends from their ranks, this type of opposition was virtually extinct by the end of the nineteenth century. There were also the conservative evangelicals, including some Anglicans, whose dogmatic system committed them to historical propositions which were irreconcilable with the findings of the new historical method as applied to the bible. Much more important, there were the Roman Catholics, who until recently took almost no part in the development of theological study in the modern universities, doubtless partly because of the commitment of their theological departments to modern historical methods; these methods seemed to imply historical relativism, in view of their assumption that theological dogmas were relative to the age in which they were formulated and could not be regarded as finally and unalterably true for all ages and situations. How far the general abandonment of the nineteenth-century view of 'scientific history' with its implied relativism will affect this situation in the future it is not for us to guess; but to those outside the Roman Catholic Communion, one of the most interesting and important aspects of Roman theological discussion today is the question how that Church will come to terms with the historical revolution which has been going on since about the end of the eighteenth century. The question whether there will be full participation by Roman Catholics in university theological departments, a thing greatly to be desired, will doubtless depend upon the outcome of current discussions about the nature of revelation. The English universities, for better or worse, are committed to the historical approach, not only in theology but also in every other discipline, including philosophy, and it is inconceivable that it should ever be abandoned. But this, of course, does not mean that they are committed to the nineteenth-century conception of 'scientific history'; it is historical method as such to which they are committed, not to any particular use or conception of it. Thus, doors are wide open for exploration and discussion.

Another disadvantage of the older type of 'historical Theology' is that it makes the study of theology rather dull. If we are allowed only to inquire into what Luther said, and how his utterance was related to the historical situation of the sixteenth century, then we are precluded from arguing about whether what he said was true or false. By removing the study of theology from the conflict of opinion, we deprive it of all 'existential' interest and relevance to our lives and beliefs. This is doubtless what those rationalists, who originally approved of theological study in university curricula, intended; they thought that theological study had no interest other than a merely historical one. But it was not what was wanted or approved of by undergraduates and others, who had decided to read theology because they were eager to find answers to real questions and to engage in an encounter with truth itself. How often has one met older clergymen who have confessed that they got very little out of their reading of theology in their undergraduate days! They had never got beyond the study of literary and historical problems, such as the date of the Exodus or the authorship of the Pastoral Epistles. They had spent long hours over Hebrew verbs and translating the First Epistle of Clement, or in trying to remember the reasons for thinking that Nestorius might not have been a Nestorian. Their theological colleges had never quite succeeded in bridging the gap between all this mass of academic detail and the practical issues of parochial life; and after they had begun to work in their parishes they had never looked into a Hebrew bible again or preached about St Clement or even so much as thought about Nestorius. And when they had come up against theological problems in their ministry, real existential questions about God's existence or the problem of evil, they found that their university studies had done nothing to help them with the answers; even if their course had included the philosophy of religion, this too was presented historically, and a knowledge of Butler's *Analogy* or of Hegel's teaching about the Absolute in which all differences are reconciled seemed to offer little assistance. It was only the very best students who had profited from their studies in historical theology; such studies had done nothing for the ordinary run of students to help them to think theologically, that is, to see all questions in the light of the christian revelation.

There is much truth in such criticism, but it is easily exaggerated. Theology is a most exacting study, requiring the mastery of several languages and of certain highly specialised literary and historical techniques, before its more interesting levels are attained. A long process of disciplined study is necessary before the student can be said to have mastered the tools of the trade. It is still true that, in certain universities, as far as undergraduate study is concerned, these propaedeutic exercises seem to occupy all the time and energy which are available in a three-year course. The fact that students nowadays usually arrive at the university with no Greek and very little Latin (and, of course, no Hebrew) means that much time has to be occupied with matters ancillary to the study of theology proper. It may be that in some departments there exists a tendency to maintain the intellectual rigour of scholarly disciplines, because of criticisms expressed in other Honours departments about Theology being a 'soft option'. In point of fact no student is likely to think that at the end of his first term in the university. But there is also an opposite tendency in many quarters to reduce the amount of sheer linguistic and critical study in order to allow more time for a consideration of those aspects of theology which are of existential concern, such as dogmatics, apologetics, the philosophy of religion and ethics. The problem is a real one. Under the conditions now prevailing in the modern universities only three years are available for a complete honours B.A.; with a discipline as many-sided and as exact as the study of theology there is simply not time to do all that needs to be done.

Since the first setting up of theological departments in certain of the older modern universities, important changes have occurred in the theological climate, and these inevitably have had an effect upon the way in which theology is taught. With the gradual waning of the old conception of 'scientific history', it has become much more usual in all university departments to encourage the free expression of personal viewpoints, and even to regard 'the conflict of opinion', not as something to be exorcised by 'the scientific attitude', but as a healthy sign of vitality and as an essential means of genuine education. In theological departments this development might be characterised as the growth of the ecumenical spirit, which outside the university world has been such a marked feature of church history in the twentieth century. The old agreement to differ is giving place to a new desire to find unity amidst differences. It is widely recognised nowadays that facts cannot be separated from interpretations in history, and every university teacher is expected to interpret the facts as he sees them. The same liberty of interpretation is, of course, allowed to every student: there is no such thing as a 'party-line' and no marks are awarded in examinations for reproducing a lecturer's views; a criticism of them would be more welcome as an indication of independent judgment. Plenty of opportunities are given in tutorials and seminars for the expression and criticism of personal and even denominational points of view. The old undenominational attitude has given place to a thoroughly interdenominational attitude. In practice it is found that this treatment of theological subjects does not lead to a decline of denominational loyalties but rather to a heightened interest in the distinctive values of the student's own tradition; he learns to discover and to appreciate what the value of his own tradition is when he tries to articulate it for the benefit of those who belong to other traditions. He understands better the meaning of his own confessional position when he has learnt something about other positions than his own. In practice, too, it is found that tensions and *odium theologicum* rarely, if ever, develop; in theology, as in life, mutual regard and respect for one's fellows breed sympathetic understanding and destroy suspicion. Above all, perhaps, the valuable truth is experienced at a formative age that we learn more from those with whom we disagree than from those with whom we agree. This is one of the chief lessons to be gained from a university education, and theological departments can become most effective in imparting it—the lesson, namely, that differences of opinion in fundamental matters can, if treated with sympathetic candour, become the means of advance towards mutual respect and a greater appreciation of the truth which we believe that we have seen.

It is to be hoped that the teaching of theology in an ecumenical way will awaken the interest and stimulate the judgment of students more effectively than the older type of 'historical Theology' used to do. Of course, there remains the hard grind of mastering the tools, of learning languages and acquiring techniques. Nothing can or should modify the rigour of theology as an intellectual discipline. But at least the newer approach enables the student to get some glimpse of the country ahead and to feel that the ardour of the struggle is worth while. Now that living questions and existential commitments are no longer excluded from teaching and discussion, the study of theology in the university has a much better chance of giving the student what he hoped to find. The twentieth-century approach to history does not forbid but rather encourages the discussion of all possible interpretations of the evidence and does not suggest that only one of them can be 'scientific'; it emphasises the importance of personal judgment and experience in the solution of historical problems. Exegesis, whether of Scripture or of the Fathers, no longer excludes the consideration of questions of existential meaning, now that it has become usual to regard all historical interpretation as a two-way traffic between the present and the past. In short, the teaching of theology is no longer 'merely' historical; contrary, even controversial, points of view are allowed full expression. No longer is it necessary in the interests of 'undenominational' teaching to exclude from the curriculum the study of dogmatics, apologetics, liturgiology and ethics, and all these subjects are taught from an ecumenical point of view in some at least of the university departments. In order to avoid misunderstanding here, it may be well to repeat that 'an ecumenical point of view' does not mean some imagined lowest common multiple upon which all denominations can agree, but rather, so far as this is possible, looking at every question from every possible confessional point of view in a determined attempt to see the truth from every side; it does not mean that either teacher or taught may not have a strong confessional conviction and loyalty of his own.

The modern universities usually have written into their statutes a clause forbidding the giving of denominational teaching or the making of appointments to the staff upon a denominational basis. The reasons for such clauses are easily understandable in the light of the denominational quarrellings of not many decades ago, which did so much damage to the cause of religious education in England. Staff is appointed and students are admitted solely upon academic ability and personal quality, as in any other university department. In the light of history and having regard to the realities of the present situation no other attitude is conceivable; it is unthinkable that credal tests of any kind should ever again be imposed as a qualification for university entrance. A university is an open society of teachers and students who come together in uncoerced association for the common pursuit of knowledge and with the single purpose of learning from one another. This is as true of a theological department as of any other department in the university. The pursuit of truth, including theological truth, requires just such a free community of scholars for its furtherance; this is the Western university tradition, and so long as free institutions remain amongst us, it is unlikely to be modified. The only people who are excluded from the university community are those who exclude themselves by being unable or unwilling to learn from or with those who are not of their own convictions. It is, of course, open to the Churches to appoint chaplains and moral supervisors for their own students, whether of theology or of other subjects. The right chaplain, himself a theologian, could do much to help the undergraduate to think theologically and to understand his studies in the light of his own tradition. The staff of the university department would not merely agree to such an arrangement; they would welcome it. A fruitful co-operation with the chaplains appointed by the churches has already developed in many modern universities, and this kind of mutual sharing of the educational task is likely to be carried considerably further in the future.

The situation in the universities is not basically different from that in the state-supported schools, where Mr Butler's Education Act of 1944 made it possible (indeed obligatory) to include instruction in Religious Knowledge in a manner comparable to the instruction given in any other subject in the curriculum. The implementation of this Act has created a great demand for qualified Divinity masters and mistresses, of whom today there is a shortage in the schools second only to the shortage of Mathematics and Science teachers. It is the theological departments of the modern universities which are chiefly helping to meet this need, and every year graduates in Theology proceed to the Education departments of the universities to read for the Diploma in Education. This explains why many undergraduates in the departments of Theology are women, who for the first time in the history of English education are now enabled to study theology in appreciable numbers. Thus today by no means all theological students are ordinands; apart from the intending teachers, others hope after graduating to enter the civil service, the social services or industry (personnel officers, etc.). The training of lay theologians is thus a new contribution which the modern universities are making to the general cause of theological education in modern society. Since it cannot nowadays be assumed that all or, in some departments, even the majority of theological students will proceed to theological colleges for further instruction, it is obvious that some place must be found in a full curriculum for the study of such subjects as dogmatics, apologetics, liturgiology and ethics, because if the student is not introduced to these subjects at the university, he (or in this case more probably she) will never have the opportunity of the academic study of them. In general, the teachers in the theological departments are fully conscious of the fact that they have only a very short time in which to cover a great deal of ground, and there is considerable discussion and experiment today in the matter of what should be put in and what left out. For instance, how much Hebrew should be taught? Should some subjects (e.g. liturgy, ethics or nineteenth-century theology) be left as optional courses for those who elect to take them?

Indeed, few today are satisfied with things as they are and many are prepared for change. The type of courses which used to be suitable

for boys coming up to the ancient universities with a good classical
education behind them, and who then expected to go on to a theological college with a view to ordination, are not likely to be appropriate for the variety of students reading theology in the modern
universities under the very different conditions of today; yet on the
whole the courses in the modern universities still tend to be modelled
on the old pattern. There is widespread agreement that the *small*
honours school in a modern university provides a valuable teaching
instrument to which there is no parallel elsewhere; it constitutes a
fellowship of teachers and taught to which there is no parallel at all
in the ancient universities, and nowadays, by all accounts, the tutorial
system in the modern universities is in no way inferior to that of the
ancient ones. Yet it may be that the very excellence of the specialist
Honours school is the enemy of experiment and development in new
and needed directions. Not all students are suited to become specialists, and, though in many modern universities there are such things
as general courses and general Honours degrees, the problem of
cross-fertilisation with other departments is not easily solved. Today
there is a good deal of criticism abroad concerning the department-
alism of the modern university system, and many would like to see
a more open and fruitful intercourse between departments, so that
the so-called 'problem of communication', which is always with us in
these days of specialisation, might be somewhat eased. Various proposals have been made. Some suggest that theological departments
should become 'departments of religion' (as often in America), so
that their studies might be widened to include the study of the non-
christian religions and the phenomena of religion generally.[1] Of
course, our universities should provide for the study of religion in
this wider sense, but such a study cannot either be included in or
substituted for the study of theology in the manner which has become customary since the 1870's; if we are to understand our
Western civilisation and its humane tradition, there must be some
place in our university curricula where the distinctively christian-
theological contribution to that tradition can be studied in depth.
Others suggest that Christianity should be studied as a philosophy of
religion and that such study should be included in the curriculum of
the departments of philosophy; but Christianity is not a philosophy

[1] *v.* Note on *Theology and the new universities*, p. 188 *infra.*

of religion, and in any case the notion would be totally unacceptable to departments of philosophy as at present constituted.

One possible line of development in some universities would be the provision of well-designed introductory theological courses as options for a general degree course. It is difficult to write in general terms about this subject, because there is already a very wide variety of such courses in the different universities, ranging from pass degrees to general Honours degrees, Joint-honours degrees, and so on. In many universities it is already possible to take some kind of theological course or courses for such degrees; they are usually based on the bible and perhaps early church history and doctrine. They might be supplemented by courses designed to introduce students to the great streams of theological thought and to the living issues of theological discussion today. Their aim would be to help those who are not specialists to understand the bearing of christian faith and morals in their wider relation to other disciplines, scientific, social, historical, literary, and so on. They should be designed to help the maximum number of students to gain a real measure of theological insight without in any way diminishing the academic rigour of the study of theology; such courses would help to create an informed lay opinion upon theological issues, so desirable in an age in which many half-digested theological ideas are discussed in the press, on television and in popular paperbacks.

Another promising suggestion is that new departments of 'the History of Ideas' should be set up within the faculties of Arts. At present there is no place where this very important subject can be studied systematically in our universities, yet the need is constantly expressed for a school which would transcend the well-worn specialist grooves in a comprehensive study of the history of thought. It would include the history of philosophy, science, literature and, of course, theology; it is now generally recognised that theological convictions have had a great deal to do with the development of Western society, its values, art, politics, morality and science, to say nothing of its literature and philosophy. Such a study might rescue the ancient and the modern classics from becoming the property of a decreasing number of specialists (even if ancient and foreign classical literature had generally to be read in translation); it might introduce many to the literature of the bible and of the Church, and to the *philosophia perennis*; it might integrate these studies with the story of man's scientific achievements and especially with an understanding of scientific method itself, which is so essential to the wholeness of outlook of an educated person today; it might relate all this, in however tentative a manner, to the general social and political development of our modern world; and thus it might show that there is, after all, only one 'culture', so far at least as the Western world is concerned. It is to be hoped that the very new (or projected) 'modern universities', which have thus far signified no intention of setting up departments of Theology of the type which have now become traditional, may become interested in such a project, provided that they can rid themselves of the rationalist prejudice that nothing which was said before about 1750 is worthy of the attention of modern undergraduates. There will, of course, be many who will exclaim that such a proposal is far too wide to be practicable and who will shrink from the task of setting up such a bold and integrating school of modern 'greats'. However that may be, it would seem that new experiments in the direction of more integrated studies are likely to be attempted sooner or later, and when the time comes it is to be hoped that theologians will be ready to take the current when it serves.

(IV) ROMAN CATHOLIC PARTICIPATION IN A MODERN UNIVERSITY

H. FRANCIS DAVIS

Definitions and distinctions

First, a word about terms. The word 'Theology' in English universities is wider in its connotation than in Catholic universities and seminaries. 'Theology' tends in England to cover everything studied in the Theology Department, especially Scripture and Church History. It does not necessarily include Doctrine or systematic theology. At the present day, as other contributors have emphasised, there is a wide and growing demand for the inclusion of the latter in the theology curriculum. The formal study of Doctrine has not always been considered respectable, especially in the Free Churches. Two reasons have been brought up against it; (a) that doctrine is a private matter, and can only be privately accepted on faith, but hardly taught; and (*b*) that it is an impertinence on the part of any professor or lecturer to tell his students what doctrines they will find in the text of Scripture. The latter objection arose out of the persuasion forced on us through long years of christian division that the interpretation of Scripture texts depended mainly, if not exclusively, on the light of private inspiration or the authority of ecclesiastical tradition.

However, there is today a far healthier atmosphere in the field of Scripture interpretation, and in the attitude to doctrine. No longer is it assumed as normal that Protestant and Catholic Scripture scholars will differ as to the meaning of a passage, nor is it assumed that there is no objective doctrine implied in the Scripture. There is, moreover, more mutual understanding of the function of ecclesiastical tradition in its interpretation. It is becoming more and more clear that the christians who study theology do so in most cases because they are committed christians, and that this is not mere sentiment, but involves some previously accepted conviction. It is really for this reason that they not only decide to study theology, but also have chosen for their special study the christian literature and history.

We have today reached a stage where most people recognise doctrine, therefore, as a fully respectable and important part of 'Theology'. This has, of course, a certain ecumenical importance, in the sense that no Catholic could even remotely conceive of a theology course without doctrine; and indeed, traditionally, doctrine has more often than not been the most important subject in the School. So much so, indeed, that for a Catholic the word 'Theology' connotes the systematic science of christian doctrine more directly even than it does Scripture and History.

A word about the term 'Doctrine', as contrasted with dogmatic theology. There is much to be said for retaining the English word 'Doctrine', and recognising that it has a peculiar English connotation. You can have a Thomist and Scotist theology; but you cannot have Thomist and Scotist doctrine. Thomists and Scotists each have their own method of explaining the one christian doctrine about which they agree. In practice, however, the word 'theology' is often enough used in the same sense as 'doctrine'; and a book with the title 'The Theology of the Incarnation' would not necessarily differ from another with the title 'The Doctrine of the Incarnation'.

The distinction here suggested between Doctrine and Theology might enable us to clear the ecumenical hurdle about titles, that is—

should a Catholic lecturing on doctrine at the university call his lectures 'Catholic Doctrine' or just 'Doctrine'? It is my claim that the second title is preferable. It is not, of course, that I, as a Catholic, would admit that there is another kind of christian doctrine which is not Catholic.

When I began lecturing in Doctrine at Birmingham in 1947, the Head of the recently organised department, Professor H. F. D. Sparks, had recently come from Durham—a university where systematic theology had been taken for granted through the tradition set by Canon Quick. He therefore took for granted it should form part of the curriculum. He made it clear to me that he looked upon theology as a science of truth not of opinion. One was bound therefore to teach it as such. One could not appear to prejudge the issue by calling it Catholic, Protestant, or even neutral. One just taught the truth as far as was possible, and did not label it.

He followed here the tradition of the English universities, which differs from that of Germany. Germany has two departments, one of Catholic, the other of Protestant theology. This offered a comfortable, practical solution to an awkward situation of mutual distrust. Yet, even in Germany, I presume, it would hardly be supposed that the Evangelical, on principle, teaches a doctrine of the Trinity and Incarnation different from that taught by the Catholic.

At Birmingham from the beginning, of course, it was known I was a Catholic, and assumed that I would approach the doctrine as a Catholic, and that I would loyally point out if, in some aspect, my Catholic standpoint would not appear acceptable to someone of another tradition. In 1947 the situation of a Catholic lecturer in the theology department was exciting, but even at that less ecumenical time it worked perfectly. Although there was some initial shyness, I have always been grateful to the Anglicans for their lack of inhibitions; and from the start my lectures were advertised as a recommended course in the Anglican theological college. But there was for a while some hesitation among those of other traditions.

From the beginning the title of my course has included the word 'doctrine'; e.g. The Doctrine of the Trinity, of the Incarnation, of the Atonement, of Grace, or of the Eucharist. In each case I do all I can to help my listeners to understand the doctrine in question, professing what I believe it to be in its fullness.

The title 'Doctrine' enables me to regard it as a revealed insight into God's nature and activity—and to keep the term 'Theology' for human attempts to systematise or explain it. There have been various Eastern and Western theologies. Some have been Catholic, some Orthodox, and some perhaps Anglican, Lutheran, or Calvinist. These theologies will have value in so far as they throw light on the christian doctrine, or make it easier for christians to defend it.

Certain distinctions are, however, necessary. It would not be true to say that Catholic, Orthodox and Calvinist have at present no different convictions in matters of doctrine. Unfortunately, Christendom is still divided both in the range of doctrinal convictions and in the importance attached to them. As a lecturer, I make no secret of the importance to me of the revealed truth or insight as I see it. As a lecturer to a mixed audience, I have to make clear those instances in which someone of another tradition may be unwilling to accept what I regard as essential to the christian message.

Let us take an easy example. Do christians differ with regard to the Trinity? Are there as many doctrines as there are denominations? If the latter were true, then clearly the cause of ecumenism would be a hopeless one. In this case, at least, we can confidently assert that all christians believe that Christ was the Son of God, one with his Father, in the unity of the Holy Spirit. It is not even easy to discover a distinctive theology that is Catholic, and not Protestant, or vice versa. It may be a fact that the majority of Catholic theologians follow the Thomistic theology in expressing and systematising this doctrine, but it is also true, however, that some Catholics prefer a more Eastern Trinitarian theology, while some non-Catholics prefer a Thomistic theology. Barth has a modern theology of his own, but not all Calvinists would accept it as preferable to more ancient theologies.

But, whether one is a Barthian, a Thomist, or an Eastern, whether one bases one's theology on the analogy of individual or social psychology, there is a basic christian doctrine of the Trinity that the various theologies are trying with varying success to systematise, interpret and make, as far as the mystery allows, acceptable to human understanding. I would state emphatically that we are all still concerned with the same vision of the Godhead, that we still, at least on principle, agree on the creeds and basic conciliar declarations. All our hopes for unity depend upon there being a basic revelation of the Trinity, as of the Incarnation, which in technical terminology, we call the orthodox christian doctrine.

The same basis, which is at the root of our hopes for unity, gives us our possibility of theological dialogue and common study of the divine insights conveyed to us through Scriptures and christian tradition—a dialogue such as has existed at Birmingham for the last fifteen years.

Since the time of Newman at least, there has been a double approach in Catholic theology. Newman was utterly convinced that formal terms or propositions are incapable of conveying more than one aspect of a truth. The more important the truth, the more it is bound up with life and the universe, the more concrete and personal it is, the more existential, the harder it is to convey it adequately in any human words—least of all technical words. God came to us existentially, in the history of a people. He came to us over a period of many centuries. After long preparation of the scene, he lived among us in human form. And by means of all these activities, and by means of the words of countless prophets, psalmists and wise men, and finally through his own Word made flesh, that Word was implanted in human minds.

The Word was made flesh. In a sense these words could apply to all God's dealings with us, though in a very special way they apply to Christ. To Newman's mind it would have defeated God's purpose if he had revealed himself to us propositionally, that is to say, in the form of a catechism. He would immediately have been transplanted from the real, concrete, personal and existential to the abstract. Worse than this he would have become a multitude of propositions instead of a real unity.

It is of the essence of Newman's *Essay on Development* that the original impression, insight, idea, or 'Image of Christ'—as he varyingly calls it—which is the whole christian revelation, and which itself he elsewhere compares to a colourless medium through which we see Christ himself and contemplate Christ and nothing else—this original Image is one—not many—like the Christ it represents. But just as one cannot depict a human person except by an infinite number of words—and even then one's expression remains inadequate—still less is it possible to depict Christianity—the Christian Idea—in any one set of words. We have been studying the Scriptures for nineteen centuries, and their meaning is inexhaustible.

By means of these words—these infinite aspects—and with the help of God's grace and the gifts of the Holy Spirit, brought home to us in our own lives and those of consecrated christians, a divine seed—the image of Christ—is sown. We call it the Faith. We see it and cling to it with the help of another word of God speaking in our hearts, a word calling forth a trust and confidence in him, which we also call faith.

This divine seed grows—if it continues to live—fed by prayer and contemplation. It is protected and fed from outside by continual reference back to the word of God in Scripture. It is helped by the words of christian Fathers and theologians. As it lives and grows it finds new ways of expressing itself, adapted to each succeeding age and culture. And this is what we call the development of doctrine. It is not a growth of one explicit proposition out of another, but a development of new expressions of the same original truth, which for all times remains at a deeper level than all its expressions. We need to watch that our new expressions remain faithful to the original idea, insight, or revelation. But they do not have to follow logically from any one explicit statement of the original.

The recent council has shown us that the contrary idea—that of a revelation made in so many propositions—still persists; and the great controversy concerning the schema on revelation in Vatican Council, session one, seems to many to have hinged on this. It was a pleasant surprise to many at the Council to find that the majority of Catholic theologians today follow Newman in this understanding of christian doctrine.[1]

Catholics, however, have never gone to the extremes found in some non-Catholic circles of denying all truth to propositions. This would, first, nullify all Scripture teaching and tradition. After all, a truth lying at a deeper level than propositions cannot be taught except with propositions. Secondly, it would exclude the possibility of any ortho-dox christian doctrine concerning the christian events. We could not know that God the Father sent his only-begotten Son into the world

[1] Professor Körner's distinction (pp. 245–6 *infra*) between the richness of reality, which we can only describe but not scientifically define, on the one hand, and the scientific definition, on the other, seems to correspond with Newman's distinction between the basic Christian Idea, which Scripture described authori-tatively and we are ever describing anew in sermons and by example in our living, on the one hand, and the credal and conciliar formulations which are useful but only give us an approximate view of one aspect cut off from the continuous mass of reality, on the other. Newman, however, went further, since no one sentence or even series of sentences of the original description exhausts the reality to which the whole description points. The reality is one, the descriptions without limit.

that the world might be saved by him, without having heard this divine fact by means of words. This would seem to exclude the possibility of a theology which was based exclusively upon events. An even more dangerous reaction to propositional theology or doctrine was the modernist one in the early part of the century. To this view, propositions might express religious experiences or attitudes, but could not give a genuine message of truth.

It is an interesting fact that, while Newman believed that the christian truth lay deeper than any or every formula, he was utterly convinced (a) that formulas could validly express an important aspect of the truth, and (b) that certain formulas, notably the creeds, did so do. For him, as for us, it will always be true that Jesus Christ is both true God and true man, even though we shall never fully understand the meaning of the terms 'God' and 'man'.

I would like to say something here about the problem of the 'liberal' theologian, using the term in Newman's sense, as it still often is. In this sense it is almost identical with either 'rationalist' or 'modernist' according to context. The 'liberal' theologian's reaction against anything in the nature of fundamentalism has led him to dissociate himself, partially or wholly, from the original insight as existent or normative. The Image of Christ—as living in the whole of bible revelation (as already expressed), as living in the martyrs, doctors and faithful children of the Church in every age, as expressed in the Church's creeds—is what Newman calls at once a great divine fact and a great divine philosophy poured out in the midst of human history. This image is weakened or lost—and in its place we have some modern philosophy or abstraction—a new example of the wisdom of man being chosen before the foolishness of God. Newman already knew it, and feared that religious liberalism was the great internal disorder in English religion, which would dissolve christian orthodoxy from within. It was responsible for driving him and his friends from the Church of England. It grew considerably in power after the decline of the Oxford Movement. It made Manning, though not Newman, despair of Oxford. The reason why Newman did not despair was that he thought it could never permanently destroy the christian faith in the Church of England.

On the other hand, the kind of common theology and dialogue previously mentioned, which is an actuality at Birmingham, and has made it possible for several Catholics to take the course there, supposes an atmosphere of what I might call orthodox and committed Christianity among the majority of professors and students. It supposes a common living acceptance of the idea of revelation, and a common recognition that its source is Jesus Christ, God's word. It supposes christians anxious to live by the christian faith, as represented in the creeds, who have a sense of responsibility for the word of God handed down in Scripture, and are in the main stream of christian tradition. Such christians, though some may be Catholics and some Protestants, are capable of having responsible and prayerful dialogue together. They would all be sensitive to the danger of heresy. They would not wish to drift into pelagianism or Sabellianism or adoptionism. They are eager to work together to penetrate more deeply into the Gospel of the Word.

Where the doctrinal liberals are the exception rather than the rule, dialogue between orthodox christians is often stimulated by their aberrations. Where, for instance, the christian and scriptural notion of atonement through sacrifice is attacked, the reaction of the orthodox christian is not unlike that of the Catholic student at a Catholic university or even at a seminary. Such attacks are recognised and discussed among Catholics as much as anywhere else. They do not dry up the wells of theology. On the contrary, they often have a healthy effect in stimulating deeper research into the origins of christian doctrine. It will probably be found that the person attacking the notion is misunderstanding its christian meaning, or perhaps is only attacking certain caricatures of the doctrine that he has heard in the mouths of christian apologists. The first result, however, where liberalism becomes universal is that true christian dialogue becomes impossible, because there is no sharing of christian insight. Another kind of dialogue no doubt takes its place; but it is rather a dialogue of philosophical attack and christian defence, and ceases to be creative. Further, as in Tillich, it usually takes refuge in new abstractions which mystify the faithful and confound the learned, but do not give confidence as an interpretation of the Gospel by which christians live.

A department entirely composed of 'liberal' theologians in this sense might well present dangers to the faith of a young Catholic student, especially if he were, as yet, not well instructed; but the majority of the lecturers in a university theology department are orthodox christians; and if there were available at least one competent Catholic lecturer, the dangers presented to faith especially in view of the now widespread ecumenical outlook, would be no greater in a department of theology than in one of philosophy; in fact they are likely to be less.

In such conditions, experience at Birmingham would suggest that a Catholic has nothing to lose; whether he would have much to gain depends on the organising of the curriculum. If Catholics fail to get the curriculum they want, they probably will have none but themselves to blame. Modern English universities are anxious to support the kind of curriculum favoured by their students. Catholics, in their preoccupation with the dangers and inadequacies of the English university set-up, may have been victims of a defeatist mentality—terrified lest they lost what they have, instead of recognising that they also have something to give.

My experience is that the orthodox christian, whether Catholic or Protestant, is anxious to learn of the value of the treasure committed to his care in his faith. One Anglican told me her reasons for studying theology. She had been teaching catechism and had been asked questions on the christian teaching on the Trinity which she was unable to answer satisfactorily. It was this that determined her to come to study theology at the university of Birmingham. For many years I was teaching at a Catholic theological college at the same time as at the university. I could not help remarking that my non-Catholic students were as committed and as eager to learn about the faith, to live it and love it as were their Catholic counterparts. They were aware that they were going into a world which would challenge their faith, and were determined to protect it.

To protect his students against this danger of rationalism, it has always seemed to me that a lecturer must not be afraid to keep his audience conscious that they are speaking about the all-holy God, and his life-giving sacred Word. One must avoid not only flippancy but an excessively abstract approach, as though one were discussing mathematics rather than the Godhead—unless of course one really does wish one's students to identify God with mathematics. We should never let our students forget that ultimately, what we are studying is Jesus Christ, the word made Flesh—the word living till the end of the world in ourselves through his Holy Spirit. We should never let them forget St Thomas's words in relation to the Eucharist—that our faith is a perpetual recalling of his passion, a pledge of future glory which is given for the filling with grace of all those around us at the university, of all those they will one day teach, or to whom they will one day preach.

Methods of teaching

I think that various methods of teaching doctrine are possible. Since we are dealing with present-day life, it is often good—especially perhaps with the Incarnation and Trinity—to show people early on to what an extent these doctrines are already intrinsic to their lives. I like Karl Adam's method, for instance, of reminding his students that they had already accepted the christian tradition that Christ is the Son of God, and had already been convinced of his presence with them, before ever they opened their bibles to find what the Scriptures say about him. This could lead one on to a simple statement of what are usually regarded as the basic elements of the doctrine, faith, insight, or Idea, which, by the common consent of christians, forms the orthodox creed.

I am sure it is possible to do this without being in the least unfair to either Protestant or Catholic. If it should happen, as in some doctrines it might, that there is still an unresolved difference of conviction about what is the orthodox christian doctrine, one just says so honestly and clearly: 'For Catholics, the orthodox doctrine includes so and so; for Protestants this is not generally admitted.' But I find that, at least on the main doctrines, this is not often necessary. Usually it is possible to say quite clearly: 'The doctrine that the Son of God became truly man, without ceasing to be the Son of God, is central to the christian doctrine of the Incarnation. If you deny this, or find that you cannot make this statement, then at least be quite clear that you no longer accept the orthodox christian faith in the Incarnation.' In an English university, I cannot insist that my students be orthodox. I can however insist that, where they depart from christian orthodoxy, they do so consciously and responsibly.

Usually the only cases where I might feel bound to point out that orthodox Catholic theology, at least in practice, is more rigid than Protestant would be on secondary questions such as Christ's knowledge. On a matter like this, one must be scrupulously fair and be ready to admit (a) that many Protestants hold that Christ assumed human ignorance, even to the possibility of error, without their denying either implicitly or explicitly Christ's divinity, or even without necessarily their admitting true kenosis; and (*b*) that very little has been strictly defined even on the Catholic side. The biggest distinction here is that Catholics temperamentally are nervous of the results on their faith in the Incarnation of denying Christ's inerrancy; while Protestants are temperamentally more nervous of appearing to be not completely honest and unbiassed in their interpretation of the Scripture text. There is probably at the same time a tendency among Catholics to be more anxious not to compromise Christ's true divinity, and among Protestants not to compromise Christ's true humanity. It has always seemed that there is a possibility of genuine dialogue here, provided that both sides recognise that these, even though concerning the faith, are of secondary importance to the doctrine of the Incarnation itself. In other words, Catholics and Protestants ought to be far more grateful to feel at one in professing the faith of the Incarnation, than disturbed at a disagreement over what usually appears to the Catholic, but not to the Protestant, as a logical consequence of that belief.

The same sort of distinction applies to the relationship between the Incarnation and Mariology. Protestant minimisation with regard to our Lady appears to a Catholic inconsistent with a true doctrine of the Incarnation. But it should be borne in mind that Catholic maximisation may appear to the Protestant almost equally inconsistent with that doctrine. These matters, though they still involve different views on the faith, are based on a common orthodoxy on the central doctrine. And it is this latter fact that makes dialogue possible.

Because of the nature and unity of God's revelation as defined above, and before discussing new formulations of doctrine, we must first try to introduce people in the most living possible way to the manner in which this doctrine was mediated to us through real personal encounters with Christ, and events as recorded in Scripture. In the doctrines of the Godhead and of Jesus in the atonement, one can only give some indications of how this is the subject of the whole of revelation.

Secondly, before coming to the theologies and other formulations one will take the best of the Fathers and see what the doctrine meant to them in the age of the martyrs and doctors, how vital it was to their faith and preaching, and in their own life and liturgy.

Thirdly, it is far more theologically important to show how the doctrine is part of a living whole than to spend a great deal of time

G

on its secondary details. One will try, therefore, to make clear that the Trinity cannot in real life be cut off from the Incarnation, or from the Atonement, Grace, Baptism, or the Eucharist. It is just a convenience of the schoolroom that the one basic revelation, Jesus Christ, should be taught gradually under these differing aspects now consecrated by long-standing tradition. This is one of the ways in which the student is given a sense of responsibility. We want him to realise that it is not just a formalistic demand for orthodoxy which makes us respect the orthodox tradition. It is not just that, for some unrealised reason, acceptance of this article or doctrine is one of the passwords demanded, without which one will not be admitted to eternal union with God. On the contrary, one tries to show that the reason for the Church's insistence is a realisation that the rest of christian belief and practice depends upon it; that, if one rejects it, one should consider whether one is not rejecting the whole fabric. As St Anselm said: 'If anyone thinks that sin can be lightly dismissed and forgotten, he should understand that he has not yet even begun to realise the gravity of sin, and the greatness and holiness of God.'

One will especially consider its relation to doctrines with which it might seem incompatible. How far is the Incarnation or Trinity an essential part of a religion based on monotheism and on God's greatness, transcendence and other-worldliness?

Next, one will consider the main attempts to develop a theology of this doctrine. This section could cover many lectures, according to the time available.

Finally, one will consider the position of this doctrine in the modern theological world, both Catholic and non-Catholic, as well as in the modern secular world. One will try to fit one's theology to the world of philosophy, to show how philosophy can help by indicating how reason can remove the obstacles to an understanding of revelation that reason had first placed there.

In the case of the Sacraments, I have often followed a different method. Here the Scripture material is so limited that it has usually seemed wisest to begin with a consideration of this. Even here, it seems that the lecturer should then face the challenge of working out with his students, as fairly as he is able, what is the christian doctrine. We are living in an age where Catholic and Protestant theologians are drawing nearer together. This has come about partly through a more objective and soundly critical biblical approach on both sides, and partly through the growing tendency of Protestant and Anglican theologians to admit the importance of tradition in this field. We have already reached the stage where the lecturer can state quite definitely and constructively that some doctrine of the real presence of Christ's body and blood, in close relation to the elements, is generally accepted as essential to the orthodox christian doctrine. The lecturer will of course forestall any accusation of narrow-mindedness or unfairness by pointing out, to the best of his ability, if there do exist any groups of responsible and believing christians who would deny this. He would however be entitled to add comments of two types: (a) such a view would not be regarded as christian or orthodox by Catholic theologians; and (b) in the light of christian history, he personally did not think that such a view, whatever its merits, could be regarded as christian orthodoxy.

The Catholic lecturer in the presence of non-Catholics, will clearly not pretend that no interpretation of the Scripture text but his own is scientifically admissible. He may state openly, as Benoît has done for the words THIS IS MY BODY, that these words in their present minimum of context and background are patient of either a Catholic or a less-than-Catholic interpretation.[1] Like the Catholic theologians, he will then have to appeal to christian tradition. He may claim, for instance, that the interpretation which was traditional during the early centuries is that which has always been accepted by Catholics; and, to us, this is the key to Christ's own meaning. He will have to admit loyally whatever historical lacunae there are in his argument, so that the student who is not a committed Catholic can make his own decision, and even the Catholic can be clear in his mind exactly what is the foundation for his belief.

Once what is the orthodox christian doctrine has been made clear, one cannot, as I have already stated, insist that one's students accept it; but one can insist on their knowing it, and being fully responsible in whatever attitude they take in its regard. Part of their criticism of any book should be to discover how it stands in relation to the orthodox tradition. It would, for instance, be theologically undesirable to accept a new work on the Incarnation which happened to be Apollinarian without realising that it was so. In other words,

---

[1] P. Benoit, O.P., 'The Holy Eucharist'—II, in *Scripture*, IX, no. 5 (January 1957), p. 5.

one should not depart from the accepted tradition of christian ortho-doxy without realising it, and doing so responsibly.

This will mean that either as part of the doctrine course, or as a complementary study connected with it, there will have to be a study of the more vital stages of doctrinal history, with special reference to the chief heresies and definitions during the first five centuries. It will be important to discover what is the doctrinal reason for the con-demnation or definition.

It is possible to show that all the technical words used in early councils and creeds are so uncertain in their meaning, and we are so unacquainted with their ancient usage, that no abstract statement of doctrine in the early centuries means what we think it means. Conse-quently, one can come away from a critical study of early documents convinced that we don't really know what was meant by Nicea, Constantinople, Ephesus or Chalcedon, or any of the other councils of the Church. Further, we can be persuaded, the creeds are only formulas for worship, not in any sense statements of doctrines. The teacher of doctrine has to get himself and his hearers away from such abstractions into the concrete. He has to take himself and his hearers back into a world which had intense doctrinal convictions, and never doubted that the maintenance of the christian faith in the world depended upon the clear formulation of those convictions. At Ephesus or Chalcedon they were not merely defining abstractions, nor were they trying merely to win a victory for one school of thought over another. What then were they trying to say? They certainly used terms that we cannot understand fully today, and we certainly do not realise the full connotations of these terms. But is it really true that christians do not realise what the Fathers were trying to safeguard at Ephesus? Somehow we must bring our students face to face with the concrete truth that the terms they used, whether abstract or concrete, wanted to safeguard. At Ephesus, it was the unity of Christ, God and man, a unity such as is implied when we ascribe many activities or other predications to one individual. In Christ, there is as close a oneness of God and man as there is in myself between the one who reads and the one who thinks while he is reading. There is a oneness sufficient to say of Christ—God, and of Mary—Mother of God.

It will be seen that the approach in a theology course in a modern university as elsewhere must be, so it seems to me, primarily

Newmanic or concrete. Abstract technical formulations may traditionally be necessary to the understanding of the concrete situation.
But the more abstract the theology, the more second order a question
it becomes; and we have too little time to consider it in the curriculum
of an English university. Much as I appreciate St Thomas, it would
never do to begin with the Thomistic article: 'Whether there are
processions in God.' This supposes an enormous background of
knowledge of Scripture, faith and tradition, so that right from the
beginning, one would give an impression of abstraction and artifici-
ality. One must prepare the way with the background of Hebrew
monotheism, the flesh and blood of the God-man in the Gospel and
his relations to his Father, and his teaching about his Father, and
about the Spirit they would send, in the context of the controversy of
many christian centuries, before one can ask the question seriously
and responsibly and with a sense of reality: 'whether there are processions in God.' I have found in practice that it takes a long course
of lectures to prepare the way to ask the simple questions that St
Thomas frequently poses in the *Summa Theologica*. What is true of
the students in an English university is probably more true than we
think of our own seminary students. I was taught the Trinity on a
theological plane from the *Summa*; for some years this was the
kernel of my Trinitarian teaching, when I was teaching in the seminary. It seemed better, and still seems better than the Trinitarian
approach of many modern scholastic textbooks. At least it did not
claim to be more than a summary of the reasoning systematisation of
Trinitarian doctrine in christian theology. By claiming to cover the
doctrine adequately at a university level, the modern textbooks often
claim to be much more.

One's method of teaching in an English university is, of course,
only partially by lectures. In many respects more important is the use
of tutorials. We certainly depend considerably upon these at Birmingham. We have admitted Doctrine as an alternative main subject
of examination, so that a fair proportion, sometimes more than half
of our students, take a specialised study of a doctrine in place of the
more traditional Reformation period. At first students were allowed
to choose between the Trinity, the Incarnation, the Atonement and
the Eucharist. The Department now, for practical reasons—chiefly of
the staff, insists on all the Doctrine students in one year taking the
same Doctrine paper. This is decided partly on the basis of an

exchange from year to year, and partly on the wish of the majority. It is not so bad an arrangement when one realises that any one christian doctrine, for its acceptable understanding, requires some understanding of all the central doctrines of the creed. The Eucharist which I do next term, supposes the Trinity, Incarnation, Atonement and Grace.

For the tutorials, students are given a weekly essay and a bibliography; each week one, two or three students will meet for an hour with their tutor to read the essay one of them has prepared, and to have general discussion.

Over the years the Birmingham arrangement has worked. It has been a better practical exercise in ecumenical understanding, I feel convinced, than most self-conscious dialogue. It is never possible for anyone at Birmingham to forget our common christian baptism and common christian loyalty. It has inevitably led us to see the good in one another's tradition, without sacrificing anything that we regard as essential to the faith. Several Catholics have taken the course preparatory to teaching. I might add that neither these Catholics nor indeed any others of our students who have taken good degrees have failed to get positions. Many of our students are hoping to teach religion as a graded post—we cannot produce enough to fill the posts offered.

The encouragement of more Catholic participation would fulfil a need, if it can be satisfactorily done. It is unfortunate that in this country theology seems to be a university degree subject open to the laity of all denominations except ourselves. Germany, America, and other countries are doing what they can in Catholic institutes. Might we not do something more fitting to the English situation, more ecumenically fruitful, if we can find a way of co-operating more uninhibitedly with the christians in our universities?

NOTE

THEOLOGY AND THE NEW UNIVERSITIES

Conditions and organisation vary so much from university to university that very few generalisations are more than roughly valid. Hence the practical approach to the question of developing the university study of theology must differ with each university. Much of what has been discussed above may well be appropriate with regard to many univer-

sities. But considering the topic as a whole and looking to the future it would be as well to enter a caveat; and the following note has been contributed by Hilary Armstrong, *Professor of Greek, University of Liverpool:*

The questions which arise if it is proposed to establish an entirely new faculty or department of Theology in a new university, or in one in which theology has not been established as an academic subject before, are different from, and more difficult than, those about the development of an established faculty of Theology. The christians who wish a new centre of theological teaching to be set up in their university must first ask themselves on what grounds they have any right to claim that a university which is, and should be, religiously neutral, should endow and include in its curriculum a specifically christian kind of study and teaching. They must be prepared to meet the objections which will be raised, that a faculty of Theology will be an 'enclave of the Church', a centre of christian propaganda rather than of properly academic teaching and research, that there is no reason, if you have a department of christian Theology, why you should not also have a department of Marxism or Scientific Humanism and so on. In order to satisfy both ourselves and others that it is right and desirable to establish new faculties of Theology, we shall have to think out very clearly what we mean by theology and what we think a university School of Theology should do. One way of answering the objections would be to show the purpose of the new faculty to be, not to teach christian doctrine, but to show what christian doctrine is; to study in an objective and scholarly manner as much as possible of the whole range of christian beliefs and practices, past and present. This is obviously a serious and academically respectable field of study, and one which is of interest to many other disciplines. However, consideration needs to be given to the argument that such a course should be expanded to include, where practicable, the study of other religions besides Christianity, and so become a faculty of Religious Studies rather than of christian Theology.[1]

Another way of answering the question would be to show that the

[1] See Professor Ninian Smart's *Religion as a Discipline* (Universities Quarterly, vol. 16, no. 5, December 1962, pp. 48–53) and his reminder that 'it is precisely when, in a Department of Religion, theology is liable to be subjected to the cold winds of criticism and to the need to respond to the challenges of humanism, Marxism and the like, that serious theology gets done.'

university theologian has something to contribute, along with psychologists, sociologists etc., to the solution of various ethical and social problems which are appropriate for study and discussion in a university. But it remains to be seen whether any proposals which are practicable and likely to commend themselves to academic opinion in general can be worked out on these lines.

While it is reasonable that this symposium should, as its practical side, be concerned with possibilities in already existing faculties it is necessary to point out that the whole topic of Theology and the university has a dimension which has not been *specifically* dealt with in a practical manner, although the relation of Theology to, and its place and nature in, a secularised society has been the main underlying concern of the whole symposium.

Other nations of different habits are not enemies: they are godsends.— *A. N. Whitehead.* One needs the enemy.—*T. S. Eliot.*

IV

THE CREATIVE CENTRE—
exercises in open dialogue

8. Theology and Literature

(I) NATURAL THEOLOGY AND ITS RELATION TO POETRY

DOM ILLTYD TRETHOWAN

It is not to be expected that in a paper like this I should undertake the defence of natural theology against the opponents of metaphysics in general or a certain sort of theologian in particular. But it is clearly necessary for me to say what I mean by natural theology and thus to make certain claims for it.

To put my position as briefly as possible, I would say that a knowledge of God is so far natural to man that it is involved in any specifically human act: any serious inquiry into the truth of things, any genuinely moral choice. It is, I think, our moral experience which presents us with the most accessible evidence—not the obligation to do particular acts but the obligation to do *something* with our lives, whatever that may prove to be, and not just to drift. This awareness of a claim upon us, a recognition of our absolute dependence is, I believe, the recognition of an absolute principle in such sort that the 'good atheist' or 'good agnostic' is a crypto-theist. As Pascal said, 'God is always known but seldom recognised.' This is not a vision of God, in any ordinary sense of that expression, but it is what I am accustomed to call a 'cognitive contact' with God in his action on the mind. It tells us not only that he exists but something about him.

I should like to suggest that theologians who are inclined to leave the subject to the philosophers might ask themselves whether this will really do in our circumstances. Academic philosophers, in general, are still very suspicious of metaphysics. Those of them who are christians, with few exceptions, if they are not content simply to fall back on faith, skirmish ineffectually from time to time with their non-christian colleagues. If they are Catholics, they do not deny that a natural knowledge of God is possible—for that would be heresy—

but they usually dispense themselves from further inquiry. The Thomists, it is true, continue to insist that there is an inferential demonstration of God's existence, but they do not succeed, I think, in producing one which works. So the theologian who wants to make contact with the agnostic typical of our society may well feel called upon to do his own thinking about the matter unless he is content to fall back simply upon faith.

I should like to put to you one consideration—it will help to bring out my own position—which seems to recommend natural theology to the theologian. Most of us, I think, would agree that faith is something which is *offered* to us, not forced upon us. When it has been offered but not yet accepted, what is the position? Faith, fundamentally, is not the acceptance of a set of propositions but the acceptance of God in Christ. It is this implicitly even when it is not recognised as such, for it must be available to all men of goodwill. They must have the opportunity of choosing God in Christ even if they do not recognise that it is God who summons them. The knowledge which they have, when the offer is made to them, must be in fact a knowledge of God, whatever they think about it, because otherwise they cannot choose him. They do not as yet possess faith, and the knowledge which they have is therefore natural—it is a summons to grace. Of course, if we wish, we may give the name of 'faith' to all knowledge of God, but the consideration which I have just put before you, tells, I think, against such a usage.

From this point of view, the approach of God to man, his offer of himself, is the philosophical question on which all others turn. If one concludes, as I do, that this approach is made in terms of our everyday judgments of value, if God's existence is really made known to us in this way, then all that we say not only about ethics but also about aesthetics must be wholly controlled by our apprehension of him, understood in the light of it. And to discover whether we should reach this conclusion or not, all we can do, in the end, is to consult our own experience. (I may add, in parenthesis, that if our knowledge of God has in fact this basis, we must allow that faith is in some sort a matter of experience, and this must affect our attitude to theology in general—if we accept this conclusion, we may be saved from a good deal of nonsense in the field of dogma.)

It seems to me strange that people should be content sometimes to regard this as a plausible suggestion without feeling the need to go further into it. It seems equally strange that theists who hold another view of the case should not be more anxious to convince us of it. Nothing is of more importance for the theologian in the post-christian world than to make up his mind, if he still needs to, about the way in which the knowledge, and so the choice, of God arises. For the choice of God is the only question which is in the full sense a question of life or death. Is the theologian to persuade crypto-theists that they have in fact this knowledge and those who have rejected it that this is indeed what they have done? Or is he to rely on logical arguments? (These have their uses, of course.) In the last analysis there are only those alternatives, as it seems to me.

At last, having explained, in this absurdly hasty fashion, what natural theology is, so far as I am concerned, I can turn to the subject of poetry. It is impossible to avoid repeating the conclusions of the paper on aesthetics and metaphysics which I contributed to the symposium volume *The Arts, Artists and Thinkers*. I shall do it, in fresh terms, as rapidly as possible and then pass on to some related questions which were not discussed in that paper. There I was concerned with aesthetic experience in general. Although most contemporary British philosophers assume that it is impossible to discover a common element in our reactions to works of art, I might in reply invert a scholastic adage: *quod gratis negatur, gratis asseritur*. But I cannot see that it is implausible to assert that there is a specific type of reaction to the beauty of a poem or a symphony or a painting, one which has so often been pointed to (admittedly it cannot be precisely described) and which lovers of the arts can recognise as pointing to their own experience. They would agree, with a quite sufficient unanimity, that there is a peculiar tautening of our faculties, a peculiarly vigorous activity of the mind (or the imagination or whatever) accompanied by a peculiarly intense satisfaction. And I think it would be generally agreed that this experience is also credited with a peculiar *value*. There is no way of demonstrating that this is true. But even if the experience is unknown to one, it would be reasonable to conclude, from the mass of testimony in its favour, that it must exist.

Contemporary philosophers would tend to disapprove even more strongly of an attempt to find a common element in the works of art themselves. But, if the common element in the reactions be allowed, it is surely reasonable to assume a common cause of them. And my conclusion was that this common element, the element of beauty, may be indicated by speaking of an 'organic whole'. Here I was drawing on two books by Mr Harold Osborne, *Theory of Beauty* (1952) and *Aesthetics and Criticism* (1954). Although this view has been anticipated by a good many thinkers, and in particular by Coleridge, I am not aware that it has been worked out before in a systematic way. Here I can only give a mere inkling of Mr Osborne's procedure by quoting at some length one passage not quoted in the previous paper:

> For example . . . Dr Leavis argues that the philosophic symbolism of Blake's poetry is inessential to its poetic excellence but points to the 'direct evocative power' of certain words as an integral element in that excellence. Elsewhere he invites us to admire the poetry of Donne because it reproduces the cadences of normal speech. Yet, neither of these qualities could be generalised into a norm of beauty. . . . Yet in these two instances once accepts the rightness of Dr Leavis's perceptions. The truth of the matter is that neither these nor any other isolable qualities are themselves either constitutive of beauty generally or constitutive of the specific beauty of the objects where they are detected. They become elements in the beauty of aesthetic objects only by a relation of congruence in which they stand to the organic whole which is the object in its totality. . . . Criticism should, ideally, not only indicate features which contribute prominently to the excellence of specific works of art but also indicate how they are contributory in this specific instance (but not in that) by reason of their organic relations to all the other qualities which together constitute the totality of the object.[1]

It seems to me that these words have only to be sufficiently pondered for us to perceive the cause of the specifically aesthetic reaction to poetic excellence. This grasp of the organic whole is a contemplative activity. If this is so, if it is the peculiar appropriateness of the words to their whole context which moves us in this peculiar way, not *what* they say—that is, not what is paraphrasable—but just this particular way of saying what is now to be said—these words as part of the poem in this order and in this particular pattern of rhythm, rhyme and so forth—then we may wonder whether there is any great value in aesthetic experience. It may seem to be just a luxury for sophisticated persons. But I think not. The conclusion to which I came at this point is that this peculiarly intense activity of mind (and I think we must call it that, for this is a *cognitive* experience) is of the greatest value because it makes us aware of *ourselves* as we never are

---

[1] *Aesthetics and Criticism*, p. 34 n.—the reference is to Dr Leavis's essay 'Literary Criticism and Philosophy' in *The Common Pursuit*.

in other circumstances. By raising our powers to this extraordinary level it shows us what they are to an extraordinary degree. We really 'come alive', as we might put it. It is not merely that we are enjoying ourselves enormously. We are aware, vaguely but most strikingly, of the capacities of the human mind. We find ourselves transported into a mysterious region of *value*, and at the same time it is a sort of home-coming or an intimation, of a peculiarly dynamic or (it may be) even of an overwhelming kind, that there is a goal which seems to recede even as we approach it. And this may occur when the poem isn't *about* anything which in the ordinary way affects us at all closely. What is this *value*? No doubt the reductive analysts and the psy-chologists between them could settle with it to their own satisfaction. But if in fact God is always acting on our minds and can be known as acting on them, then, it seems to me, the explanation is rather obvious. The more active they are, the more we are aware of them and of God's action on them. And it is only in contemplative activities that they are thus active.

So far, then, if this hypothesis can be entertained, the value of poetry seems to lie not in itself but in what it enables us to be. Beauty is food for the mind—it is necessary if the mind is to achieve full health in the natural order. There is no need to emphasise the im-portance of such a conclusion for the theologian. But of course this is only one side of our subject. Poetry is not just an exhibition of formal beauty. And that leads me to the other feature of Mr Osborne's work which has seemed to me of special value—his forthright dis-tinction between form in art (the element, that is, which is the cause of aesthetic experience) and content (that is, the 'ideas' which it conveys, the truths which it recommends, the 'criticism of life' which it embodies). This means that the critic must bring, as a rule, a double standard to bear on literature. He must not mix up his judgment of the work of art as such, the organic whole, with his judgment on the artist's points of view. He may regard the writer as no artist, but still consider that he has expressed, perhaps very effectively, valuable points of view.

This distinction is not at all popular today, and, I think, for two chief reasons. One is that whenever a distinction between form and content is mentioned it is usually assumed that an attempt is being made to isolate the 'meaning' of, say, a line of poetry from the way in which it is expressed as if the artist first thought of a good idea and then tricked it out with a few frills. That is not the way in which works of art are made. I remember how depressed I felt when some-one told me that he had written a book but had now to 'put in the style'. The point is that a work of art, as such, has *no* meaning. This is a wildly controversial statement, but one cannot say anything on this subject without being controversial. Music, as such, in my sub-mission, has no meaning. It *is* something. When musicians try, as they often do, to give it a meaning, they appeal to the associations which certain sounds in fact have. There need be no objection to this, but it is only confusing, I think, to include such associations in a definition of music. Music is what it is without any associations—a construct, in Mr Osborne's language, of sensory forms to be appre-ciated as such. But a good poem often contains not only the essential characteristics of a work of art, as *this* combination of meaningful words, but also 'ideas'—for example, theological ideas, as in *Paradise Lost*. Here the distinction which I am recommending is surely obvious and necessary. If we are talking about a work of art as such, the meanings of the words in a line of poetry are elements in the organic whole. They must be understood if the work of art is to be under-stood. But to understand a work of art is not just to understand the sum of the meanings of the words. It is to understand them as organically related to one another and to the whole complex of meaning, sound, associations and so forth which *is* the poem and (if I may say it just once more) has as such *no* meaning. As I have tried to suggest in an earlier paragraph, that is not to say that it has no value for human life.

The other reason for the unpopularity of this distinction brings us, at long last, to ground not covered by the paper read five years ago. It is the notion that art is in some mysterious way revelatory of reality. It will be clear that my own views about aesthetic experience support the notion in a certain sense. And perhaps those who take up with it—artists in many cases—might be ready to listen to an ex-planation along those lines provided that there was no mention of 'natural theology' (theology always suggesting dogma) or meta-physics (which always suggests meaningless abstractions). But the distinction itself, and apart from this suggested analysis of aesthetic experience, would be unpopular because it seems to rob art of its mystery. Aesthetic experience, as described by Mr Osborne for in-stance, has a quite unmysterious explanation. The grasp of sensory forms as a unity, the apprehension of an organised system of relationships, the contemplation of the whole in its parts, engages and *fills* the mind. It has only to attend to the ordered richness directly presented to it by the sense organs. And this naturally gives intense pleasure. Indeed it does, but there is also the mysterious over-plus of which I have spoken, and this leads people to attribute to certain sets of words (or sounds or pigments) what I can only describe as a magical quality. One thinks especially of Baudelaire, Rimbaud and their successors. In the long run in this matter everything depends on distinguishing the specifically aesthetic emotion, aroused by the work of art as such, from the other emotions which the materials, the elements, of a work of art arouse. And some people, no doubt, will deny that this can be done. I can only tell you how it strikes me.

Literature, obviously enough, and poetry in particular, can provide us with insights of the profoundest significance—poetry in particular, because this is the appropriate medium for expressing things which we feel strongly about. But I see no reason for suspecting anything magical here or for attributing to this function of poetry any power to provide us with esoteric knowledge—knowledge, I mean, which is not provided by the words of the poem properly understood. This may seem to be begging the question: *How* is the poetry to be understood? Have we not to see through the ordinary sense of the words to something beyond? Certainly the poet will often be hinting at what cannot be *described*. But he does provide us with these hints by using words which can be understood literally or symbolically in a non-poetic context. Apart from this all that he can do is to describe the effect upon himself of what is indescribable in the hope that we shall be able to see what he is driving at because it has similar effects upon ourselves. What I am arguing against is the view that there are things which are indescribable except by poets, in the sense that the poet has a language of his own, working according to its own supra-rational laws, which can give us information not otherwise obtainable. I am not denying that certain symbols may be the occasion for our descrying the indescribable, but I am denying that the poet has any rights over them, in this matter of providing insights, which the novelist or the revivalist preacher in principle has not.

It remains that the poet is more likely to interest us in these symbols—and these descriptions of human experience—than anyone else. And this is, I think, partly, as I shall suggest later, because he has already engaged our aesthetic experience which contains non-aesthetic experience as its materials. The poet has contrived to put a peculiar emphasis on this or that word or phrase. That helps to bring home to us the importance which he attaches to it. It even gives it a special meaning—by its use in this context its meaning is 'stretched.' Our language is enriched. But it remains the same language. In this sense the area of the describable has been enlarged, but we have not been transported into a new sphere. Again, the ambiguities in which English poetry is so rich and which have been the concern of so many contemporary critics do not show that there is a poetic language capable of describing what is otherwise indescribable; in such a case they could not be successfully analysed. Perhaps I am pushing at an open door. But it seems necessary to resist any suggestion that the poetry is 'a raid on the Absolute'. We can only 'point to' the Absolute, and to do this is not the perquisite of poets.

It will be useful, I think, to consider the interaction of aesthetic and non-aesthetic experience in some detail. The poet must normally light upon some topic or series of events which are rich in human interest if he is to have the materials for that peculiar enrichment which converts them into a work of art. Our response to it will be in fact a double one, although we do not normally advert to this. Take, for example, Professor L. C. Knights's comments on Macbeth's words when the witches' prophecies began to come true:

> *This supernatural soliciting*
> *Cannot be ill; cannot be good. . . .*

This,' he says, referring to the speech as a whole, 'is temptation presented with concrete force. Even if we attend only to the revelation of Macbeth's spiritual state, our recognition of the body—the very feel—of the experience, is a response to the poetry, to such things as the sickening see-saw rhythm ("Cannot be ill; cannot be good").....'[1] Here we have a state of soul shown to us by poetic means. Shakespeare has represented its movement by the movement of a blank verse line. We experience what Mr Osborne calls 'sympathetic reverberations'. But we could experience these if Shakespeare had written in prose and informed us that there was a sickening see-saw rhythm in the movements of Macbeth's soul. But we should not be so much interested. The situation would not be so much brought

[1] 'King Lear' and the great tragedies, *The Age of Shakespeare* (Pelican), p. 230.

home to us. But why? If Macbeth had said, falling into prose, 'It can't be wrong and yet it can't be right,' should we not grasp the situation as well? Not so well because the steady swing from side to side is less well exhibited. Still, by the addition of this reference to a steady swing, we should, indeed, grasp it well enough. But there is more immediacy about the words which Shakespeare has written; they are more economical and so they bring the situation before us with greater force. We return to the conclusion that the poet provides us with no special key to the mysteries of human life but that he can describe them more effectively than other people.

Our reaction to an effective description may be a vigorous one but it is not, as such, an aesthetic reaction. I doubt whether our response to these words of Macbeth's would be a vigorous one unless we were responding not only to his situation as described by the poetry but also to the poetry for its own sake, unless (that is to say) we were regarding the words in question as contributing to an organic whole of words and sounds, a whole which includes the description of Macbeth's situation as one of its elements and consists of the full context of the words—and joins it up with the organic whole which is the *play*. And this is what I take Professor Knights to be saying a little later[1] in connection with the function of imagery in the organisation of the play. The passage must be quoted *in extenso* because it shows also that when Professor Knights speaks of the play as a whole he is directly concerned not with its organisation as a work of art (in the sense which I have recommended) but, if I do not misunderstand him, with an attitude or set of attitudes to life which are presented to us by it:

> What we attend to is not only the imagery but all the organic components of the living verse; and the verse in turn works in conjunction with the dramatic action and our sense of what the different persons of the drama stand for as each play develops. The greater Shakespeare plays thus demand an unusual activity of attention, forcing the reader to respond with the whole of his active imagination. It is only when the mind of the reader is thoroughly 'roused and awakened'[2] that meanings from below the level of 'plot' and 'character' crystallise out and form themselves into a living structure. If that structure of meaning seems especially closely connected with recurring and interrelated imagery, that is not because possible associations and recurrences are puzzled out

[1] ibid., p. 231.
[2] The reference is given to Coleridge's *Biographia Literaria*, ch. 15.

by the intellect, but because the mind at a certain pitch of activity and responsiveness combines the power of focusing lucidly on what is before it with an awareness of before and after, sensing the whole in the part, and with a triumphant energy relating part to part in the living whole. But it is only in relation to that larger all-embracing meaning— determined by the 'plain sense' of what is said, and by its overtones, by the dramatic situation and the progress of the action, by symbols and by the interplay of different attitudes embodied in the different persons of the drama—it is only in relation to this total meaning that the imagery, or any other component that may be momentarily isolated, takes on its full significance. We only hear Shakespeare's deeper meanings when we listen with the whole of ourselves.

From the point of view which Professor Knights adopts, he has said in this passage, it seems to me, precisely what needed to be said. His concern is with the 'larger all-embracing meaning'. What he says about 'a triumphant energy relating part to part in a living whole' seems clearly to include what I have tried to indicate as the specifically aesthetic reaction, but the function of this reaction for Professor Knights (if I understand him) is, in the last analysis, to rouse us to a response to the 'all-embracing meaning'. Obviously it has this function. Unless we respond to 'all the organic components of the living verse' we shall not understand what these words in this order really *mean*. Nor shall we be roused to a responsiveness to the play as a whole (I think Professor Knights would agree) unless we are responding to the 'organic components of the living verse' precisely as such, reacting to them aesthetically and so attaining 'a certain pitch of activity'. My concern here is to suggest that there is another way of looking at the play as a whole, in which we look at it as a work of art, an organic whole which, as such, has no meaning but is an object of contemplation in its own right—a contemplation, however, which is extraordinarily *not* a dead end. And in the case of *Macbeth*, and still more in that of *King Lear*, this contemplation bears upon a vision of life which is the 'all-embracing meaning' of the materials which compose the organic whole. But it bears upon them as so composing it. Taking Professor Knights's point of view, I should say that *Macbeth* and (especially) *King Lear* are outstanding instances of the way in which a poet can comment on the human situation far more effectively than anyone else, providing us with insights which in practice nobody else provides so effectively (although, in principle, they can be provided by the mere metaphysician) because they are offered to us in a rich concreteness reinforced by all the power of suggestion of which blank verse lines are capable. From the complementary point of view, I should say that Shakespeare does here what only a poet can do: he makes a drama into a thing of beauty.

I hope I shall not be seeming to suggest that Professor Knights's point of view is not a valid and most important one. I am only asking whether it is the only possible one. Later in the same essay,[1] he speaks of 'a peculiar resonance' in the poetry of *King Lear* which should leave us in no doubt of Shakespeare's intention. This is surely the case. We are forced to conclude that it is Shakespeare's vivid apprehension of *value* in human living (more and more critics are coming to realise that *King Lear* celebrates the triumph of christian charity) which provides the driving force behind this immensely rich and powerful dramatic poem. Many people still fail to see this. They are not 'listening with the whole of themselves'—or perhaps they are lacking something. But the play may give them the opportunity to acquire it, and the importance of this for our subject needs no stressing. In this sense beauty is indeed power, but it is important, I think, to distinguish this power of persuasiveness from the power which beauty has in its own right. If we confuse them we may be led to make claims for poetry which are high-sounding but vague, and perhaps misleading.

It happens that *Macbeth* and *King Lear* are interpretations of life and works of art through and through, and we may take them up (as it were) by either end. Perhaps I ought to take an instance of what I mean by a work of art. I should like to consider a well-known poem which (so far as I can see) has nothing to say about human life which is specially cogent or revealing although it deals with a human situation which is serious enough in itself. It is called simply 'Song' in editions of Blake.

> *My silks and fine array,*
> *My smiles and languish'd air,*
> *By love are driv'n away;*
> *And mournful lean Despair*
> *Brings me yew to deck my grave;*
> *Such end true lovers have.*

[1] pp. 233–4.

His face is fair as heav'n
  When springing buds unfold;
O why to him was't giv'n,
  Whose heart is wintry cold?
His breast is love's all-worship'd tomb,
  Where all love's pilgrims come.

Bring me an axe and spade,
  Bring me a winding sheet;
When I my grave have made
  Let winds and tempests beat:
Then down I'll lie, as cold as clay.
  True love doth pass away!

It is not necessary to subject that poem to a very detailed analysis if one wants to understand the general principles at work in it. It begins with a simple statement in rising rhythm and becomes exciting when and because there is a perfectly appropriate and therefore highly impressive change to falling rhythm and a longer line in 'Brings me yew to deck my grave'. The excitement is maintained by, for example, the half-stress on the second syllable of 'spring*ing*' which is again peculiarly appropriate (but it does not *reproduce* a situation like 'Cannot be ill; cannot be good . . .' which is perhaps not a group of words capable of arousing *of itself* even in its full context the *aesthetic* reaction). And then there is '*win*try cold' where the 'physicality' of 'wintry' is accentuated by its use as an adverb, and the stress follows heavily after an almost mute 'is'. When we get to the penultimate line of the stanza we expect the falling rhythm again, but no—the rising one is kept up all through. Interest is kept up, however—there is the curious picture of the shrine where love lies dead and the effective half-rhyme at the end which seems to prepare for the shock: 'Bring me an axe and spade'. The falling rhythm comes back again with redoubled force after the interval. And it continues: 'Bring me a winding sheet . . .'. But perhaps I have already said more than enough. Once the beauty of such lines has come home to one, they haunt the memory, because there is so much in them: the subtle relationships in which the words stand to one another form organisms within the organism of the poem, unities within a unity, which, without explicitly working them out, we can appreciate more and more.

This is what the poet alone can give us. And when he combines this sort of thing with the use of evocative symbols and with a description of his own profoundest insights the result is a very potent mixture indeed. There is plenty of excuse for extravagant theories of beauty.

I am getting near the end, and I have said nothing yet about these symbols. Fortunately, I can be brief about them. That does not mean that I regard the subject as a simple one. On the contrary, it is exceedingly mysterious. But there is nothing much, I think, that we can do about it. Symbols which succeed in producing concentrations or constellations of meaning in works of art I must leave on one side; they are of a great interest from the aesthetic point of view, but for our purposes the symbols which matter are those which are part and parcel of natural theology. It is a commonplace to say that we can speak of God or of our knowledge of him only in metaphors. But there is a trap here. As Mr Owen Barfield has shown,[1] it is a mistake to suppose that, for example, the word 'spirit' was applied first to breath and then to the mind of men, the original meaning being a purely material one. If a word has a *purely* material meaning, how can it come to mean something spiritual? The suggestion is, I think, that there are some words which live on two levels at once, because we, their inventors, do so. But if a man can see only the material meaning, you cannot get him to see the spiritual one merely by shouting the word at him. There are some words which ought to wake an answering echo in a man's mind, but in fact they may not do so. We have to go on trying by ringing the changes on these words which we thus rather misleadingly call 'metaphorical'. And there is another trap about 'analogy'. People sometimes seem to think that since the created world proves to stand, once we have knowledge of God, in a certain special relation to him, to be an outward showing or rather a 'reflection' of him, we can build up a knowledge of him on the basis merely of created values. This is obviously a mistake. We should indeed point to those features of the created world which reveal God's activity most readily (principally, I believe, our own minds) but this activity must itself be detected in these features.

I can touch on only one of these symbols, that of light. The word 'light' lives on two levels. On the upper one it refers to what happens

<hr>

[1] *Metaphor and Symbol*, a symposium, edited by L. C. Knights and Basil Cottle, London, 1960, p. 55.

to our minds when they achieve the success which is proper to them. And so it naturally refers also to God's glory, and is a peculiarly evocative word. It is so notably in St John of whom it has been said that he has no style at all. He is not interested in the 'physicality' of words; they are, for him, just windows through which (if we have eyes) we see. 'God is light, and no darkness can find any place in him.' It is as simple as that. When a poet takes up the theme the effect, of course, is arresting, for example, 'They are all gone into a world of light,' where Vaughan achieves by the run of monosyllables not only the sense of urgency, beloved of critics, but a great bang on the last word. Or, as in the wonderfully casual opening of 'The World', that most impressive poem:

> I saw Eternity the other night,
> Like a great Ring of pure and endless light . . .

So when Wordsworth talks about 'something far more deeply interfused, whose dwelling is the light of setting suns,' it is not difficult to understand why he produces a strong reaction. It is not, in my case, a strong aesthetic reaction.

I hope that the burden of my paper will not seem anti-Romantic. Although the Romantic movement led eventually to confusion between the natural and the supernatural and to faulty analyses in aesthetics and in literary criticism, the preoccupation of the original Romantics was, it appears, to heal the breach between religion and culture from which we have suffered so long, summed up in Burckhardt's famous remark that when religion loses touch with the arts it becomes 'rationalism for the few, and magic for the many'. Plainly, the fundamental reason why theology and the study of literature should go hand in hand is that the supernatural cannot do without the natural any more than the natural can do without the supernatural. And the fundamental activity—a contemplative one—is of the same kind in each case. The grasp of a poem as a whole, whether aesthetically as an organic whole or as an 'all-embracing meaning', is very different from the grasp of a continuous argument. It requires a particular kind of *attention*. So does that apprehension in which, as I think, natural theology arises. This is the affair of the intuitive not of the discursive reason. More properly, I would say, it should be called the affair of the intellect. (When the Romantics, having lost touch with this distinction between reason and intellect, spoke of the imagination, this was sometimes what they meant.) It should be clear from what I have said that theological apprehension, in my view, differs from the apprehension of the poem not only because it is more profound, a vertical not a horizontal movement, but because it is simpler. But it is often hard to be simple. For those who are capable of the study of literature, it should be a most efficacious propaedeutic for the apprehension of God, and (what is more to the purpose here) it should lead to an intensification of that apprehension. As we have seen, it often offers us those very media in which the apprehension takes place, the human values in which absolute value can be descried, the symbols in which the transcendent is immanent, and always, as I have especially emphasised, when we are studying poetry which deserves that name, those objects of aesthetic contemplation which can reveal to us in a peculiarly fruitful way something of the meaning of our own selves.

(II) THEOLOGY AND POETRY

L. C. KNIGHTS

I

In the previous paper Dom Illtyd Trethowan spoke of natural theology and its relation to poetry. Speaking as a theologian he claimed that the kind of contemplative activity called forth by poetry—indeed by art in general—is one of the natural ways in which a man may have knowledge of absolute value, and so of God. The theologian, therefore, far from regarding literature as extraneous or peripheral to his proper concern has a duty to cultivate an intimate and inward sense of artistic values; and he does this with a sense of genuine fellowship with all, whether believers or agnostics, who respond to art seriously and disinterestedly. My task, I take it, is to look at the same common ground, but to do so from the other end. Speaking as someone deeply concerned for literature I have to give my sense of its nature as a central human activity, and to suggest those implications of the study of literature that look towards philosophy and religion. For one who is neither a theologian nor a philosopher it could be a daunting task; but I am fortified by the thought that in a symposium of this kind—of which the essence is conversation from different points of view—honesty and a limited competence may partly compensate for a deal of ignorance. I propose to proceed by way of agreement and disagreement with the paper of Dom Illtyd.[1]

First, then, for the agreement. Dom Illtyd spoke of the aesthetic experience—the fully engaged response to, say, a poem, in all its particularity—as 'a *cognitive* experience', and he claimed that this 'is of the greatest value because it makes us aware of *ourselves* as we never are in other circumstances'. And at the end of his paper he spoke of 'those objects of aesthetic contemplation which can reveal to us in a peculiarly fruitful way something of the meaning of our own selves'. These are statements with which I find myself entirely in agreement. Ignoring for the moment the problem of the nature of the knowledge that is in question, I quote them here as a way of indicating the immensely important shared assumptions—shared, I mean by Dom Illtyd and me, and presumably many other people—against which some differences may be defined and perhaps reconciled. Art matters, not (certainly) because it indulges our feelings, not simply because it gives pleasure, but because it offers a form of knowledge.

It is however one thing to agree in a general way that art offers us a means of knowing, above all a means of knowing ourselves, and quite another thing to say what we mean—even though we may feel quite sure that meaning is there. In the contemplation of art, what do we know? How does art prompt us to knowing? How does *this* knowledge differ from other kinds? Is it *sui generis* or does it relate in significant ways to other activities and modes of apprehension—especially to those that have a special relevance for religion and theology? What is its place in our lives as human beings? I know that I have rather alarmingly taken flight into the upper atmosphere and that these questions, if asked at all, can only be answered by genius or by a collective wisdom; and the answers even of genius, even of a rich tradition of thought, are still only provisional and subject to modification. But I do not see that we can deal with art at all without having at the back of our minds some working notions about these matters. In order to bring them to the front of our minds, and to relate them to the main concern of this symposium, it is necessary to be more specific.

[1] A draft of which he kindly showed me at a time when the very scope of the subject seemed likely to inhibit all effective thinking.

—Hands, do what you're bid:
Bring down the balloon of the mind
That bellies and drags in the wind
Into its narrow shed—

From now on I shall speak of poetry rather than of 'art'; and I shall direct my attention to the kind of knowledge that poetry may be said to offer.

It is necessary to cast back to what we have already heard. A poem is an organic whole. The attempt to grasp its elements—not just the paraphrasable meaning, but the more elusive intimations carried by rhythm, imagery and so on—demands a 'peculiarly intense activity of mind'; and if this activity of contemplation feels both new and familiar, at once a revelation and a home-coming, this is because in this activity it is 'ourselves' that we become aware of: 'the value of poetry seems to lie not in itself but in what it enables us to be'. I have already indicated my agreement with this view of what poetry does and why it is valuable, and I think I understand the further claim that it is when we are thus awakened, actively reaching beyond our habitual routine selves, that we see more clearly what is meant by the action of God on our minds.

It is after this that my own doubts and difficulties begin, and in order to clarify them it is necessary to pick out what seem to me the salient points in the next phase of Dom Illtyd's argument.

> So far, then ... the value of poetry seems to lie not in itself but in what it enables us to be. Beauty is food for the mind—it is necessary if the mind is to achieve full health in the natural order. There is no need to emphasise the importance of such a conclusion for the theologian. But of course this is only one side of our subject. Poetry is not just an exhibition of formal beauty. And that leads me to the other feature of Mr Osborne's work[1] which has seemed to me of special value—his forthright distinction between form in art (the element, that is, which is the cause of aesthetic experience) and content (that is, the 'ideas' which it conveys, the truths which it recommends, the 'criticism of life' which it embodies). This means that the critic must bring, as a rule, a double standard to bear on literature. He must not mix up his judgment of the work of art as such, the organic whole, with his judgment on the artist's points of view.[2]

[1] Dom Illtyd, it will be remembered, had previously referred to Mr. Osborne's contention that the separate and distinguishable qualities of a work of art 'become elements in the beauty of aesthetic objects only by a relation of congruence in which they stand to the organic whole which is the object in its totality'. I regret that I have not read the books by Mr. Osborne to which Dom Illtyd refers.
[2] p. 197, *supra*.

My doubt is whether it is possible to make the distinction recommended here in any but a preparatory and provisional way; whether, indeed, if the distinction is developed beyond the stage of preparatory pointing (preparatory, that is, to the fullest possible apprehension of the work in question), it does not break down. Of course the value of a poem does not lie in the poet's 'points of view'—that is, in any points of view that can be asserted outside the poem: if 'content' is identified with paraphrasable meaning then we can all agree that the content of a poem is not what we go to it for. But does it follow that, as Dom Illtyd goes on to say, 'a work of art, as such, has *no* meaning'?[1] True, he admits that the poet 'can provide us with insights of the profoundest significance'; but, he says, the poet has no monopoly here, and if he in some special way interests us in the symbols through which the insights are mediated, this is because 'he has already engaged our aesthetic experience which contains non-aesthetic experience as its materials'. And here we reach the crux of the matter; for if Dom Illtyd's account is right then it is possible—indeed necessary —in our dealings with a poem to distinguish between the aesthetic experience as such and the non-aesthetic experience it contains and with which it interacts: our response to the poem 'will in fact be a double one'. If I may quote from an earlier paper from the same author, 'the appreciation of poetry (or prose) as a work of art is different from the appreciation of the truth thus communicated'.[2] It is this that seems to me wrong and misleading.

For me—coming as it does from a critic with whom I find myself so often in resonance—it is also perplexing; and I think I can best resolve my perplexities, and perhaps advance the argument, by taking up what Dom Illtyd says about some remarks of my own—by letting the anvil, as it were, have its turn as hammer. What is in question is the possibility of distinguishing between 'the aesthetic experience'— the experience of poetry as poetry—and any content, vision or message that it may be said to contain. For Dom Illtyd (though he says it politely) in my writing on Shakespeare I am too much con-

[1] Naturally, after the sentence just quoted, Dom Illtyd first instances music, where paraphrase—except in the form of programme notes—is clearly impossible. But even music, it seems to me, has 'meaning' in the sense that what Suzanne Langer would call its symbolic presentation of emotional life has *some* bearing on our life outside the concert hall and may offer insight into it.

[2] 'Aesthetics and Metaphysics', *The Arts, Artists and Thinkers*, edited by John M. Todd (Downside Symposium, 2), p. 321.

cerned for the latter at the expense of the former: 'when Professor Knights speaks of the play as a whole he is directly concerned not with its organisation as a work of art . . . but . . . with an attitude or set of attitudes to life which are presented to us by it'.[1] For me the distinction is unreal; but if I may now try to say why it is so certain of my contentions will, I think, nevertheless be found to be very close to Dom Illtyd's central positions regarding the function of poetry and of art in general. Since I am concerned not to plead a case but to disentangle meanings, some indirection of approach may perhaps be allowed.

II

In the Philosophical Lectures, Coleridge speaks of the inexhaustible power of great works of art.

> The same unwearied form presents itself, yet still we look on, sinking deeper and deeper, and therein offering homage to the infinity of our souls which no mere form can satisfy.[2]

He is here speaking of the great paintings of the Italian Renaissance, but as is clear from an earlier passage,[3] the idea is one that he is prepared to apply to all the arts, and it is important for our present purpose. Coleridge does not only capture in a memorable phrase the capacity of art to 'make us aware of ourselves', he directly relates this power to 'the unwearied form' of the work in question. What, then, is this form that both prompts and withdraws?[4] What—to be more specific—are those formal elements of poetry, brought together in 'a relation of congruence' by the poet's unifying imagination, and, as Dom Illtyd would have it, prompting in us an activity of aesthetic contemplation—'the power which beauty has in its own right'—that has no meaning beyond itself?

It is my contention that ultimately there is no such thing as a purely aesthetic experience or a purely formal structure. The formal elements—'these words . . . in this order and in this particular pattern

---

[1] See pp. 201 ff., above.

[2] S. T. Coleridge, *Philosophical Lectures*, 1818–1819, ed. Kathleen Coburn, p. 194. The passage should be read in its context.

[3] op. cit., pp. 167–9.

[4] 'This value have the images of form as far as they make us forget ourselves, and become mere words unnoticed in that which they convey.'—op. cit., pp. 168–9.

of rhythm, rhyme and so forth'—are, from the start, elements of meaning or significance, so disposed in relation to each other as to reveal what could not otherwise *be* revealed. The form is soaked in, one with, the insight which is known only in the activity of mind generated by the precise particulars of phrasing, rhythm, tone, and so on. In other words, the form *is* the content; we concentrate on form because it allows us to perceive matters of human import that could not otherwise be so securely or so fully or so subtly grasped.[1]

Perhaps I can clarify my meaning with the help of two examples— one small and fairly easily manageable, the other a leviathan that cannot be hooked but that may be briefly observed. The first is Blake's Song, 'My silks and fine array', instanced by Dom Illtyd as a poem which 'has nothing to say about human life which is specially cogent or revealing although it deals with a human situation which is serious enough in itself'.[2] I am grateful to Dom Illtyd for making me read this poem—really read it—and for the subtle delicacy of his analysis of its musical effects. But—'nothing to say about human life'? Surely, like other of Blake's poems, it is a self-placing dramatic monologue in lyric form. As a first approximation I should say that it offers, without overt comment, a contrast between true and spontaneous feeling and feeling that is not quite true but *tending towards* self-dramatisation. What love has driven away is the girl's consciousness of her charms ('My smiles and languish'd air'), but as despair takes over the feeling begins to slip into a different but complementary kind of self-consciousness, marked by the falling rhythm ('Bring me yew to deck my grave'), on which Dom Illtyd rightly comments. The second stanza is straightforwardly poignant; but with the return of the falling rhythm in the third stanza ('Bring me an axe and spade') the poignancy is again qualified by a literary heightening: it is not only Blake, we feel, but the imagined speaker, who has read *Hamlet*. This of course is a simplification: the strength of this remarkable little poem lies in the representation of an inextricable blend of true feeling and a half-conscious *dressing* of that feeling, even though the whole is suffused with the bleak and touching quality of the end— 'True love doth pass away': but this is not to say that evaluation of

[1] I am not of course denying that it is often necessary to use the language of formal or technical criticism, though the extent to which it is necessary varies between the different arts, music and literature being in this respect the two extremes.

[2] The poem is quoted on pp. 203–4, above.

the feelings expressed has no part in it.[1] Of course the poem is more
than moral or psychological analysis, if only because of the tenderness
and delicacy of its music, but it shares the same ground of observation
and insight; there is no absolute discontinuity between the poem's
beauty and the world in which we live and sympathise and observe.
Indeed to speak of the beauty of the poem, it seems to me, is only to
refer to it as a device of concentration: meanings come together in
this lens of the poet's making and then, as we read and assimilate, ray
out over a world that is both familiar and, if ever so slightly, trans-
formed.

My second example—the leviathan—is *King Lear*; and here indeed
we need to acknowledge the foolishness of any attempt to harness
this thing of power to our own limited predilections: that is, to make
it the vehicle for a 'message'. The danger is, in Dom Illtyd's terms,
of concerning ourselves with a set of attitudes to life extracted from
the play rather than with its 'organisation as a work of art'. When,
a few years ago, I tried to give my sense of the value of some of
Shakespeare's plays, and especially of *King Lear*, one critic, Miss
Barbara Everett, accused me of precisely this—of confusing poetry
and morality, of killing the poetry in the pursuit of an abstraction;[2]
so it seems I must state the obvious and say that I do indeed regard
King Lear as a great work of art, a highly wrought formal structure
that engages our attention no less for the minutest parts than for the
whole; no less for the precise way in which things are said and
presented than for what we may call the substance. But what we call
formal structure is not an end in itself; it is a means of simplifying,
concentrating, enriching. When we attend to the play's 'organisation
as a work of art'—whether to such devices as the parallel plots and
the juxtaposition of scenes or to the power and complexity of the

[1] Too subtle for a poet not yet—as the Preface to the *Poetical Sketches* tells
us—beyond his twentieth year? Not, I think, for a poet of Blake's genius. Besides
the fact that the *Sketches* contain many direct anticipations of Blake's later work,
there is the psychological insight of 'Mad Song' and the literary insight of 'To the
Muses'. Of 'Love and harmony combine' and 'Mad Song', H. M. Margoliouth
says, 'there is no real difficulty, but there is need for the most wide-awake attention. This is no facile warbler.'—*William Blake* (Home University Library), p. 50.
For what I mean by a self-placing dramatic monologue in lyric form see 'The
Angel' ('I Dreamt a Dream! what can it mean?') in *Songs of Experience*, and
J. H. Wicksteed's commentary in his edition of *Innocence and Experience*, pp.
158–9.
[2] In a review of *Some Shakespearean Themes* in the *Critical Quarterly*, Vol. II,
No. 1, Summer 1960.

spoken poetry—we find, inevitably, that we are dealing with *meanings* related one to another in a continually widening context. These meanings of course are not definable units in a common currency (as when we speak of 'the dictionary meaning of a word'), they are thoughts, perceptions, feelings, evaluations, that only exist for us in so far as, our minds and imaginations fully alert, we actively apprehend them, bring them home to such knowledge of ourselves and the world as we may already possess. If we do not so bring them home we may have some very powerful feelings—whether about the harshness of the world or the grandeur and misery of man—but we are not exactly reading Shakespeare.

One example must serve in place of many. Early in the storm Lear says that now is the time for the gods to find out their enemies.

> *Let the great Gods,*
> *That keep this dreadful pudder o'er our heads,*
> *Find out their enemies now. Tremble, thou wretch,*
> *That hast within thee undivulged crimes,*
> *Unwhipp'd of Justice; hide thee, thou bloody hand,*
> *Thou perjur'd, and thou simular of virtue*
> *That art incestuous; caitiff, to pieces shake,*
> *That under covert and convenient seeming*
> *Hast practis'd on man's life: close pent-up guilts.*
> *Rive your concealing continents, and cry*
> *These dreadful summoners grace . . .*

Our response to these lines is certainly an 'aesthetic' one. The poetry simultaneously 'frames' the feelings expressed, holds them at a distance from 'real life', whilst making us aware of them, in some sense share in them, with unusual force and immediacy: our imagination traces the pattern of an emotional upheaval that gathers momentum with each heavily stressed imperative—'Tremble', 'hide thee', 'shake', 'Rive your concealing continents'. On a first reading that may be enough. At some time in our subsequent readings, however, we are bound to make the connection between 'Unwhipp'd of Justice' and the later references to the whipping of vagrants (III. iv. 137–8) and to the whipping of prostitutes by the parish constable (IV. vi. 162–5) —legal procedures which the play surely forces us to question. And if we question the procedures, what of justice itself? What of distributive justice, the apportioning of reward to merit (for that is what

Lear thinks it is) in the love-test at the beginning of the play? What of retributive justice, parodied in the mad mock-trial of Goneril and Regan? We need not hesitate to say that these are shown as worse than inadequate, for the play is explicit: 'see how yond justice rails upon yond simple thief. Hark, in thine ear: change places, and, handy-dandy, which is the justice, which is the thief?' But this does not mean that we have come away with a bare moral formula, for the play has likewise insisted on our linking all these references to—and enactments of—an inadequate 'justice' with the varied perversions and self-thwartings of the inner life.[1] At the end of the play we have been too actively engaged in understanding a vastly complex presented experience—an experience that is simultaneously 'out there' and yet an intimate part of ourselves—to find any formula an adequate substitute.

And yet we have to use the formula, the short-hand, if only because it is a necessity of our nature to exchange with others our sense of why we value the experience of 'great tragedy' or 'great art'. It is a formula to say that in *King Lear* all the forms of self-protective legalistic justice are shown in their utter inadequacy when contrasted with the reconciling and transforming justice of Cordelia's free forgiveness of her father; but I can't see how I could—or why I should—avoid it. So too, in writing about the play, I summed up my sense of its total significance by saying: 'at the centre of the action is the complete endorsement of a particular quality of being. We may call it love so long as we remember that it is not simply an emotion, and that, although deeply personal, it has also the impersonality that comes from a self-forgetful concentration—momentary or enduring —upon the true being of "the other".'[2] Miss Everett found this a formula—a pious sentiment completely out of scale with the greatness of the tragedy. What she failed to notice (and I am not going to pretend that I had not made it clear) was that my summary only made sense as springing from an extended analysis in which what was most insisted on was the mind's activity in increasing the range of its imaginative understanding. And I do not see what that understanding can be 'of', if not those permanent aspects of life—calamity, conflict,

[1] For a somewhat fuller account of the play's varied dealings with the theme of 'justice', I may refer to my essay, '*King Lear* as Metaphor', in *Myth and Symbol: Critical Approaches and Applications*, ed. Bernice Slote (Bison Books: University of Nebraska Press).
[2] *Some Shakespearean Themes*, p. 118.

H

loss—and those permanent possibilities of human nature—self-love, self-deception, charity—that the play concentrates in a single, almost infinitely complex, image. But what finally matters is not the image— not even *King Lear*—but the life that it enables us to see and the powers of vision that it calls forth.

III

I have tried to define and to justify certain beliefs about the way poetry works. I conclude by drawing out some consequences and implications.

1. In spite of some (not negligible) disagreements with Dom Illtyd, I have, I think, supported his claim that the experience of poetry is a cognitive experience. The knowledge in question, as he also insists, is not 'knowledge about' but lies in the particular activity generated by the poet's art. So we may surely agree with Suzanne Langer when, speaking of the view of tragedy as a breach in, and restoration of, the moral order, she says, 'All this concern with the philosophical and ethical significance of the hero's sufferings . . . leads away from the artistic significance of the play, to discursive ideas about life, char- acter, and the world.'[1] But there is no need to accept an absolute dichotomy. When Mrs Langer goes on to say, 'Macbeth's fate is the structure of his tragedy, not an instance of how things happen in the world,'[2] we say that surely it is both. It is precisely the controlled, complex and unified activity that, for each of us, *is* the play that keeps us from *substituting* for 'the artistic significance', 'discursive ideas about life, character, and the world'. This activity can of course only be fully known in its own terms, but it does not cease when we leave the theatre or close the book.[3]

2. Because the knowledge gained through art is not 'knowledge about', but lies rather in the growth of intellectual power, what we

---

[1] *Feeling and Form*, (Scribner's, 1953) p. 358.

[2] op. cit., p. 360.

[3] The—to me—unnecessary dichotomy appears also in the following passage by Mrs Langer: 'Poetic criticism, more than any other, is torn between the judgment of artistic aims, means and achievement, and the judgment of what *the poet* is "telling" the reader; between the evaluation of something created and something asserted. Matthew Arnold's "criticism of life" is such a discursive message. Perhaps he himself was misled by an unhappy phrase. Poetry does, indeed, *make life appear in certain ways*, but it is not commenting on it.'— *Problems of Art*, (Scribner's, 1957) p. 122.

know is no mere object to our subject. As may be already apparent, I think that art has many functions: it may increase and heighten our understanding of other people and our sense of the world; it may sharpen our powers of direct introspection (as in reading, say, Jane Austen's novels); by means of images and symbols it may offer means of handling and making more manageable our unconscious conflicts; and so on. But always in the contemplation of a work of art the awareness thus aroused is essentially *of* those very powers of knowing and responding through which alone the awareness comes into being: it is knowledge of ourselves in the full depth and range of our subjectivity, of potentialities only known as they are activated and harmonised in a living response to living form.

3. On both these points there is a considerable measure of agreement between the views expressed here and those expressed by Dom Illtyd in the last paper. The difference centres on my rejection of anything that could be described as the aesthetic realm, of 'the power which beauty has in its own right'. For me the imagination is not a special faculty, but simply life coming to consciousness.[1] And the advantage of this way of looking at things is twofold. First, it suggests a significant analogy between the disciplined experience of art and other creative disciplines of the mind and spirit (such as, I suppose, the practice of meditation), where—to borrow a phrase from Whitehead—'rightness of limitation is essential for growth of reality', and where—Coleridge again—'the sensation of *self* is always in inverse proportion' to the 'clearness and vivacity' of the thoughts and images.[2] Secondly, it not only brings into view a relation between poetry and the widest possible range of human activities, it intimates a quality of living that is very far indeed from being the exclusive concern of poets and of people who happen to like poetry. Edwin Muir says that

[1] This, I think, was what Coleridge meant when, having spoken of the power of music and of the connection between creative power and joy, he went on: 'We feel therefore that our being is nobler than our senses and the man of genius devotes himself, to produce by all other means, whether a statesman, a poet, a painter, a statuary, or a man of science, this same sort of a something which the mind can know but which it cannot understand, of which understanding can be no more than the symbol and is only excellent as being the symbol. *It is this same spirit, still craving for something higher than what could be imagined in form,* (this value have the images of form as far as they make us forget ourselves, and become mere words unnoticed in that which they convey), *which works in all men more or less. . . .'—Philosophical Lectures,* ed. Kathleen Coburn, pp. 168–9 (italics mine).
[2] A. N. Whitehead, *Religion in the Making* (Meridian Books, New York), p. 146. Coleridge, *Biographia Literaria,* ed. Shawcross, Chapter 2, Vol. I, p. 30.

the poet is one who cannot use the language of the public, 'which is the language of the third party and the onlooker', because 'he is not concerned with life in its generality, but in its immediacy and its individuality'.[1] If poetry is conceived in this sense, as an apprehension of things in their depth and presentness—an act of knowing which is simultaneously a self-forgetful self-knowing—then the experience that it offers, far from being *sui generis*, appears as a quality—or potentiality—of life as a whole. Perhaps another name for immediacy is the religious dimension of ordinary living. But what the implications are for the relation of poetry (thus conceived) to natural theology I must leave to others to determine.

NOTE

LITERATURE AND THE THEOLOGIAN

The foregoing dialogue between Dom Illtyd Trethowan *and* Professor L. C. Knights *touched off a question of particular importance, namely, what is the value to the theologian of a more exact understanding of the nature of literary judgments, and what is the relationship of such judgments to his own?*

David Jenkins *has contributed the following note by way of a summary of the ensuing discussion:*

It is not the job of the theologian to 'pass judgment' on any piece of writing which has claims to be considered a work of art.

Rather the theologian has the responsibility, and the need, to seek to stand in the same relationship to a work of art as any other man who is seeking sensitivity and integrity. The nature of that relationship may perhaps be indicated thus. An authentic work of art does not so much stand to be judged by us as stands in judgment over us. This holds in so far as it is 'authentic', that is, arises from, and points us to, genuine and valid insights into, and responses to, some aspect of the reality of the world and of human life in the world. Thus questions, say, of moral and doctrinal 'orthodoxy' do not, or at least should not, arise during the moment of our contact with a work of art. We are simply to be open to whatever illumination the work has to give us concerning the reality of things.

This sort of illumination stands in judgment upon us. It poses the

[1] See Edwin Muir, *The Estate of Poetry*, pp. 101–2.

question to our attitude to life, to our christian faith: 'How does this attitude, this faith *now* look in the light of this heightened apprehension of what it is like to be alive?' It is only when *this* question has been fully and unreservedly faced that the theologian (or indeed any christian) can go on (or go back) to his task of 'theological' understanding.

For example, the theologian (simply as a man) may be struck by a note of despair and monotony deeply felt and deeply moving in the work of Samuel Becket. He must *not* cut that despair and monotony 'down to size' by a facile application of categories from his customary talk about sin, redemption and forgiveness. Rather he must face up, as a man who is one with those for whom Becket speaks, in the human situation, to the reality and authenticity, to the dimension, of this despair. And *then* he must seek to shape his understanding and systematisation of, say, the Doctrine of Redemption and of the new life in Christ in such a way as to speak relevantly to, and take undiminished account of, the reality and validity of the despair experienced and expressed. Only thus will he be at all true to the theological insight that in Christ there is a new creation (II Cor. 5).

The dreadful thing about so much theology is that, in relation to the reality of the human situation, it is so superficial. Theological categories (really mere theological formulae) are 'aimed' without sufficient depth of understanding at life insensitively misunderstood. Theologians need therefore to stand *under* the judgments of the insights of literature before they can speak with true theological force of, and to, the world this literature reflects and illuminates.

The wisest of the Ancients consider'd what is not too Explicit as the fittest for Instruction, because it rouzes the faculties to act. I name Moses, Solomon, Esop, Homer, Plato.—*William Blake.*

9. Theology and Philosophy

(I) THE USE OF LOGICAL ANALYSIS IN THEOLOGY

ANTHONY KENNY

British philosophy today seems ill-fitted to play handmaid to theology. In an age in which most professional philosophers are atheists and few theologians are conversant with professional philosophy there appears little hope of co-operation between the two disciplines even on terms of equality. Yet the gulf of incomprehension between them is not as great as it was thirty years ago. In the thirties the philosophers of the tradition now dominant in England were, for the most part, both ignorant and contemptuous of systematic theology. One of the most brilliant of them, Frank Ramsey, summed up their attitude in a notorious remark. 'Theology and Absolute Ethics,' he wrote, 'are two famous subjects which we have realised to have no real objects.'

In 1936, Professor A. J. Ayer dismissed theology in six pages of his book *Language, Truth and Logic*. According to Ayer there was no way of proving that the existence of a God, such as the God of Christianity, was even probable. When a christian speaks of God, he intends to talk about a transcendent being which cannot be defined in terms of any empirical manifestations. Therefore, said Ayer, the word 'God' was a metaphysical and meaningless term. 'No sentence,' he concluded, 'which purports to describe the nature of a transcendent God can possess any literal significance.' (*Language, Truth and Logic*, p. 115.)

The philosophy presented in *Language, Truth and Logic* was called by its author 'logical empiricism'. 'The views which are put forward in this treatise,' he wrote, 'derive from the doctrines of Bertrand Russell and Wittgenstein, which are themselves the logical outcome of the empiricism of Berkeley and David Hume.' Ayer accepted the central doctrine of empiricism, which is that all our knowledge derives from sense-impressions. But he restated this doctrine as a theory of meaning. A word is meaningful, according to *Language, Truth and Logic*, only if it is possible to give rules for translating any sentence in which it may occur into a sentence which refers to sense-contents. Into this restatement of empiricism Ayer incorporated many elements which he had taken from the writings of Russell. Ayer was wrong in regarding Wittgenstein's *Tractatus Logico-Philosophicus* as an empiricist treatise; but he did find there one doctrine very congenial to empiricism. This was the thesis that all the necessary truths of logic and mathematics were tautologies. Earlier empiricists had argued implausibly that mathematical propositions were open to refutation by experience. Ayer felt himself able to preserve the necessary nature of mathematical truth without infidelity to his empiricist principles, because he asserted that the necessity of such truths was guaranteed solely by our conventions concerning the symbols used to express them. It was for these reasons that Ayer described his version of empiricism as 'logical empiricism'.

In recent years there have been several attempts to present an account of religious belief which would be compatible with some form of logical empiricism. Such attempts may be found in some of the contributions to the symposia *New Essays in Philosophical Theology* (1955) and *Faith and Logic* (1957). Two of the best-known attempts of this kind are Professor I. T. Ramsey's *Religious Language* and Professor Braithwaite's *An Empiricist's View of the Nature of Religious Belief*. One of the most recent is John Wilson's book *Philosophy and Religion*. In that book it is suggested that religious assertions about the supernatural are factual assertions which are verified by religious experience in the way in which statements about physical objects are verified by sense-experience. A statement such as 'there is a God', Wilson suggests, means that certain experiences of vital interest and importance are permanently available at least to certain people under certain conditions. In this way, the word 'God' would be made to conform more or less to the conditions of meaningfulness laid down in *Language, Truth and Logic*. Rules would be given for translating any sentence in which it occurred into a sentence which referred only to sense impressions, though these would be impressions of an inner and mysterious sense, rather than of sight or hearing or touch.

Attempts to reconcile theism with empiricism seem to me misguided. If I suggest that philosophy and theology are less far apart than they were it is not because I hope for success in any such attempt. Professor Ayer seems to me quite correct in believing that the philosophy which he inherited from Hume is incompatible with any theology worthy of the name.

However, since *Language, Truth and Logic* was first published, the philosophy of logical empiricism has been shown to be untenable by thinkers holding no brief for theology. That philosophy, we have seen, contained two major theses. The first was a logical one, that all the truths of logic and mathematics are tautologies. This thesis was refuted by the work of formal logicians in the 1930's, who showed the discontinuity between those parts of logic (such as the propositional calculus) in which the validity of formulae can be checked by mechanical tests and those other parts (including many parts necessary for the formalisation of mathematics) for which no such decision procedure is possible. The second thesis was the epistemological thesis that all our knowledge begins with sense-impressions, restated as the theory that only those sentences are meaningful which admit of restatement into sentences referring only to sense-contents. This thesis was refuted by the later work of Wittgenstein, who showed in his posthumously published *Philosophical Investigations* that the notion of a sense-content, conceived by empiricists as an essentially private and incommunicable entity, was itself a radically incoherent one. To say this, of course, is to take sides in a dispute that is not yet over. But many philosophers in this country and the United States would agree with Alasdair MacIntyre's judgment: 'Wittgenstein's philosophy renders empiricism no longer viable.' (*The New Statesman*, 2 April 1960, 491.)

The decline of empiricism must not be seen as a victory for its traditional opponents, idealism and rationalism. Wittgenstein's arguments, if they are valid against Hume's impressions, are equally valid against Descarte's *Pensées*. The *Philosophical Investigations* contains little comfort for those theists who seek to establish the existence of God by appeal to an intuition of Being, or who find proof of the immortality of the soul in the contemplation of their own Cartesian ego. Those who accept the conclusions which Wittgenstein reached towards the end of his life are committed to the belief that modern epistemology since Descartes has rested on a very fundamental misconception. Professor Ryle's book *The Concept of Mind* is a well-known attack on Cartesianism which has enjoyed great influence in this country since the war. One philosopher summed up his deep dissatisfaction with post-Renaissance epistemology in the slogan: 'Back to Aristotle'!

Certainly it is possible to find in several recent philosophical publications evidence of a quickening interest in Aristotelian ideas. Three examples which have appeared in the last few years are Miss Anscombe's *Intention*, Professor Hampshire's *Thought and Action*, and Professor von Wright's *The Varieties of Goodness*. This is no doubt partly due to the fact that Oxford has since the war replaced Cambridge as the centre of philosophical activity in England. Oxford, unlike Cambridge, has long had a tradition of Aristotelian scholarship of the kind illustriously exemplified in the work of Sir David Ross. But Aristotle appears to be taken seriously now by philosophers as well as by historians of philosophy in a way which contrasts sharply with the attitude, say, of Russell and his immediate followers.

Interest in Aristotle's medieval successors has been stimulated from a different quarter. The great advances which have been made during the last hundred years in formal logic were made largely in ignorance of the work done in this field in the Middle Ages. Recently, however, logicians have come to appreciate the achievements of their medieval predecessors. Recent writers have studied in particular the medieval work on questions of modal logic and tense-logic, which is often discarded as sterile by neo-scholastics. (For references see Prior, *Formal Logic* and *Time and Modality*; Geach, *Reference and Generality*; Kneale, *The Development of Logic*.)

It is, no doubt, a contingent fact that much of systematic theology was worked out by thinkers trained in Aristotelian philosophy. But given this historical fact, the circumstances I have mentioned are of significance for the relationship between theology and philosophy. The decay of empiricism has weakened one of the greatest *a priori* obstacles to the construction of a natural theology; the revival of interest in scholastic writings and terminology lessens one of the great practical difficulties in communication between professional philosophers and professional theologians. The renaissance of formal logic has placed within the bounds of possibility a philosophical theology more rigorous than any known to the Middle Ages. But this possibility has not yet been explored. The interests of logicians have been hitherto almost entirely mathematical; only recently has attention been turned to modal and epistemic logic and tense-logics.

Yet such branches of logic are important for an assessment of the validity of proofs for the existence of God and for the consideration of the classic problems about his omniscience and omnipotence. The theologians, for their part, have hardly responded to the opportunities open to them: it is still rare to find a theologian fully aware of the progress made in logic since the time of Kant. Until a rigorously formulated natural theology has been constructed, there seems to be little hope of commending theism at a serious level to a philosophical public. The construction of such a system will naturally be an enormous task, and the qualifications which it will require are formidable. Fortunately, it is not the purpose of this paper to put forward even prolegomena to such an enterprise.

Dogmatic Theology is not in the same position as Natural Theology. The dogmatic theologian does not have to wait for the natural theologian to be in a position to convince unbelieving philosophers of the existence and attributes of the one true God. It is already possible for him to apply the results of those philosophers' labours to assist him in his own thinking. Thirty years ago, such a thing was impossible, not so much because of the unbelief of philosophers as because of the irrelevance of their interests. Now the situation has changed. Philosophical discussion is not, in general, much more favourable to theism than it was, but it is greatly more relevant to it. Many examples could be given of contemporary philosophical discussions which are of immediate relevance to well-known problems of theology.

It seems to me important that theologians should be familiar with the work of their philosophical contemporaries on topics which fall within the interests of both. It is not, necessarily, that present-day philosophers are more acute or profound than their scholastic predecessors. It is rather that the modern theologian is unlikely really to get to grips with the thought of the classic scholastics unless he has been brought by the study of contemporary philosophy to a genuine appreciations of the problems in these fields. A man who cannot understand and evaluate the work of philosophers close to him in time and culture is unlikely to interpret without parody the difficult and remote thought of the scholastic doctors.[1]

I do not intend to provide a list of recent discussions which have an interest for the theologian. Instead, I intend during the rest of this

[1] cp. Charles Davis, p. 129 (*supra*) (33), and David Jenkins, pp.150, 160 (*supra*).

paper to show, with regard to a single topic, how much theologically relevant work is being done by philosophers working in the contemporary Anglo-American tradition. The topic I shall choose is transubstantiation, a subject which above all others seems at first glance medieval and remote from twentieth-century philosophical concern.

II

The doctrine of Transubstantiation is stated by the Council of Trent thus. In the sacrament of the Eucharist, when the bread and wine are consecrated the whole substance of the bread is thereby turned into the substance of the body of Christ our Lord and the whole substance of the wine is thereby turned into the substance of his blood. This turning of one substance into another, the Council affirmed, was aptly named by the holy Catholic Church: 'transubstantiation' (Session XIII, cap. 4).

This doctrine is expounded as follows in the twenty-fifth section of the second part of the Catechism of the Council of Trent. 'Now there are three wonderful and stupendous things which in this Sacrament, Holy Church without all doubt believes and confesses to be wrought by the words of consecration. The First is, That the true Body of Christ, that very same which was born of the Virgin, and now sits in Heaven at the Right-hand of the Father is contain'd in this Sacrament. The Second is that no substance of the Elements remains in it: Altho nothing seems more strange and distant to the senses. The Third, which is easily gather'd from both the former, tho the words of Consecration fully express it, is that what is beheld by the Eyes, or perceiv'd by the other Senses is in a wonderful and unspeakable manner, without any subject matter. And one may see indeed all the Accidents of Bread and Wine, which yet are inherent in no substance, but they consist of themselves; because the Substance of the Bread and Wine is so chang'd into the Body and Blood of the Lord, that the substance of the Bread and Wine altogether ceases.' (English edition of 1687, 208.)

In discussing this doctrine I wish altogether to abstract from the question, whether there is any good reason to believe it to be true. In particular, I wish to abstract from the question whether the exposition contained in the Tridentine Catechism is the only possible orthodox interpretation of the teaching of the Council. I wish to consider the purely philosophical question, whether the doctrine stated in that Catechism is or is not self-contradictory. If it is, then of course there can be no good reason to believe it true, no matter how august the authority which affirms it. On the other hand, if it does not appear self-contradictory, the question of its truth remains open for the philosopher. We cannot rule out from the start a philosophical position which accepted the coherence of the notion of transubstantiation, but rejected the possibility that it might be a doctrine revealed by God, on the grounds that a contradiction was to be found not in the notion of transubstantiation but in that of a divine revelation.

It might be thought that a philosopher could have no possible interest in investigating the concept of transubstantiation unless he already believed it to be revealed by God. For the occurrence of transubstantiation, even if not logically impossible, is surely extremely improbable. But it is wrong to suppose that a philosopher should be interested in analysing descriptions only of states of affairs which are likely to obtain. Contemporary philosophers, like philosophers in all ages, frequently use the consideration of very improbable suppositions in order to throw light on concepts of great generality. Thus Strawson, in his book *Individuals*, devotes a whole chapter to the discussion of purely auditory experience such as would be enjoyed by beings who lacked all senses but that of hearing. Logicians talk of empty universes, and of the possibility of changing the past. In Wittgenstein's *Philosophical Investigations* we read of lions which talk, of dolls in pain, of disappearing chairs and languages of fantastic structure. The ability to imagine outlandish states of affairs is indeed a necessary skill for a philosopher. There is therefore no reason why the possibility of transubstantiation should not be investigated as a philosophical question in its own right, for the sake of the light such an inquiry might throw on concepts such as that of *material object*.

At the outset, it is obvious that if the true account of material objects is a phenomenalism such as that of Professor Ayer, then the notion of transubstantiation is self-contradictory. In his book *The Foundations of Empirical Knowledge* Ayer wrote as follows in the chapter entitled 'The Constitution of Material Things'. 'As for the belief in the "unity" and "substantiality" of material things, I shall show that it may be correctly represented as involving no more than the attribution to visual and tactual sense-data of certain relations which do, in fact, obtain in our experience.' On this view, to assert that a certain substance, e.g. bread, is or is not present in a certain place is to make a statement about what relations may be expected to obtain between sets of visual and tactual sense-data in our experience. But it is clear that a believer in transubstantiation who denies that the substance of bread is present on the altar after the consecration is not denying that all the relations between sense-data will obtain which would obtain if the substance, bread, really were present on the altar. As the Tridentine Catechism puts it: 'If the Faithful perswade themselves, that those things only are contain'd in this Sacrament, which are perceiv'd by the senses; they must needs be led into the greatest impiety, when with their Eyes, their Feeling, their Smell, their Taste, perceiving nothing at all, but the Species of Bread and Wine, they will judge that there is only Bread and Wine in the Sacrament.' If Ayer is right, therefore, the believer in transubstantiation is easily convicted of contradicting himself.

Since *The Foundations of Empirical Knowledge* was written, however, the doctrine which it contains has been severely criticised by people with no brief for transubstantiation, such as the late Professor J. L. Austin, whose posthumously published *Sense and Sensibilia* is almost entirely devoted to a refutation of Ayer's phenomenalism. Not all Austin's arguments are conclusive, but probably today most philosophers would agree with him in rejecting Ayer's claim that 'to say anything about a material thing is to say something, but not the same thing, about classes of sense-data' (Cf. *Sense and Sensibilia*, 119).

If we reject phenomenalism, it might seem that we must say that behind the perceptible phenomena of any material object, there is an imperceptible part of it which is its substance. And indeed the Council of Trent, when it speaks of the substance of bread and wine, has frequently been taken—by believers and unbelievers alike—to have been speaking about a *part* of the bread or wine. The teaching of Trent is often expounded with the aid of a doctrine of substance which goes as follows. There are some parts of a loaf of bread, such as its shape and colour and taste, which can be perceived by the senses; but the substance which is beneath these outward parts is not perceptible to the senses. The perceptible parts or accidents of the bread may be pictured as concealing the inner reality which is the substance of the bread rather as a layer of paint may conceal the wood of a table. Whatever may be perceived of a material thing is only accidental to it: for each of the perceptible qualities of a thing may change and yet the thing remain the same. The substance of a thing is that in which these accidents inhere, the subject of which they are predicated. It is itself both imperceptible and indescribable: imperceptible, because all perceptible qualities are accidents; indescribable, because to describe a thing is to record its attributes, and attributes are what a substance has, not what it is.

I think it will be agreed that the doctrine of transubstantiation is often explained in this manner. Many who, like myself, find this account unacceptable, therefore reject transubstantiation. In fact it is very unlikely that the Council of Trent meant anything like the thesis we have just stated. It was not Trent, but Locke, who defined substance as some thing, we know not what, which supports the sensible qualities we find united in things. The account of substance accepted by the scholastics who worked out the theology of transubstantiation was not Locke's theory but the quite different one of Aristotle. The views of these scholastics are surely more relevant than those of Locke in determining what is likely to have been in the mind of the Fathers of Trent.

Commonly, in their Eucharistic theology, when these scholastics spoke of 'substance', they had in mind what Aristotle in his *Categories* called 'first substance'. The doctrine of the Categories has been stated in modern terms by Miss Anscombe. '*First substance,*' she writes, 'is explained in the first place as what neither is asserted of nor exists in a subject: the examples offered are "such-and-such a man", "such-and-such a horse". A "first substance" then is what is designated by a proper name such as the name of a man or of a horse, or again, if one cared to give it a proper name, of a cabbage. A proper name is never, *qua* proper name, a predicate. Thus what a proper name stands for is not *asserted of* a subject.' A surface, such as the surface of a particular wedding-ring, is not *asserted of* a subject, but in Aristotle's sense it is *in* a subject. First substance, therefore, is described by contrast with what is *asserted of* and what *exists in* a subject (*Three Philosophers*, 7–8).

In the Categories, Aristotle lists ten different types of predication. A predicate may tell you what kind of thing something is, or how big it is, or what it is like, or where it is, or what it is doing, and so on. We may say, for instance, of Christ that he was a man, that he was

six feet tall, that he was a good man, that he was younger than John
the Baptist, that he lived in Galilee, that he lived under Pontius
Pilate, that he sat upon Jacob's well, that he wore a beard, that he
healed the sick, and that he was crucified. The predicates which we
use in saying these things belong to different categories: they belong,
respectively, to the categories of substance, quantity, quality, relation, place, time, posture, *habitus*, *actio* and *passio*.

'Substance' is here clearly being used in a sense different from that
in which it occurs in the phrase 'first substance'. Geach, following
Aquinas, has recently drawn a distinction between substantival and
adjectival terms. 'Aquinas calls our attention,' he writes, 'to a feature
of Latin grammar—that substantives are singular or plural on their
own account, whereas adjectives "agree in number" with substantives
(*Summa Theologica Ia*, 39, 3c and *ad* 1; 5 *ad* 5). This suggests to him
a logical distinction between two sorts of terms: substantival terms,
to which the question "how many?" applies directly, and adjectival
terms, to which this question applies only in so far as they are used
to add a qualification to substantival terms. One may ask how many
cats there are in a room; but not, how many black things there are
in the room; only, how many black *cats* (say) there are in the room.
The basis of this distinction is that the sense of "cat" determines a
sense for "one and the same cat", whereas the sense of "black thing"
does not in the least determine what shall count as one and the same
black thing.' (*Three Philosophers*, 86; *Reference and Generality*, 39–
40.)

Geach's distinction takes us only part of the way to understanding
Aristotle's distinction between predicates in the category of substance
and predicates in the other nine, accidental, categories. A substantival
term is not the same as a substantial term. 'Gold' is a predicate in the
category of substance; yet we cannot ask 'how many golds are there
in the room?'. On the other hand, the noun 'city' determines a sense
for 'one and the same city', yet 'city' does not stand for a kind of
substance.

The notion of a substantial predicate, as Miss Anscombe has in-
sisted, is closely connected with a particular sense of the question
'What is that?' which might be asked while pointing to something.
'We can pick out that sense of "What is it?" that is answered by the
name of a kind of thing or of a kind of stuff: "That is sulphur",
"That is an oak-tree", "That is a hyena".' ' "Substance",' writes Miss

Anscombe, 'is a classification, but whether of things or of concepts (or words) seems difficult to determine. If we ask what falls into the category of substances the answer is "e.g. men, horses, cabbages, gold, sugar, soap". This answer mentions things, not concepts or words, so substance might seem to be a classification of things.' On the other hand, we cannot ask: in virtue of what characteristics are these things all substances. For a description of their characteristics would already be a description in the form: description of the properties of substances. It is not just a well-established hypothesis that gold or a cat is a substance: that e.g. the question 'What is it made of?' has an application to a cat or a lump of gold. (*Three Philosophers*, 13.)

Aristotle devoted much thought to the relationship between first substance and predicates in the category of substance. Consider a sentence which contains a predication in the category of substance, such as 'Socrates is a man'. The name 'Socrates' stands for the individual, or first substance, Socrates. Now what does the predicate '. . . [is] a man' stand for? A Platonist might say that it stands for humanity as such. But this answer is not open to an Aristotelian: he rejects the idea that there is such a thing as humanity as such. The answer which Aristotle gives to this question is that the predicate stands for exactly the same thing as the subject does; that is to say, it stands for, or refers to, Socrates himself.

On the other hand, in a sentence containing a predication in one of the other categories, such as 'Socrates is white', the subject and the predicate do not stand for the same thing. The subject, 'Socrates' stands for the man Socrates; but the predicate '. . . [is] white' does not stand for Socrates. Does it stand for whiteness? Only a Platonist could say this. The answer given in the Aristotelian tradition was that it stood for the 'individualised form', the whiteness of Socrates.[1]

Such was the interpretation given by scholastics of the doctrines of Aristotle in Metaphysics *Δ* and Z. If we seek a definition of 'sub-

---

[1] A modern philosopher would speak naturally of the predicate of 'Socrates is a man' as being '. . . is a man'. Aquinas, though in his commentary on the *De Interpretatione* he recognizes the use now common, usually spoke of a predicate as a single term like 'man'. In a sentence such as 'Socrates is a man', if 'Socrates' and 'man' both stand for Socrates, what, if anything, does 'is' stand for? Aquinas's answer was that 'is' stood for *esse*—an *esse* which differed systematically accordingly as the predicate following the 'is' differed in category. (*In V. Met*, Cathala 890.)

stance' and 'accidents' in this tradition, we must say that the substance of a thing is what a predicate in the category of substance,
which is true of that thing, stands for; and the accidents of a thing
are what true predicates of it in the other nine categories stand for.
Thus, if it is true that Peter is a man, then the substance of Peter is
what the predicate '. . . [is] a man' stands for, to wit, Peter himself;
and if it is true that Peter is clever, then among the accidents of Peter
will be whatever the predicate '. . . is clever' stands for in the sentence
'Peter is clever'.

Now most modern philosophers would object to saying that predicates of any kind, whether substantial or accidental, *stand for* anything at all. Names stand for, or refer to, what they name; but there
is nothing which '. . . is a man' or '. . . is clever' stands for in the way
in which 'Peter' stands for Peter. To be sure, '. . . is a man' and
'. . . is clever' have meaning. But so do 'if' and 'but' have meaning;
they are not empty noises. But no one supposes that they stand for
some ifhood and butness existing in the world. So many philosophers
would argue: a typical example is Quine in his essay 'On What There
Is' (*From a Logical Point of View*).[1]

I am inclined to accept their argument, for the following reason. It
seems clear that all the words in a sentence must stand for the same
thing whether the sentence is true or false. If a question admits of the
answer 'Yes' or 'No', the reference of all the words in the question
must be the same no matter what the answer may be. But if the
sentence 'Peter is clever' is false, there is no such thing as the cleverness of Peter for the sentence to be about. Therefore, the sentence
'Peter is clever', whether true or false, cannot contain any phrase or
word which refers to the cleverness of Peter.[2]

For this reason I find it difficult to accept that accidents are the
references of accidental predicates. But although many of the
scholastics accepted such a theory, it does not seem necessary to do

[1] On the other hand, there *are* modern philosophers who are prepared to
accept the idea that predicates have references. Strawson, (*Individuals*, p. 144),
considers whether in 'Raleigh smokes' the expression 'smokes' can be said to
stand for smoking, or the habit of smoking. He says: 'I know of no rule or custom
which makes it always senseless or incorrect to say this, any more than I know
of any rule or custom which would make it always senseless or incorrect to say
that an assertion made in the words "Raleigh smokes" was an assertion about
smoking.'

[2] The form of this argument goes back to Buridan (Geach, *Reference and
Generality*, xi).

so in order to make sense of the teaching of Trent. All that it is necessary to believe is that the wisdom of Socrates, say, exists if and only if Socrates is wise. It is not necessary to believe, as these scholastics did, that this wisdom is actually referred to in the sentence 'Socrates is wise'. It is not difficult to find modern philosophers who are prepared to subscribe to the much more modest thesis that if Socrates is wise then there is such a thing as the wisdom of Socrates, and if Socrates is not wise then there is no such thing as the wisdom of Socrates.

Mr Strawson, for instance, in his widely acclaimed book *Individuals*, discusses ways in which particular and universal terms may be tied to each other. We may distinguish, say, particular utterances, and particular catches at cricket. We can then group together some particular utterances as wise utterances, and some particular catches as difficult catches. We are in that case grouping particulars by means of universals which are attached or 'tied' to them. But we may also group particulars by tying them to other particulars: as we may group together Socrates's utterances, and Carr's catches. In cases where we have two particulars tied together in this way, we often find that one particular will be an independent member of the tie, and the other particular a dependent member. For instance, Socrates may be tied to many particular utterances, but any particular utterance of his cannot be tied to any other particular person. Particulars, such as Socrates, which are the independent members of all such ties as they enter into, are called by Strawson: 'independent particulars'. As he explicitly recognises, Strawson's notion of *independent particular* is very close to Aristotle's notion of *first substance*.[1]

To an Aristotelian, the natural meaning of the decree of Trent which states that the substance of bread and wine turns into the substance of Christ's body and blood, is not that some part of the bread and wine turns into some part of the body and blood, but simply that the bread and wine turns into the body and blood. Following Aquinas (in 1 Cor 11: 24), the Fathers of Trent used 'the substance of Christ's body' and 'Christ's body' as interchangeable terms. According to scholastic theory, substance is not an imperceptible part of a particular individual. It is not a part of an individual; it *is* that individual. And it is imperceptible by the senses only in the following sense: I do not see *what kind of a thing* something is with

---

[1] op. cit., pp. 167–70.

my eyes as I see *what colour* it is with my eyes, any more than I see *what it tastes like* with my eyes. For all that, substances may be perceived. I can see, say, sulphuric acid with my eyes; though it is not just by looking, but by intelligent use of hypothesis and experiment and information, that I know that the stuff I see is sulphuric acid. Similarly, when I see sugar, what I see is sweet, though it is not with my eyes that I discover this. *A pari*, before the consecration the substance of bread is *not* imperceptible: what I see is bread; the substance which I see is the substance, bread.

Transubstantiation is a *unique* conversion, a turning of one thing into another which has no parallel. In all other cases where A turns into B there is some stuff which is first A-ish, and then B-ish. As scholastics would say, the same matter is first informed with the form of A-ishness and then informed with the form of B-ishness. (This sentence is merely a restatement, not an explanation, of the sentence which precedes it.) But in the Eucharistic *conversio* there is no parcel of stuff which is first bread and then Christ's body; not only does one form give way to another but one bit of matter gives way to another. In an ordinary change, when the form of A-ishness gives way to the form of B-ishness, we have a trans*form*ation—substantial transformation, or accidental transformation, according to whether the forms in question are substantial forms or accidental forms, that is to say, according to whether the predicates '. . . is an A' and '. . . is a B' are accidental or substantial predicates. In the Eucharist we have not just one form giving way to another, but one substance giving way to another: not just transformation, but tran*substant*iation.

It may well be asked at this point: what is now left of the notion of *turning into* here? To my knowledge, no completely satisfactory answer to this question has yet been given; nor do I think that I can succeed where others have failed. But it may help if we explain how the notion of *turning into* came to have a place in discussion of the Eucharist at all. There is no mention in Scriptural references to this sacrament of anything turning into anything else: why is there in Trent?

Aquinas introduces the notion of *turning into* as the only possible explanation of the presence of Christ's body under the appearances of bread and wine after the consecration. After the consecration it is true to say that Christ is in such-and-such a place. Now there are only three ways, says Aquinas, in which something can begin to exist in a place in which it did not exist before. Either it moves to that place from another place; or it is created in that place; or something which is already in that place turns, or is turned, into it. But Christ's body does not move into the place where the Eucharistic species are, nor is it created, since it already exists. Therefore something—to wit, the bread and wine—is turned into it.

It is essential to St Thomas's account that the bread and wine should cease to be, not by being annihilated, but by being *turned into* the body and blood. Transubstantiation is sometimes explained thus: the bread and wine are annihilated, and in their place Christ's body begins to exist. But for St Thomas there could be no sense in saying that Christ's body existed *in such-and-such a place* if the bread and wine formerly existing in that place had been annihilated. For, he would ask, how is the connection made between the body on the right hand of the Father and this particular altar? The connection, for him, is this, and only this: that the accidents of what has been turned into Christ's body are in such-and-such a place. Take away the transubstantiation, according to St Thomas, and you take away the presence.

The accidents which remain, says the Tridentine Catechism, following the Council of Constance, remain without a subject. Believers in transubstantiation are sometimes wrongly thought to hold that the accidents after consecration inhere in the substance of Christ's body.[1] If this were so then, for example, the whiteness which the bread once had would become the whiteness of Christ. And thus all the accidental predicates which are true of the sacramental host would become true of Christ: it would be true that Christ was white and round and two inches across and smaller than an orange.

When we consider the concept of accidents inherent in no substance, examples come to mind which are either incredible or too straightforward. The idea of the Cheshire cat's grin without the cat seems the very quintessence of absurdity. On the other hand there is nothing miraculous or mysterious in there being a smell of onions after the onions have ceased to exist. The smell of onions is just the sort of thing which St Thomas meant by an accident in this context. When he discusses the question how accidents without substance can nourish and inebriate he considers the suggestion that it is the smell of wine which inebriates, as the smell of wine in a full cellar may

[1] cf. Hobbes, *Leviathan*, I, viii (Everyman edition, p. 40).

make you feel dizzy before you broach a cask. He rejects this suggestion, not on the grounds that an accident is a different sort of thing altogether, but on the grounds that you can get far more drunk on consecrated wine than you can by going into a cellar and sniffing. But perhaps a better example of an accident without a substance than any known to St Thomas is the colour of the sky. When the sky is blue, its blueness is not the blue *of* any substance. 'The sky' is the name not of a substance, but of a phenomenal object (like 'the host') and there is no substance *in* the sky which is blue.

The principle that the accidents of the host do not inhere in the substance of Christ's body is one which is often violated in popular preaching of the Eucharist. '. . . is moved', '. . . is dropped', '. . . is spat upon' are accidental predicates. Consequently, if the host is moved, Christ is not moved; if the host is dropped, Christ is not dropped; if the host is spat upon, Christ is not spat upon. In the words of Cardinal Newman: 'Our Lord neither descends from heaven upon our altars nor moves when carried in procession. The visible species change their position but he does not move (*Via Media*, 1877, ii. 220).' The principle to which Newman alludes is violated in popular devotions to 'The Prisoner of the Tabernacle'; it was violated also by Cardinal Pole when he forced an unfortunate heretic to repeat the words of the recanting Berengar: 'The real body and blood of our Lord Jesus Christ . . . are held and broken by the hands of the priests and are crushed by the teeth of the faithful.'[1]

The principle that the accidents inhere in no substance, however, leaves one problem with which I shall conclude. Among the accidental categories of Aristotle is the category of place. '. . . is on the altar', for instance, is an accidental predicate. But if the accidents which once belonged to the bread do not inhere after consecration in the substance of Christ's body, then it appears that it by no means follows from the presence of the host upon the altar that Christ is present on the altar. Thus the doctrine of transubstantiation appears in the end to fail to secure that for which alone it was originally introduced, namely the real presence of Christ's body under the sacramental species. I do not know of any satisfactory answer to this problem. If I did, I would give it. Since I do not, I must leave it, as the writers of textbooks say, as an exercise for the reader.

[1] I am indebted for these last two references to the Rev. H. Green, C.R.

(II) ON MAKING ROOM FOR FAITH

A Humanist's View

STEPHAN KÖRNER

In this paper I wish to discuss the problem of the compatibility or incompatibility of science on the one hand with morality and religion on the other. I shall in particular try to answer the following questions: First, are scientific theories compatible or incompatible with ethical beliefs, especially the belief that man is responsible for his actions? Second, are scientific theories compatible or incompatible with a religious cosmology to the effect that God has created the world and occasionally suspends the operation of the laws of nature in it?

To a humanist the two questions are logically independent since his moral beliefs are logically independent of the acceptance or rejection of a religious cosmology, which to him seems incapable of any proof or disproof. To a religious person, religious cosmology and moral beliefs are closely interrelated, and there are religious persons who hold that morality can be based only on religion.

I shall proceed as follows: After a brief examination of two important attempts at establishing the compatibility of science with morality and religion, I shall make some remarks about the logical structure of scientific theories and their relation to experience. From these remarks I shall draw the conclusion that science and morality are compatible; and that science is compatible with some parts of religious cosmology, but incompatible with others. I shall conclude with a personal observation.

Kant and Peirce on the relations between science, morality and religion

Both Kant and Peirce see the root of a merely apparent incompatibility between science on the one hand and morality and religion on the other, in a misunderstanding of the nature of science. For our purpose an outline of their views and of the reasons for their inadequacy will suffice.

Kant's argument rests on the distinction between the phenomenal and the noumenal world. The phenomenal world is fully describable in terms of *a posteriori* concepts, categories and mathematical notions which are characteristic of the structure of space and time. The laws governing the external world are expressed in terms of these concepts, and coincide to a large extent with Newton's deterministic physics. On the other hand, statements about the freedom of the will and the existence of God do not have the phenomenal world for their subject matter and cannot thus be incompatible with Newtonian physics or science in general.

It is not necessary here to examine in detail Kant's transcendental argument from the actual adoption of certain concepts and principles to their 'necessary' adoption as a pre-condition of all objective experience and all science. That the argument has failed becomes clear from a consideration of the post-Kantian development of mathematics and the natural sciences; the failure affects the validity of Kant's general procedure of reconciling science on the one hand with morality and religion on the other and calls for a fairly extensive reconstruction of the Kantian philosophy.

There is, moreover, another feature of the Kantian position which, though logically unobjectionable, is difficult to accept—at least for many people. Most people's belief in their freedom to make decisions is based on what they would call self-observation. But self-observation is observation of the phenomenal world, which according to Kant, is a wholly deterministic system. Kant's argument, then, that we are noumenally free implies that any alleged introspective evidence of freedom is illusory and that consequently the notion of our freedom must remain forever mysterious to us.

Peirce's attempt to show the compatibility between science and morality (and other extra-scientific beliefs) rests on a bold re-interpretation of Newtonian physics.

Like Kant, Peirce has no reason to doubt that Newtonian physics is substantially true; but he holds that the truth of its laws and of scientific laws in general, is only approximate. His view is mainly based on an unorthodox interpretation of the fact that different measurements of the same physical quantity do not coincide, but show a certain spread. According to Peirce this means, not that the measurements express greater or smaller deviations from the true or real value of the measured quantity, but that there exist in nature only approximate regularities. If with Peirce we drop the distinction between the true or real value of a measurement and the values deviating from it—as is assumed by the statistical theory of errors— then the laws of nature themselves become statistical. We are here confronted with a thesis of the ultimately statistical character of all laws of nature, which in some ways anticipates Quantum Mechanics, although Peirce's supporting arguments are wholly logico-philo- sophical.

Yet the statistical character of the laws of nature, be they statisti- cally interpreted Newtonian laws or, even *prima facie* statistical, does not, as Peirce supposed, suffice to show that science and moral re- sponsibility are compatible. That the radiation of certain substances conforms to statistical laws concerning random processes does not imply that these substances are capable of choice; similarly it would not follow from man's being a system of random processes that he can ever choose freely. Free actions are not random actions and the expression 'random action' is in many senses a contradiction in terms.

Both the Kantian and the Peircean attempts at reconciling science with morality and other extra-scientific beliefs are therefore, to put it mildly, rather unsatisfactory. They are nevertheless the prototypes of most attempts at a reconciliation, apart from those which see the root of the matter in more or less trivial verbal confusion—e.g., the conflation of a spurious metaphysical notion of liberty with 'liberty' in the sense of an absence of constraint, which, for example the people outside a prison, but not its inmates, enjoy.

The empirical differentiation of the world around us

In order to understand the logical relation between scientific and extra-scientific thought and language, it is necessary to consider not only the structure of scientific theories and of the ways in which they are anchored in experience, but also the structure of pre-scientific, extra-scientific or 'ordinary' thought and language. As I shall argue that scientific theories (of a very general kind) are not only deductive unifications of experience, but also, and unavoidably, idealisations of it, I shall have to exhibit some features of ordinary, empirical thought which are modified through their incorporation into deductive systems.

In our thinking about the world around us we habitually differentiate it into individuals and classes. There are, of course, more ways than one of individuation and classification although we are naturally inclined to argue that our habits of thought and talk are the only possible 'adequate' or 'necessary' ones. The most familiar schema of empirical differentiation, and perhaps the oldest, is to divide the world into individual things which move about in space and time. Its refined counterpart is mechanistic physical theory, which for a long time was considered the only intelligible explanation of physical phenomena.

Yet the schema of things moving in space and time is not the only way of differentiating the world around us into individuals and classes. Language, philosophical speculation, and the scientist's attempts to make sense of the variety and strangeness of the phenomena give rise to other schemata. Thus, to give at least one further example, the ancient speculative philosophers sometimes conceived of the whole of space as being occupied by 'one thing', a permanent substance which leaves no room for a plurality of impermanent things. Their place is taken by distinguishable patterns which emerge from, and after a certain time dissolve into the background. Such a schema of differentiating the world reminds one of physical theories in which the permanent substance is an aether, capable of certain modifications which, like wave-packets, are travelling through it and dissolve after a time. It reminds one also of Spinoza's metaphysics with its one external substance and its impermanent modifications.

For my purpose it is not necessary to develop a typology of the various actual or conceivable schemata of empirical differentiation, that is of the methods of discovering or creating empirical individuals or of finding them in, or putting them into, various classes. Some general features of the classification of empirical individuals must, however, be pointed out if the nature of scientific idealisation (which consists in the modification of these features) is to be understood.

The definition of empirical concepts, and of the corresponding classes of individuals, in terms of other empirical concepts depends ultimately on explaining the meaning of some concept by means of standard members of the class of its instances and of standard non-members of it. This means that among the qualifications and disqualifications of an individual for membership in an empirical class there is the requirement that the individual should be similar to standard members and dissimilar to standard non-members—and that a method is available for producing standard objects which are needed for comparison. I shall call any class such that the qualifications for membership include the mentioned requirement, a 'resemblance-class' because the term 'empirical class' is often used in a wider sense.

In the present context it will be sufficient to emphasise one characteristic of resemblance-classes, namely their inexactness, i.e., their admitting border-line cases. Apart from having standard members and non-members and ordinary members and non-members (i.e. objects which are sufficiently similar to standard members and sufficiently dissimilar from standard non-members to qualify for membership, or objects which are clearly disqualified for membership on the basis of their comparison with standard members and non-members), a resemblance-class also admits of neutral candidates, i.e., objects which can with equal correctness be assigned or refused membership of the class. The reason for this inexactness of resemblance-classes lies, of course, in the fact that the required degree of resemblance in a certain respect is not capable of so sharp a determination as to exclude the occurrence of neutral candidates.

If o is an object and P is a class, only two kinds of predication are possible in traditional and modern logic, namely (i) $(o \in P)$, i.e., 'o is a member of P' and (ii) $(o \in' P)$, i.e. 'o is a non-member of P'. But if o is a resemblance-class it admits also of a third possibility namely (iii) $(o \in {}^*P)$, i.e., 'o is a neutral candidate for P'. To these three analysed elementary statements there correspond three unanalysed, atomic statements namely (i) p, i.e., 'p is true'; (ii) p', i.e., 'p is false' and (iii) ${}^*p$, i.e., (say) 'p is neutral'. To the inexactness of resemblance-classes there corresponds thus a three-valued propositional logic, where the third truth-value—unlike the third truth-value in the Tarski-Lukasiewicz type of three-valued logic—can be turned by decision into one of the other two. Suitable truth-tables for this logic and a sketch of the further development of it are contained in Kleene's *Metamathematics*.[1] The inexactness of resemblance-classes affects, of course, all those empirical classes which are, at least partly, defined in terms of them.

Just as in any schema of empirical differentiation at least some classes of individuals are inexact, so at least some individuals are

[1] S. C. Kleene, *Metamathematics*, p. 64, Amsterdam, 1952. The intended interpretation is, however, quite different.

indefinite in the sense of not being in all their parts clearly distinguished from other individuals or from their background. When precisely, does any stone, tree, man, motorcar etc. begin or cease to exist, i.e., what is already and what is no longer part of its history? When precisely does any of these things lose its individuality as a result of a successive separation of parts? How far separate must the parts of a thing be for it to cease existing, how near for it to start existing? Such questions can be asked not only about things, but about all types of individuals, such as situations or processes.

Just as in the case of inexact classes we distinguished between members, non-members and neutral candidates for membership of an inexact class, so we can in the case of indefinite individuals distinguish between parts, non-parts and neutral components, which can with equal correctness be judged to be parts or non-parts. (It is possible to define the indefiniteness of empirical individuals in terms of the inexactness of a resemblance-class, namely that of empirical part-to-whole relationships, but there is no need to do this.)

To say that an individual is indefinite is, of course, not to imply that it is without any demarcation, that it is indefinite throughout or that all its components are neutral. A man, for example, is from his birth to his death quite clearly distinguished from other individuals or from his background, although, as is recognised by most legal systems, his birth and death are not sharply demarcated. Indefiniteness in some phase or aspect is quite compatible with definiteness elsewhere. In a similar way the inexactness of a resemblance-class does not imply that all individuals are neutral candidates for membership of it. The world is neither all chaos nor all order and empirical individuation and classification are neither infinitely sharp nor infinitely blurred.

Apart from the inexactness of classification and the indefiniteness of individuation, any schema of empirical differentiation (or at least any known schema) involves a notion of empirical continuity such as we apply when we distinguish perceptually continuous from perceptually discontinuous spatial expanses, movements or qualitative transitions. This is not the place to exhibit the structure of (e.g.) an empirically continuous colour spectrum in any detail. But two almost obvious characteristics of this structure may be pointed out, namely (i) the number of different discriminable colour-classes is finite in number, since although people differ in their powers of discrimination, nobody's discriminatory powers are infinite; and (ii) that any two 'neighbouring' colour-classes merge into each other in the sense of having common neutral candidates. Similarly in the case of a continuous spatial expanse or thing (i) the number of different discriminable parts is finite and (ii) any two 'neighbouring' parts merge into each other in the sense of having common neutral components. The notion of empirical continuity is, as seen in the relation of 'neighbouring' classes or parts, dependent on the inexactness of classes or indefiniteness of individuals.

To sum up, the schemata of empirical differentiation by which we apprehend the world, and, as it were, prepare it for our activities, involves the discovery or creation of indefinite individuals (of various types), their classification into inexact classes, in particular resemblance-classes, and the notions of empirical continua. I must now turn to the deductive unification of experience in science, and in particular show how as a result of it the fundamental empirical notions of individuals, classes, and continua are modified.

Deductive unification as idealisation

Even the most superficial consideration of any hypothetico-deductive system, formulating the results, laws, and predictions of scientific investigations, shows how deductive unification enforces the replacement of indefinite individuals by definite ones, of inexact classes by exact ones, of empirical continua with a finite number of inexact or indefinite members by mathematical continua with an infinite number of exact or definite members.

In theoretical physics, and wherever the differential and integral calculus are applied, the replacement is most obvious. Empirically continuous series of a finite number of members merging into each other are replaced by continuous series of real numbers or other exact (or definite) mathematical entities conforming to Dedekind's— or equivalent—postulates for mathematically continuous series. Among them is, for example, the postulate of density to the effect that between any two members of an infinite series there is at least one other member, and therefore an infinite number of members.

The full mathematical formulation and treatment of measurements presupposes the real number system and thus the mathematical theory of continuity. But even the simple and fundamental notion of mathematical equality, e.g. of equality in weight is, as Poincaré pointed out, already an idealisation of an empirical notion. For while the relation of mathematical equality e.g. in weight is transitive so that for any three objects a, b, c—if a equals b and b equals c then a equals c—empirical equality in weight as ascertained for empirical individuals by means of actual instruments is non-transitive. For it is always possible to find for any pair of scales three empirical objects A, B, C, such that though A balances B and B balances C, A and C do not balance each other.

Since mathematically measurable characteristics have instances of which any two are in a given respect equal or unequal in the mathematical, transitive sense, and since empirically measurable characteristics have instances of which any two are equal or unequal in a non-transitive sense, the replacement of the latter characteristics by the former constitutes a transition from describing experience to its idealisation. The reason for the replacement is, of course, the suitability of transitive relations for inference and calculation.

Another, and even more, thorough-going idealisation is involved in the general replacement of inexact resemblance-predicates and other inexact concepts by exact ones. The reason for this is clear. The deductive unification of any empirical field means the incorporation of empirical concepts and statements in a pre-existing logical framework, that is to say in at least a system of elementary logic including propositional logic and the theory of quantification. For this purpose one adds to the primitive terms of elementary logic the primitive concepts of the empirical field, and to the postulates of elementary logic the non-logical postulates, required for the deduction of the propositions which are to constitute the content of the hypothetico-deductive theory. But the possible *logical* relations between the statements and predicates of the theory are not increased; and these relations are relations holding only between propositions involving exact concepts and classes. Elementary logic, and therefore the deductive theories embedded in it, cannot accommodate inexact classes but only idealised exact substitutes for them.

It needs little consideration to convince oneself that the individuals which occur in hypothetico-deductive theories are different from empirical individuals in being sharply demarcated from each other and from their backgrounds and in being the bearers of exact predicates rather than inexact ones.

The deductive unification of a field of empirical investigation by means of elementary logic (propositional calculus, quantification theory and theory of identity), which underlies every scientific, hypothetico-deductive theory, involves thus the replacement of inexact by exact classes, of indefinite by definite individuals, of non-transitive perceptual indistinguishability by transitive equality. If the underlying logic or logic-cum-mathematics includes also the system of real numbers and thus the notions of mathematical continuity, a further replacement and modification is involved, namely that of the empirical by the mathematical notion of continuity.

It is, of course, often said that a sufficiently rich hypothetico-deductive theory involves idealisation. It is, however, rarely noted that the idealisation is enforced already by the framework of elementary logic. And a most important and quite obvious consequence of this situation is either not drawn or is neglected, namely that a hypothetico-deductive theory does not describe experience except in a loose, and for the purpose of an understanding between science and extra-scientific beliefs, even dangerously loose, sense of 'description'.

The usual account of scientific prediction and explanation by means of a hypothetico-deductive theory is roughly as follows. Starting with a basic proposition, say, b_1 which we can formulate on the basis of some experiment or observation, we deduce from b_1 and the hypothetico-deductive theory, say T, another basic proposition b_2, which can again be checked against experiment or observation. The schema is $(b_1 \text{ and } T) \vdash_L b_2$, where '$\vdash_L$' expresses deducibility with respect to the underlying logic L.

But b_1 and b_2 are formulated in the language of T and subject to the requirements of L. That is to say the constituents of b_1 and b_2 are not empirical predicates and individuals but idealised non-empirical ones. In other words, the connection between T and experience is more complex than the schema: $(b_1 \text{ and } T) \vdash_L b_2$ makes it appear. In order to establish the connection with experience we must first 'identify' an empirical statement, say, e_1 with the idealised premise b_1, and an empirical statement, say e_2 with the idealised conclusion. We must, as it were, 'idealise' before and 'de-idealise', after the logical deduction. To identify e_1 with b_1 and e_2 with b_2, is not to ascertain an identity or equivalence, but to treat two different propositions *as if* they were identical. And such treatment is successful not for all, but only for some purposes, and not within all, but only within some contexts.

A scientific statement of the form: 'If, within a specified context and for a given purpose, we idealise an empirical statement e_1 describing a type of event into a basic theoretical statement b_1, deduce b_2 from (b_1 and T) and de-idealise b_2 into an empirical statement e_2 describing a type of event then if e_1 occurs, e_2 will also occur' is an empirical statement, more precisely an empirical generalisation. About it some remarks are in order: First, in verifying or falsifying the empirical generalisation we do not strictly speaking verify or falsify the theory, but a more complex statement in which the theory plays the part of an incomplete symbol. Second, the scientific empirical generalisation differs from the 'ordinary' empirical generalisation, not in being more or less empirical, but in being connected, through the theory, with other empirical generalisation and in being (as a rule) intellectually more satisfying. Third, the 'identification' of empirical with non-empirical concepts allows for great precision of reasoning and calculation within the context and set of purposes for which the identification is legitimate. Fourth, the 'identification' is limited, and every extrapolation of a scientific theory beyond these limits must be based on new reasons, in addition to those by which the limited scientific generalisation was supported.

On the logical relation between science, morality and religion

Scientific theories have as their subject matter definite non-empirical individuals which are the bearers of exact predicates and stand in exact relations only. Their subject matter is not experience but an idealisation of experience. Statements about experience must, therefore, be compatible with statements about idealised experience. The descriptions of theoretical physics are identifiable with descriptions of the world of experience only with important qualifications and limitations. (The gain in explanatory power and precision, and the price of limited applicability paid for the gain is well expressed by W. Heisenberg, *Physics and Philosophy*, London 1958, p. 171.)

Thus, *if* our bodies are subject without qualification or limitation to the laws of physics, then since we cannot act without our bodies, those of our actions which seem to us determined in part by free decisions, are in fact with certainty or probability—determined by physical antecedents alone. But, since the applicability of theoretical physics to experience, via the identification of non-empirical with empirical statements, is limited to contexts in which decisions play no part, it is not theoretical physics but an unwarranted philosophical extrapolation of it which is incompatible with the assumption that decisions for which we are responsible, sometimes determine our actions.

The compatibility between scientific theories (embedded in standard elementary logic) and moral responsibility does not imply that moral responsibility is or that it is not an empty notion. But it leaves room for the belief that it is not empty. And this belief, or faith, is as essential to the humanist tradition as it is to the Western religions.

Whatever the analysis of the relation between description and idealisation in scientific thinking may be, its subject-matter is the relation between spatio-temporal states, and not a relation between the totality of all spatio-temporal states and anything which is not spatio-temporal. Whatever is said about such a relation is, therefore, incapable of logical proof or disproof from empirical premises. The belief, for example, that God has, or has not, created the world is thus compatible with science.

Although science is compatible with the belief in moral responsibility and in God, as the creator of the world, it is not compatible with the belief in miracles. For this belief implies that there are no laws of nature in the strict sense, but only alleged laws of nature the full formulation of which requires the additional clause: 'Provided that no miracle happens'. The religious person, of course, has no qualms about adding this clause. For to be religious is to hold, among other things, that whatever is incompatible with one's religious beliefs, is false.

To me, if I may conclude with a personal remark, the main value of any religion consists in its moral teaching. If God exists, and has the perfections which are ascribed to him, then he must be much more concerned with man's fulfilling his moral duties and following worthy ideals, than with his religious belief, disbelief or agnosticism.

The foregoing paper demonstrates some of the difficulties to be encountered when we ask for a dialogue between philosophy and theology to be established as part of the curriculum of a modern British university.

Yet the case put by Professor Körner—that belief in free will is neither supported nor contradicted by the presuppositions of scientific inquiry—draws our attention to three points of importance for theologians. Firstly, the scientist, qua *scientist, has no competence to challenge the metaphysical claims of theism: it is the* philosopher *of science who is competent to dispute with theologians. Secondly, the distinction between experience and its theoretical explanation to which the paper points is one to which the theologian must be especially sensitive (See Mgr Davis, supra, p. 178[1]). Thirdly, since much of what the paper says may seem unfamiliar to the theologian, it must be seen not only as evidence of the extent of the separation of theology from its cognate disciplines, but as a reminder that whether or not there is conflict between theism and an adequate philosophy of science cannot be decided by those who are ignorant in either of these fields. Thus theologians should be wary of supposing that what is believed by faith can, by some pseudo-scientific demonstration, be 'proved' (See David Jenkins, supra, pp. 150, 160; and Dom Illtyd Trethowan, supra, p. 194).*

The symposium clearly established, however, that philosophers and theologians can still talk to each other to their mutual advantage, and that were such dialogues carried out systematically within a university, sufficient common ground might be found for the development of joint schools and other work in philosophy and theology, which might make a distinctively British contribution to European theology.

V

NEEDS AND PROPOSALS

10. The Need for Theology from within the Secular Environment

Simon Clements

It could be said that a new dimension has entered the theological scene with modern society, and that in former ages the need for theology was felt mainly by the teaching magisterium of the Church —the hierarchy and the clergy—and not by the taught—the laity. Père Congar has shown how in the past the roles of the hierarchy and the theologian have been distinct: 'The part of the hierarchy—in which they have never fallen short—is to guard the deposit of faith and to witness to the unchanging truth. The part of the theologians— in which they have too often fallen short—is to work out the implications of the christian fact in the actual conditions of its embodiment in human life.'[1] Today, with the advent of a laity capable of greater maturity in the life of faith, one needs to work out where the layman belongs within the partnership of hierarchy and professional theologian, and what are his specific needs. I want to argue that his needs are for a theology distinctly related to his situation. In his *Spectator* article, 'The same again, please', of 23 November 1962, Mr Evelyn Waugh seems to have missed the point that the life of the layman, upon which the Church's theology should bear, is not confined to his private acts of devotion and religious observances. The sphere in which the layman most needs help is exactly in his professional life as a man of the world, and it is just here that theology in its modern context needs to be directed. It is also here that the layman has most to contribute to the thought of the Church, because he witnesses most to the continual clash of reality and ideal, and therefore experiences the actual working out of the Church's theology.

The need of theology arises after I have already encountered God

[1] *Divided Christendom*—a Catholic study of the problem of Reunion, Père Congar, O.P., p. xiv (Geoffrey Bles, 1939).

in my life and have made an act of faith in the revelation of himself to me. If I have so encountered God, this encounter has been in the situation in which I find myself. The encounter, then, is partly a revelation, partly a willingness to lend an ear or obey a call, what Newman called 'an act of the will'; in any event, it involves a submission of the individual. For some this encounter may be strong, for many it is probably rather vaguely felt. The growth towards this creative encounter came for me in the situation of my work, as a teacher in a school, a non-Catholic comprehensive secondary school for boys and girls run by the London County Council and set in an intensely sooty, urban area of crowded, decaying streets and eroded tenement blocks, whose only open spaces are scrofulous bombed-sites. The vigour, response and endlessly fresh relationships of the children against this background began to declare for me something of the mystery of the incarnation and redemption.

I began to understand that Christ was met quite simply in the children I taught. I tried to remember to reply to their breezy greetings of an early morning, to inquire after the health of a child returning after a few days' sickness before asking for an official note; for in every situation I was required to respond, and I realised that God could not do without me, that God needed me precisely because I was the only person there to reply 'good morning' to my class. In other words, I saw how everyone of us fits into the divine scheme of things and somehow realises it, not necessarily through pious acts and prayers but through being fully human.

This breakthrough from a nominal to a real belief comes from an encounter with God in a given situation. It would seem from the evidence that the breakthrough is possible only when the encounter is recognised as an invitation to become involved in a divine plan, in certain well-defined circumstances such as the field of one's work. Henceforth the need for theology makes a great jump forward. Up to that moment a systematised assembly of formulae about the nature of God and his plan was absorbed parrot-fashion, was rationalised as in apologetics in order to secure a nominal faith against adolescent doubts, and to assure the pupil of a juridical existence in a christian assembly. A science of faith as clarifying an encounter and invitation, as the meeting of two persons (God and man), as the call of deep to deep—God calling from his depths to the inner depths of personal life—did not seem necessary, because the child was not at the stage when such an encounter could be experienced. It was only possible when the child had grown to take up a new and more responsible relationship with his parents and other people somewhat on the basis of adult equality. In other words the nature of the encounter between God and the person stems from personal human relationships.

This change, one might say, is a moment of maturity. It is the period when the adolescent is experiencing many new-felt needs of both a secular and spiritual nature. One speaks often today of young people giving up their faith in God and his plan at this point in their personal growth, of lapsing from the 'practice of their faith'. What this usually means is that the person finds that the faith, as he has been taught it, is quite inadequate to explain his newly discovered situation; and at the first opportunity he therefore discards the dead bones of doctrine and moral teaching, in order to experience a phoenix-like new freedom and responsibility. A minority however do not suffer from this loss of nerve, this inability to rise to the occasion and rediscover faith at a new level of operation. They wish to follow St Paul's advice to the Corinthians—to do away with that which is only in part, and to put away childish things. Their need is for a deeper theological interpretation of their newly found life. The need of a theology felt at this stage of personal growth corresponds to the natural need of the person to throw himself into life and work, and particularly into the life of his times. For the apprentice it may be any time after sixteen, for the graduate it is probably delayed until his twenties. A need of theology arises from the situation, therefore, but in the sense that the person has become more vividly aware of his situation and feels the need of doing something to make his impression on it. This need however is not felt by everyone. There are many, I suspect, who refuse to face the reality and implications of their situation for fear that they might lose their faith. Because their derived notion of God is wholly inadequate, they prefer to keep their idea of God intact rather than become committed to their work in life. Their spiritual growth becomes stunted in a blind imbalance. I am worried that this might be the lot of very many practising Catholics today.

Finally I want to suggest that the discarding of faith may not necessarily be a negative act. For many it is often intrinsically bound up with a quest for a core of principles that *will* suffice; the Church having failed these people because her image hid what she had to offer. 'Organisation Man' is concerned today about de-personalisation and is searching for a set of values which will restore meaning to a situation which looks like becoming a dreary, contented process of acquisition, and of desiring a steadily rising salary, a status and a pension at an early retirement. The danger is that things lesser than himself are satisfying man. Indeed many of us recognise that unless man is disturbed in his life, he does not find his fulfilment. The lack of willingness or ability for this rigorous questioning is probably fundamental to many modern neuroses. Few admit that theology has the power to interpret the situation and disturb man that he might find his completion.

I shall now go on to describe how my situation and theology became so interrelated and the sort of theology I needed. Because my work happens precisely to be the job of communicating ideas to young people and encouraging in them thoughtful response, I want also to put before you a brief analysis of the process of communication, as I have found it between teacher and taught; because I think it has something to say about the contact the Church has to make with her faithful, that is the problem of putting over her theology.

The Crisis

The Catholic Catechism and the Anglican Agreed Syllabus, which are commonly accepted in the schools as representing the conventional christian teaching, are a distillation for the laity of a professional theology. Today these summaries seem critically inadequate. The crisis is the Church's failure to present her true self, to offer an adequate lay theology to christians attempting to rediscover their faith at a more mature level. This breakdown of image and of interpretation means that people are discarding a parody of Christianity rather than the true Christianity and without realising that this is so. The crisis appears even more acute when the Church attempts to meet the widespread loss of a religious disposition in our society. We may suggest, therefore, that the Church's mission at all levels of the community is critically dependent upon her central and highest forms of theological research. If her theology fails to develop, her contact with society will shrivel.

The infidelity of the day, producing widespread apostasy and subtle disbelief, that Newman devoted a paper to in *The Idea of a University* is not an isolated christian problem, but is, I believe, part of a more general cultural crisis in our English society and must be seen as part of that. This is the importance of such writers as Hoggart, Raymond Williams, Tawney, and Galbraith; and I refer throughout this paper to the English scene. The problem is seen clearly in the secondary schools where we are often faced with a cultural gulf between teacher and taught—the image of 'Them and Us'. The efforts to bridge this gap need constant inventive renewal, for the teacher and the Church both appear to be standing one remove from the society they are hoping to influence. The task is one of gaining acceptance. The manifestations of this gulf and the distractions aggravating the issue are all too numerous. There is the debilitating effect of mass media upon response, on which the Pilkington report (para. 102) had this to say: 'Our own conclusion is that triviality is a natural vice of television, and that where it prevails it operates to lower general standards of enjoyment and understanding. It is, as we were reminded, "more dangerous to the soul than wickedness".' Then there is the loss of a sense of sacredness and reverence, epitomised by transistor sets in wild open spaces, speculative land grab and capitalist attitudes towards landscape, which it is worth remembering William Blake characterised simply as, 'A fool sees not the same tree as a wise man sees.' I might also mention an apparent lack of gratitude or concern for the values held by our forefathers in their struggle for social justice; and I would even dare to suggest a detectable growth of resentment, particularly for tradition. I feel the present education offered by Local Education Authority night schools is particularly significant of much of this, where the desire is either for knowledge and technique in passing examinations, related to increased status and salary, and regardless of evaluating the content of what is learned, or for a fashionable variety of craft skills which, while desirable and valid in themselves, are no substitute for intellectual and moral discipline. It is a commonplace within Adult Education that W.E.A. classes are not what they were—the fire is lacking, and so is the fierce concern for standards—whilst a comparable crisis within sixth form education is epitomised in what passes for 'English' in the new *Use of English* examination for potential Oxbridge candidates.

All these observations ought to be intrinsic to a theological frame of mind and need to be the concern of a modern theologian.

K

In addition to these elements withdrawing people from the idea of a Church, the Church herself must accept some responsibility for the growing gulf. She no longer offers visibly a living culture; her very life itself suffers from a fossilised liturgy; she is bogged down by a false sense of respectability, and she appears to offer a Christianity based upon injunctions and a negative feeling of guilt, rather than a positive intellectual grasp of sin.

It is my contention that this common deadness in society may be owing to a lack of response, a virtual deafness. It is for this response as a schoolteacher I teach; and it is that which is called for in the encounter at depth with the divine. Indeed there is a creeping shallowness and self-consciousness in people that is cutting them off from being part of a collective body, of belonging to a community, a kind of isolated individuality that prevents them from approaching the very idea of a Church.

Secular Counterbalance

In the last pages of *The Uses of Literacy* Richard Hoggart did not despair of these elements I have alluded to, but observed that 'working class people, though they are in a sense being exploited today, at least now have to be approached for their consent.' I feel that in the schools we are concerned to create this freedom for real assent to moral and aesthetic values to which Hoggart refers, and that we have some understanding of the new society and its educational needs, to which the theologian will need to look for the counterbalance to the problems he faces.

The Pentecostal wind is stirring with the Second Vatican Council, and the Church is on the verge of recreating herself. But her future development is not simply a matter of formal christian restoration, or of shifting the blame for a deficiency of response or right attitude upon individuals. The problem of providing for man is far more complex and extends throughout the entire cultural pattern of man's society. My religious understanding and responsibilities became completely redirected when I discovered this complexity, on coming down from university and while working for four years in a crowded urban comprehensive school, whose children came from tightly developed nineteenth-century streets, and preserved a vigour and culture divorced from anything I had met before. My religious education had not prepared me for this shock, because it had laid disproportionate emphasis on the notion of individual responsibility regardless of a man's situation, whereas I have grown to realise over the last four years through my daily work how deeply man is part of his environment, indeed grows out of it, is shaped by it and bears distinct characteristics as clear as the streets and houses he lives in. Only the reality of experience could properly impress this upon me. We are familiar and happy with the rural version of man's dependency upon his background and the need to have and to recognise his roots—the essential key in much of the thought that runs through Thomas Hardy's novels. We are perhaps less easy about the urban form of it, yet it is the forbidding fascination of this interrelationship that has provided such rich material for exploration by the directors of contemporary cinema. For illustration we should look at the recently published evidence on the discrepancy of educational attainment between different sections of the community. When an urban school-child fails to present her homework on the following morning, she may provoke bourgeois indignation in her teacher at her personal failure. On further investigation it may well be found that the child was expected to set herself to written work in the midst of a lively and crowded family evening, where quiet was unattainable through lack of extra rooms and cramped living conditions. In other words this episode suggests that the schoolteacher will not succeed by ignoring the setting as a whole from which his pupils come, since their own intellectual and personal growth is circumscribed by material and cultural conditions. The same situation applies to the work of the Church. Such realisation had for me frightening theological ramifications, that the pressures of environment affect the growth of a man's soul and his eventual salvation. I suspect that the Church's response to social conditions has been too legalistic, the 'give them instruction and they'll be all right' type of approach, which completely avoids any examination or questioning of the roots, and avoids the simple truth that the only cure for the effects of bad housing upon people is good housing, not prayer meetings, or religious instruction.

I have hinted through my own experience that this might be the discovery that a graduate makes for himself when beginning work in the community, and that it can only be learnt by doing just that. Much more far-reaching, however, in its effects upon one's religious outlook and limited understanding of christian responsibility, is the realisation of the extent to which many spheres of secular activity are inherently theological, without overtly referring to christian principles. I would cite as examples the Pilkington Report with its indictment of the triviality of bad advertising and mass media; the countless social planners, researchers, and architects who emphasise the vital implications of environment; and the men in industry and education who realise that technical proficiency alone is not sufficient, but that the economic health of a society also depends upon the spiritual sanity and fulfilment of its workers. The importance in saying this is not that we should agree with these as solutions, but that we should realise that they represent areas of secular responsibility that are concerned from a specific angle with exactly what the Church should be concerned with—the personal worth of individual people and their salvation in all its aspects; and that as christians we have a direct responsibility to support this work and concern ourselves with it. So often I have felt that Roman Catholics do not see this as at all relevant to the practice of their religion.

Indeed my experience took me further in the understanding of what I may term the cleavage between the strictly catechetical attitude to life and the secular grasp of its issues. I soon discovered that the fully professional man was a much more moral and fundamentally christian man than the 'religiously' trained man who practised his morality in isolation. I was continually meeting men and women in a professional capacity and working alongside them, from whom I derived a deep respect for the reality of the values they held. Their values of justice, integrity, intellectual honesty, hard work, self-sacrifice and love, were frequently held without any defined religious premise. I am not suggesting the absence of these qualities among christians; I am more concerned to note their presence among formally non-christians as being the values of primary concern to these men and women. The sanity of their secular morality threw into distinction the notional values that my conventional religious teaching had inculcated. The morality I had derived from the manuals had been abstract and legalistic—attendance at mass, chastity, no meat on Fridays, states of grace and grades of sin—which seemed to me to be introverted and self-seeking, and largely not the sort of morality that a professional life and responsibility could be built on. I can add to these values a notable enthusiasm for their professional discipline that few christians hold for their Christianity. Many of them had a dynamic sense that things were not right, but admitted that they had not got the answer, and therefore struggled and investigated on all fronts, prepared to accept whatever might seem relevant without preconceived judgment. What I think had happened to me is that my Catholic education had not prepared me to recognise the valid theological properties of the natural realm, or that a fully professional man of integrity might be a theologically formed person.

The Secular Situation

The degree to which this cleavage extends is well shown in a comparison of approaches, between the 'Roman Catholic' teacher and his secular professional counterpart. While teaching in my non-Catholic school I had regular meetings with a group of Catholic teachers. These teachers were very worried about the state of their Catholic schools, and we came together to find some way to recreate our situation. But from these discussions and from reading Catholic educational journals we grew to the conclusion that perhaps a preponderant amount of energy and time was spent in sorting out the religious education of the children in isolation from the rest of the school curriculum; that there seemed to be too much concern with finding the right answers, preventing the children from 'lapsing', accounting for Mass attendance, banning pornographic literature, and pursuing Roman Catholic rights in non-Catholic schools, that it was hardly surprising that this gave little satisfaction. The approach was much too purely denominational to reach the heart of the problem.

Much more to the point were my experiences with a secular, professional body of teachers in English. Here was another group of people looking for a similar sort of recreation, but this time finding it. Their concern was with the response and growth of the child, a thoroughly christian and theological matter, but in their case freely approached without the inhibiting jargon that a 'religious' group tends to bring with it. Both groups, then, were basically involved in the same problem, the salvation of a child's soul, but one starting with the interpretation of doctrinal formulae, the other from the situation of the child.

The discoveries of these teachers in English are relevant to the teaching of theology. Because the teaching of English is concerned with the growth of response, it goes far to the heart of the theological education of the person, for it must be understood that the teaching of language, in particular the mother tongue, can only arise properly out of formed experiences, and that language and experience are interdependent for their development. In other words the formalistic teaching of language as grammar does not begin to meet the linguistic sensibilities and needs of the person. I quote from professional evidence submitted recently to the Central Advisory Council for Education which supports this vital extension of the sphere of English teaching: 'Room must be found in English lessons for pupils to express sincerely their experience, to consider the problems which arise from it, and to read those works which speak to their experience and extend it. We would expect English work to be rooted in the concerns, hopes and fears, and daily lives of the pupils. Stereotyped procedures and condescending text-books cannot touch these vital areas.'

For a moment I want to examine the process of creative writing, because it is through their writing that children are helped to see themselves, and because I believe that much of this English teaching that I am referring to may well be a substitute for the conventional religious education lesson.

First, a right moral attitude on the part of the teacher is vital, if he is to encourage the freely given response of the child, to persuade the child that personal writing matters, because honesty and sincerity are essential to good writing: it is these qualities that must characterise the relationship between teacher and taught.

The stages worked out are interesting in their theological implications, and go some way towards restoring that sense of reverence, the lack of which I referred to earlier in this paper. The children must quickly learn to accept each other's ideas, and to have simple respect for each other's work. Constant freedom of discussion is essential, so that there can be an acceptance of each other's experience; and humility must be learned in the face of criticism. In turn the teacher has to avoid moralising about some of the surprising experiences that are related and that are perhaps contrary to a bourgeois or conventional social code; for instance, one must be concerned, first with the *experiences* of such a pastime as 'Knock Down Ginger' (knocking on doors and running away), and then only afterwards does one let the class comment on its possible social implications. To establish this sense of trust the teacher must show concern in the little everyday things of the children's lives. Commenting on written work is not solely a matter of literary judgment, but—and this is more important—a time for discussion about content: the difficulties of housing a bicycle in a flat; mum grumbling about the smell of nail varnish in the middle of a meal; and the feelings experienced on first bringing a boy or girl friend home. Together the class explore themselves, their families and their street through common experiences. And through awakening them to the richness of the world in which they live and precisely as they know it, there will be some chance of leading them to a reverence for areas wider than they yet know, from the neighbourhood to the whole city, from the city to their national and ultimately international situation. Throughout this one will have been working for deeper and deeper critical thought, for some simple objective appraisal towards a natural respect and need for symbol and sign; at first, in their writing, the factory in their street was simply black and dirty, but later the same factory stood for the realms of work and, to the more highly sensitive, the poisonous smoke for social irresponsibility.

In this way the school and its work can become acceptable, the gulf may be slowly bridged. From the children's own world a sense of wonder is aroused, and the moment arrives for them to meet their cultural heritage. In the discussion of literature the whole process is reinforced, and response considerably developed. One is continually tapping a deep-rooted sense of values held without necessarily christian overtones; for instance in discussing the problem of conscience and attitudes towards stealing between Huckleberry Finn and Tom Sawyer, when they run away to the island having hooked a ham, the teacher strikes upon a surprisingly developed conception of natural law among the children. The idea of sin and expiation comes across vividly in the *Rhyme of the Ancient Mariner*. One does not need the stereotyping of the catechism; its truths are far better learnt in terms of real experiences, for the discussion of all literature must always lead back to a discussion of the children's similar experiences, if they are to find an interpretation of life. Then it is poetry above all which holds the key to a sense of wonder and preserves a clarity of feelings, symbol and commentary; for, after all, feelings are highly developed in the adolescent, and it is so often through them that we have to educate towards the truth.

Yet this whole educational theory cannot succeed apart from a light and happy atmosphere in a class. If their response is striven for in the light of a self-conscious moraliser, it will inevitably fail, for this sort of work is deeply concerned with very personal things. The sacredness of personal relationships matters most of all, and that in itself is something of great influence. This ultimately could be the antidote to that moribund boredom and resentment that produces the juvenile delinquent. I am thinking of a certain intelligent thirteen-year-old boy, for whom school with over thirty in his class could never provide the intensive challenge and absorption in experience that crime offered him with its opportunities for pioneering. Secondly, the content of such creative writing must be rooted in what they know—the street—in order that they can achieve a reverence for what has borne them; only then can that reverence for that which is greater than themselves possess reality and avoid the danger of degeneration into pious formality and bourgeois convention. For the children learn that they depend upon men, communities, and eventually a Being greater than themselves; and it is all this which liberates them from the limitations of their environment.

I believe that much of what I have described to you is partly the working out of the task that Pius XII described thus: 'from being inhuman, the world must be made human; from being human, it must be made divine; that is according to the will of God.' This observation supports the view that education needs to be more than just technical, mechanical and vocational; that we have a responsibility to educate the whole man and to provide for what Maritain has called 'his need for resources'. Arthur, the main character in *Saturday Night and Sunday Morning*, represents this need when, as he walks out of the factory and into the evening, he says, 'you stepped out into a cosy world of pubs and noisy tarts that would one day provide you with the raw material for more pipe-dreams as you stood at your lathe.'

But the education of the feelings and the development of a creatively critical response is by its nature nebulous and unpredictable. It has not got the neatness of the teaching of a body of knowledge. Modern man likes the cut and dried, and will resist a more creative approach with its inherent uncertainties. Education is not a matter of instruction and cramming but is essentially a matter of leading out, and I feel that the Church needs to adopt this approach more consciously. I do not wish to claim that this secular approach easily solves the problems of the cultural gulf, antipathy or deadness of response, but I do claim that it makes more sense. Yet again it will fail if, like conventional religious training, it goes over in isolation. It is more than a subject; it is about a person's whole field of response. We are seeing today the refraction of the sciences, the atomisation of subject matter, over-specialisation within education. These depth studies are in one sense illuminating the person, but in another are fragmenting him and leaving him abandoned. The schoolteacher at all levels is uniquely at the centre of all this and is expected to synthesise such studies for the pupil. He is professionally concerned with the integration of the personality, and must establish an inner order. This is where he realises his need of theology for himself and his pupils.

I am dwelling on the secondary school, because it has been my situation, and because I believe it can be held that what we discover in the secondary school teaches us much that is universally applicable to universities, higher education and the Church, about the nature of communication, response and development.

Theology and the Layman

I have now emphasised at some length how a theological disposition in a person can be encouraged; how it tends to be dependent upon the method, nature and approach of his early education; that just as the sphere of an individual's responsibility to God lies in his daily relationship with society, so his discovery of the divine must come through the whole of his social experience, and the relevant preparation for such a deference through the whole secular pattern of his educational growth; and that the fundamental purpose of education might be to prepare a person to respond creatively to his own discoveries. I am sure that it is this disposition and power of the person that Dr Leavis has in mind when, towards the end of his 1962 Richmond Lecture, he says:

> that mankind . . . will need to be in full intelligent possession of its full humanity (and 'possession' here means, not confident ownership of that which belongs to *us*—our property, but a basic living deference towards that to which, opening as it does into the unknown and itself unmeasurable, we know we belong). I haven't chosen to say that mankind will need all its traditional wisdom; that might suggest a kind of conservatism that, so far as I am concerned, is the enemy. What we need, and shall continue to need not less, is something with the livingness of

the deepest vital instinct; as intelligence, a power—rooted, strong in experience, and supremely human—of creative response to the new challenges of time.[1]

This is essentially a theological statement about man's situation today, and I would like to think it summarises the direction in which the Church's mission of ideas must work. Therefore, in conclusion, I want to describe how a man might come to recognise that such a statement made at the secular level can be theologically pertinent, and show why the preceding part of the paper has been relevant.

Every man who has had some formal religious education meets his situation with some ready-made theological terms and ideas. The process is at first one of matching up those received concepts with the new experiences being encountered. Some of those ideas which had been given me clear and undistorted I found helpful in throwing light on my situation, but for the majority I had to expurgate the peculiarly Catholic ethos in which they became enshrouded. A technical term like 'redemption' made sense only in terms of meeting the activity of redemption in relation to the moribund lives and condition of the children of an underprivileged area among whom I worked. I can indicate some depressive aspects that I found affecting their lives which made sense only if I realised all were redeemed: the cheapness of life, a breakdown of sexual morality, hard bargaining between men, the morality of the van driver who deliberately disregards the safety of his community, prejudice, resistance, massive indifference, and a common disregard for such traditional sanctities as landscape and culture.

The daily process was one of trying to make sense of the religion I had been taught. Formal proofs for the existence of God seemed meaningless in the context of the social problems I was meeting. I only came to understand how God exists and why he is a God of love by means of widening my understanding of the mystical body, as something which includes all the children in a school, Catholic and non-Catholic, Christian and non-Christian. When I discovered some Catholic teachers trying to organise Catholic teachers in non-Catholic state schools to hold their own morning assemblies apart from the community, and then when I found a Catholic boy using his so-called 'rights' to opt out of the non-Catholic Religious Education lesson in order to go stealing, I began to wonder just how exclusive the

---

[1] *Two Cultures?* The significance of C. P. Snow, p. 42 (Chatto and Windus, 1962).

mystical body should be. So often Catholics use the term 'our parish' to mean their fellow Catholics who live around and attend their parish church. The extensive nature of my work and the structure of the city complex in which I lived, prevented me from even belonging in this sort of customary way, and I could never see that such an idea of a parish could ever contribute to the community at large, or could even sensibly exist. What I could see, however, was that if the parish comprehended the whole borough in which it was set, then my neighbours, my professional colleagues and the children I taught would be my fellow parishioners, so that it would become my task to represent those that I knew and worked with, 'whether Jew or Greek', at the parish Mass. In fact I understood how there was so much preventing them from accepting the universal invitation to the Mass, that it was in fact simpler for one, for me, to represent them. In this dynamic and real way the fact of the mystical body acquired definition and the idea of the sacraments took on significant purpose.

I am not suggesting that the layman needs to produce a whole new existential theology from his situation, but I do say that, for example, in the secular school the teacher has to recreate theology for himself in terms of the reality he has to grapple with. For instance, I found that my inhibited bourgeois attitudes were divorced from the morality I met in a number of the children who were of a different culture. In simple everyday occurrences, such as unconscious habits of swearing or limited manners, it would have been presumptuous for me to have become indignant, as perhaps my social formation might have considered advisable. A recent incident occurred in which a very difficult teenage girl said to her teacher, 'Cor mam, i'n't your arse getting fat!' To which the teacher quietly replied, 'Yes, dear, I'm trying to cut down my weight.' Vituperative indignation would have solved nothing for that girl; the natural acceptance of her precocious language, however, helped to sustain a human relationship. This was the clue I found; every child was Christ in a unique way, everything suddenly appeared as a matter of personal relationships, so that love and patience and compassion became my guides, and in small ways I tried this out. I tried standing aside at doors to let the children through first instead of insisting upon my adulthood, and at assemblies I tried to remember to fetch chairs for children when they arrived late. For surely Christ is met in terms of those he came to redeem, that is everybody. The process was not a matter of creating a theology from life without reference to what already exists; it was a matter of relating and developing what had been taught me. The example of the term 'grace' will serve to show this. The account of grace given in the schools and pulpits was meaningless and untheological. What was meaningful was that acts of charity, such as being kind to the children and the creation of happiness in the classroom rather than mere discipline, were the way by which grace might be communicated to the secular environment, in my case the school. Thus it was that I grew to discover that theology could offer the illumination I needed, not in terms of devotional practices, but in my secular life; that our secular responsibility is one of service as was Christ's, when he washed the feet of his disciples at the Last Supper; and that to hold authority means to hold a responsibility for the growth of those under one, whether children or adults, not to lord it over them, for the mission of the diaspora situation is essentially one of personal example and sincerity of witness.

In turn, I was finding that my experience was giving me a wider vision and understanding of theological truth. This is what I want to call 'creative theology'. It contains something of the similar localised response that one finds in the paintings of Stanley Spencer. This has been for me no more than the discovery of the natural realm, that the supernatural has life within the natural, that the natural is disposed to the supernatural. The important thing is that the activity is reciprocal and complementary, with theology declaring the clue to one's living situation, and the working environment completing the sense of theology. But I have found that many of the existing formulations of doctrinal and moral theology have lacked a comprehensiveness that would satisfy my needs. What does meet my needs is the study of the scriptures that puts back life into the theology I possess, for in the scriptures are echoed those same experiences as mine, but with God's comment already on them. I find that the richness of revelation goes far beyond anything the manuals can give.

Only this last term I became involved in a discussion with a twelve-year-old class about the relative merits of a scientist's needing to read the bible. One non-Catholic boy had this to say: 'The bible teaches you to have faith in yourself, and a scientist above all needs just that, because he will always be inventing and exploring things. You can't experiment without faith in yourself.' I think several significant things emerge from this answer; that the boy, through not being given a catechetical definition of either faith or the purpose of the bible, was free to comprehend a much richer idea of faith, and the bible remained unlabelled for him. I think this shows the response that is demanded of one in scriptural study; and theology based on the scriptures can never be confining.

All that I have said in delineating a theological way of thinking has radical consequences far outweighing any immediate effects. I am thinking of the consequences that such aspects as the validity of experience will have upon the authority of conscience; of the frequent apparent clash between reality and theological statement; of the results of allowing the contemporary scene to structure one's theology; all of which could have an unnerving effect upon a conventionally Catholic mind. For a soundly educated layman, born of and enjoying the freedom of intellectual integrity, must become deeply involved in his society; since, as a christian, he has a deeper sense of social responsibility than that possessed even by the social scientist, because his outlook is based upon a theology of personal relationships. So he comes to understand that a snob cannot be a christian; that a professionally responsible man is more of a christian than he supposes; that a christian should feel that what he does, matters, and is, in itself, its own reward; and that a Church, which takes on the same characteristics as the bourgeois, capitalist society in which it exists has little chance of carrying out the christian mission. For, ultimately, this social and intellectual freedom of the educated layman, in Newman's use of that term, gives him the opportunity to carry out the mission of the new Church of the diaspora; since the position in which the layman is honest to his situation is essentially missionary and dynamic. No longer will he be motivated by a capitalistic, safety-first mentality, but he will be animated by the livingness of what it means to be a member of the redeeming community and to respond to the task therein that falls to him.

Today, society does not want the Catholic Church doubling up on similar institutions. The community requires the Church to produce fully christian men, who will contribute to the great secular institutions as men, and not as 'swordsmen of the spirit'. Therefore, this man of the diaspora Church requires a kind of theology and religious education that will enable him to perform fully and efficiently that missionary vocation, which ultimately means nothing less than becoming involved in the open society of his day.

11. Proposals for the Teaching of Theology in an English University

Laurence Bright, O.P.

Some time ago I was asked to take part in drawing up a plan for theological teaching at an English university, in which Roman Catholics could take part on equal terms with Christians of other denominations, both as lecturers and as students. We worked instinctively: in this paper I shall try to set out explicitly the principles which lay behind the plan that emerged. The principles are not new; most of them have in fact been expressed by other speakers at this symposium, where there has been, I am sure all will agree, a most impressive unanimity.

Our idea was to produce a plan based on existing university practice, in order to satisfy ourselves that there would be no problems from the Catholic point of view. For we felt that it would be of immense benefit to Catholics to be able to enter into an existing situation, to join something which had been proved to work and was thoroughly English in character: at the same time we believed that here, too, Catholics had their own specific contribution to make, as in those other areas of English cultural life to which they have gradually returned. We had no wish to set up a separate Catholic department; the problem we set ourselves to solve was how Catholics could, without compromise, collaborate in the working of a university theological department *on its own terms*. Needless to say these have not been the terms on which up to now Catholics have studied theology in England; they were not our concern. Enough that in practice their effect has been to exclude an important section of the Catholic community—educated lay people—from benefiting from, or contributing to, the study of theology, and that we believed it was time alternative possibilities were investigated.

Three main principles seemed to emerge:

1. There must be a combination of teaching and research: this is the basis of English university studies, and theology should be no exception.

2. In teaching theology, lectures should be combined with seminar discussions: this is essential for theology because it is concerned both with what is given in divine revelation and with what is found in human experience. This has some bearing on the complex problem of collaboration in teaching between the clerical and lay sections of the christian community.

3. The whole faculty must be ecumenical in spirit; not simply because this is demanded by circumstances, but because the divided christian communities are not self-sufficient: each needs the others.

I shall now comment on these three principles in turn, and draw some practical conclusions from them.

(1) A combination of teaching and research has so long been taken for granted as the ideal in our universities, that it is difficult for anyone trained there even to consider the possibility of their separation. A mere teaching establishment, we are clear, will lack that important dimension which teaching only gets when it is done by men directly acquainted with creative work at the growing front of knowledge. A university must never become a place in which the mere handing-over of facts is of central importance. Such a place would begin to rely on the textbook rather than on primary sources: its examiners would start asking for the exact regurgitation of what had been dictated in lectures. No one would claim that English universities are ideal in this respect, but faced with absurd demands to double their student-teacher ratio, or to work on a shift system, they are prepared to fight to the death for the fundamental principle that there can be no culture without leisure. Leisure is needed to think towards the ideas which shape the future and, taught to pupils, prepare them for that future. Where there is no freedom from the burden of continually imparting information, where teaching is divorced from research, the dead hand of traditionalism lies heavy on the entire institution.

I have spoken at some length about what may well seem perfectly obvious to most of us, yet it seems to have been far from obvious to those who drew up the programme for theological teaching currently followed in Catholic seminaries, and in England on the whole that is the only theological teaching which takes place. There are people for whom the very idea of theology as a research subject, not merely repeating the past but having a developing life of its own, is somehow paradoxical. Even where the need for research has been felt, the natural solution has seemed to be the creation of a separate establishment devoted purely to higher studies. But this would impoverish teaching without providing the necessary safeguard of trying out speculative ideas on real people. By contrast the British university system, with its healthy empirical outlook, has always resisted such a solution. There is danger in the kind of speculation which never meets the challenge of being put over in terms that the ordinary educated man—the student—can understand and criticise. If a university became no more than an institute for higher studies, those studies themselves would suffer, while ordinary teaching, done elsewhere, would degenerate into sheer cramming.

It is, I am sure, because Catholic theology has had to be taught in this way in England that there has been so negligible a contribution on our part to its renewal in Germany, Holland, Belgium and France. Our great theologians have tended to be brilliant amateurs —and how few names there are, in any case, after one has thought of Newman's. If we in England can enter fully into the tradition of our universities in the matter of research and teaching, we may at last begin to play a real part in the theological life of the Church as a whole.

One practical consequence of this first principle must be mentioned. Theological research takes place in a tradition: of its nature it depends on the witness of the past, on scriptural revelation and on the understanding of that revelation by the faith of the Church in different times of its history. The witness is a written one, and books are bulky objects; hence the requirement of a well-equipped library. Excellent departmental libraries exist in our universities, but the past isolation of the Catholic community from other christians may well mean that these libraries are incompletely stocked with Roman Catholic books, particularly in French and German. To remedy the situation would put a strain on departmental resources in both space and money. Catholics might therefore feel that one of the specific ways in which they could immediately make their contribution to the development of theology (using the term now without denominational qualification) would be by a grant of money (perhaps from the educational funds of the diocese in which a university is situated) to be used for buying Catholic theological works.[1] It might even be possible to establish a subsidiary library within reasonable distance of the main one and of course available to all students who wished to make use of it. In the genuinely 'open' spirit which prevails in a university there is often advantage, rather than danger, in retaining denominational differences for practical purposes. Such a Catholic library would form a centre round which could then be organised research projects in Catholic theology to be undertaken by Catholic and non-Catholic alike, just as one envisages similar provision on the part of Anglicans and Free Churchmen. I shall return, in my last section, to the necessity of this kind of co-operation within the department as a whole.

(2) I now turn to the teaching course itself. We have considered only the general degree; a degree, that is, in which three subjects (four in the first year in some universities) are read. Theology would be one of these. The aim of such a theological course is not to turn out specialists in theology who might go on to do research, but men and women who will take ordinary jobs as teachers or as civil servants or perhaps especially in commerce and industry; and who will follow their avocation all the better for being theologically literate christians. The task of running a course to achieve this purpose is in itself of the highest importance; but for Roman Catholics there is the added advantage that if this is a way by which we can come in on the ground floor we feel that we will be able to prove our worth, and show that we are capable of collaborating in a small-scale enterprise in a manner that our university colleagues will accept. Later on we may receive an invitation to collaborate in a specialist course. (First perhaps in a joint school of Theology and say, English, if there is a tradition of running such courses in what are sometimes called modern 'greats'.) But at the moment we are hardly in a position to offer men with sufficient experience of university Theology to take part at a higher level than the general degree: the experience gained there, particularly

---

[1] Pusey House was established at Oxford in this way: founded in 1884, its basis was Pusey's Library of biblical, patristic, and Hebraic literature. Similarly, St. Deiniol's was founded at Hawarden by Gladstone in 1896 as a residential library for students in the arts. Its basis is 30,000 volumes from Gladstone's collection.

No real theological work can be done without a well-stocked library (*v.* Fransen, p. 83 f. *supra*). To found such a library would, incidentally, be one of the surest means by which an Institute of value to a university might be established.

if combined with research, will be the necessary preparation for a further step to be taken some time in the future. In the meantime we shall have got to know our non-Catholic colleagues, and they us.

In order to explore the possibilities, we set out to devise a scheme of teaching which we thought would be acceptable from the Catholic point of view, and would form a point of comparison with existing practice in the open university, on which it is largely based. This also has a practical value in that not every theological department runs a general course, and where there is one it is not always suitable for training lay people to be theologically literate—too often it is no more than a laundry-shrunk specialist course. But I must emphasise that this course represents only one possible solution. There is no such thing as 'the' solution: there are real advantages in matters being organised differently in different institutions and comparison made of the results.[1] But we believe that what we are proposing is at the same time rooted in the nature of theology and in the English approach to academic growth.

The central principle we relied on was that teaching ought to be divided equally between lectures and seminar discussions. Though this is normal university practice, it has special significance for theology. For the contents of a theological course are both given and discovered. They are given as the revelation of God's word in scripture and its tradition in the Church; they are discovered in the experience of men living in an actual cultural context. If men restrict their attention to what is given, their theology becomes a dead system to be 'looked up' in textbook or even the bible; English Catholic theology has in the past all too often seemed to be of this kind. It is only brought to life, changed from a series of answers to questions people have ceased to put, when set in a living context. Yet if we restrict attention to the cultural context, we may well be left with a series of questions to which no answers whatsoever can be given, and it is part of the christian faith that God has given an answer, though one which each man must earn by listening in trust to his word. We believe that in the exploration of key texts having a critical and philosophical nature, by the method of the seminar, students will be led to ask the questions to which the lectures will indicate some way to understand the answer given by God in Jesus Christ. Lecture and seminar are necessary complements of one another.

[1] See Fransen, p. 95 (*supra*).

To take the lecture course first. We have allotted two periods of lecture per week over the three years, and one period of seminar. This is as much as we felt could be allowed to one subject among three. It has led us, somewhat reluctantly, to exclude the requirement of Greek and Hebrew. If additional room could be found for the teaching at least of Greek, this should of course be done; but we felt that with only three periods a week available we could not take up time that would, in the case of those not gifted with a flair for languages, perhaps cut an already limited course by one-third. On the other hand we consider that a qualification for entry into the course ought to be at least one A-level subject in, say, French or German, since so much important modern work exists only in those languages.

Next we have proposed that the first year should, in the lectures, be devoted entirely to a preparatory course that in some sense covers the field. Theology cannot survive the process of fragmentation that is possible with other disciplines, since it is of its essence to transcend the division between speculative and practical, the 'is' and the 'ought'. Catholics are only too well aware of the disastrous results that have followed on the divorce of scripture and doctrine or of doctrinal and moral theology, or of both these and the study of liturgy. We are less sure about just how such a preparatory course could be organised.[1] One solution, the one we have actually put forward, is of a survey type of course, to which later studies in depth, by an examination of the sources at a particular number of specified points, could then be related by the student. This has the further advantage that where the subject is taken for one year only, by students going on to other subjects, they will at least have been shown something complete in itself. Clearly it has its difficulties, and an alternative suggestion might be of something more methodological in character.[2] Here the student would be introduced to the various ways in which Scripture and doctrine are approached, and perhaps the teaching could be shared by members of different denominations, term by term.

Though we are by no means committed to the survey type of course, it may help to assess its usefulness if I quote my own experience in the matter, of course from a Roman Catholic point of view. I have been teaching just such an introductory programme at King's College, London, to Catholic students during the period when others

[1] v. Charles Davis, pp. 125, 130 (supra).
[2] v. note on following page 274.

attended the general A.K.C. lecture. My course extended over three years, but for one period a week only, and as time had to be allowed for discussion, the lectures themselves were not much more than half an hour in length. I used a traditional three-fold division, the first year being given to God the creator, the second to the work of the Son, the third to the sacramental moral life of the christian. The approach was entirely biblical; the first year explored the revelation of God in the Old Testament, and gave me the opportunity to talk about the nature of revelation and inspiration as themselves part of the pattern of saving history; the second year led on to the Christology revealed by the New Testament, the nature of the mission of the Spirit and the Church living by his life, all this being then related to the definitions of the early Councils; in the third year I discussed the nature of the chief liturgical sacraments in relation to Christ the primordial sacrament of the Father, and drew more explicitly the practical consequences for the moral life of a christian in the world of today, though this had always been to the fore in the earlier talks. My approach was rooted in experience; for example I discussed the Eucharist at length as memorial and as meal before going on to speak tentatively of its sacrificial aspects. The course was not entirely successful, since Catholics have so often been systematically unfitted for grasping theology by the doctrine classes they get in their schools; but about half came to realise what we were up to and to like it, while the rest took notes.

Note to p. 273. The Rev. Kenneth Grayston, Deputy Head of the Special School of Theology, Bristol University, suggests that a course on the following lines might be considered as an alternative:
1. An introduction to the biblical languages for students who have neither Greek nor Hebrew, by means of:
    (a) An examination of the various uses of language—e.g. conceptual, metaphorical, analogical and typological.
    (b) English, Greek and Hebrew described and compared as languages.
    (c) Further studies in the languages of the bible—sources, problems raised by translation, the advantages and limitations of theological word studies.
2. An introduction to the study of the principles of exegesis (hermeneutics):
    (a) Common presuppositions described and examined: the main denominational approaches; fundamentalist and liberal approaches; the historical approach and its limitations etc.
    (b) An examination of the various methods by which a biblical theology might be constructed, especially whether it is built up from within the bible or imposed.
3. An introduction to the textual, literary and historical criticism of Scripture preparatory to the study of christian doctrine.

To return to our proposed university course. Two years remain, and two lecture-periods are available in each. We therefore devised four courses. Two of these should be devoted to the deeper exploration of Old and New Testament topics, from a theological rather than a merely exegetical point of view. Here it is essential to have a sensitive study of definite texts. In many ways it is unfortunate that such studies must be based on the English text alone, but at least students will be spared texts interesting only for their grammatical or philological complexity. In detail our proposals are extremely tentative. One might take an important complex of biblical writing: the Pentateuch, the Deuteronomic history, the prophetic writings, the synoptic gospels, the Pauline and Johannine writings are obvious groupings. Yet even one of these would form too large a whole, and careful selection is needed. The texts, we feel, ought to be used to explore the theological preoccupations of their authors or strands of authorship. By coming to recognise, through detailed work, the complex of ideas represented by, shall we say, the Yahwist author, students will be in a position to read other parts of scripture for themselves, so that it can at last begin to deliver its saving message with the full intelligibility that modern scholarship has released. An alternative method of procedure might be the discussion of certain key concepts through their various manifestations over the range of Israel's history, but this would lead to greater practical difficulty by obscuring the convenient division of the two Testaments.

A third course should be given on the development of a particular doctrine through the Church's history. Unless we can see squarely how any part of our faith has developed the particular form in which it is expressed today—unless, that is, we can distinguish what is essential about it from all that is merely the manner of expressing it for our time—we remain fixed in our own particular systems of thought, unable to enter into dialogue with others. Hence discussion should not be restricted to doctrines that seem to have been settled long ago, and are common to all christians—the Trinity, for example. From time to time (for all these courses should run cyclically, the same theme not recurring for at least three years, so that the lecturers do not get bored with their work) more controversial subjects, such as the theology of the Eucharist, would have to be dealt with. Since each lecturer must naturally be faithful to his own tradition, this will raise denominational difficulties, but I will deal with those later.

The fourth course could well be a study of liturgy, again treated historically; not merely as a description of what once took place (an archaeological treatment) but as relating the theological outlook of the Church at different periods to its liturgical expression. Again this would have the effect of tying in theology with life, even if with life at a rather happier period than our own. Perhaps this course could also run cyclically, different periods being chosen year by year.

So much for the lectures. Yet however well they relate theology to life, something more is necessary if the student is really to find it from his own cultural experience. It is not enough for us to say that theology must be at the creative centre of human experience if we do not learn to feel it there on our pulses. The solution we suggest is a somewhat novel one, and not unattended with risk, yet one we believe well worth trying out. It is to make use of the seminar method for a discussion, involving students of all three years, of texts that are not in any sense overtly religious. The study of a text of creative literature, for example, is a thoroughly religious activity, so long as we allow it to judge us and our lack of moral insight, rather than sit in judgment upon it.[1] What we have to avoid is any notion of 'applying' a cut and dried theology to the text. But in these discussions the student will learn to 'discover' theology for himself as a further dimension to the human world of art and literature and science. Again, the study of social–political questions raised by texts from a particular period of history would be useful—the relationship between religion and society in the early nineteenth century as instanced in texts of Coleridge, Bentham and Mill, for example. But we must be careful to avoid doing a bit of this and a bit of that, or of prejudging the issues by choosing texts that obviously 'give their message'. One way of avoiding this would simply be to take texts proposed by, for instance, the department of English for study in a particular year, and to examine—for this course must be rigorously examined, the results being given equal importance with those based on the lecture-material in assessing the student's capacity—with the help of members of that department. Another year the texts selected by the departments of Philosophy or of Sociology might be used, and so on. Obviously this course is going to be peculiarly exacting on both lecturer and student; yet if it could be made to work, it could meet

[1] v. note on *Literature and the theologian*, p. 218 (*supra*).

the demands of those who seek to recognise the christian dimension in their lives.

One can see immediately how a sensitive critical response to the text before them, learned in these seminars, could also change the students' response to the text of scripture worked on in the lectures. And the theologian would be profiting fully from his position in the context of the university; he would be drawing fully on all that is best in the other disciplines being studied and brought to the help of the community as a whole.

The balance between lecture-course and seminar is, as I have suggested, the balance between the two sides of the single discipline of theology, given from above and drawn from our human world; wherever one side has been developed at the expense of the other there has been distortion. The distortion to which we as Catholics are peculiarly prone is that of a false 'supernaturalism': the world is passing away, we say, and so anything can be done in it and to it. This shows in such things as our cavalier attitude to natural justice or truth-telling: the vice that rightly or wrongly has gained the name of 'clericalism'. I do not wish to enter now into the peculiar difficulties of sorting out the difference between two attitudes towards the world, the clerical and the lay;[1] sufficient to say that the world and its values are especially, if not exclusively, under the care of the layman and it seems right that the seminar should normally be in his charge. To divide out rigorously one area for the laity and another for the clergy would merely be to perpetuate an unhappy divergence, and it is unfortunately true that some of the most vicious exponents of the anti-humanist attack on the sacredness of the world in which God has placed us are really 'priests' in lay clothing—here too *cucullus non facit monachum*. Priest and layman are both needed in the unity of the Church. Any great enterprise within it must be the work of the whole body of the Church, a partnership of cleric and lay, and it could well be that we shall, in the open society of the university, manage to achieve something of the balance that is, for example, notoriously lacking as yet in the context of our Catholic schools.

(3) The third principle I spoke of was the *essentially* ecumenical nature of the work. Ecumenism springs from something deeper than the mere wish to get together; it springs from the realisation that no

[1] See note on the distinction cleric and layman, *What is a layman?* p. 63f *supra*.

man, no Church, possesses the fullness of theological truth or evei will: that fullness resides in the mind of Christ who is Lord of all, and in this life our share of it is only partial, until we know as we are known. But each christian community bears witness to important truths which in other communities are neglected and obscured, and so each must learn from dialogue with the others. Each must remain completely faithful to its own traditions, but each must seek to renew its thought and bring it closer to the mind of Christ with the help of others, thereby naturally growing towards that unity which all recognise as the will of God. This is the great discovery of our own times, and the spirit which lies behind all we have tried to do in this symposium.

It has important consequences for our teaching in the proposed course. The safe way would be to stick to neutral topics, to Scriptural exegesis and Church history; to doctrine presented not as true or false but merely as held by certain people at certain periods of history. No doubt it is possible to teach a 'highest common factor' theology in which all matters of controversy are suppressed. This is not what we envisage at all. We want each man to teach what he sincerely believes; but a man teaching as a Catholic, for instance, must then show why an Anglican or a Presbyterian would disagree with him. This ought not to turn into the presentation of a set of opinions, leaving the student bewildered, wondering which to choose; properly done, it will leave the student who is, say, an Anglican, more deeply committed to his own tradition because now more aware of how it stands in relation to others. Openness and commitment are correlative, not contradictory; a man who believes deeply and personally can afford to be sensitive to the deeply held personal beliefs of others. Now if the teaching is to be done in this way, those who are teaching will naturally feel the need of constant discussion with their colleagues. A man who thinks he is presenting the Methodist objections to his own position will have to consult his Methodist colleague to find out if this is really so; he may well have to engage in a small piece of research, or help his pupils to do so, in order to find out what christians of another denomination do in fact believe. Obviously this will never be done in a polemical spirit, but as part of the common search for the fullness of christian truth. We believe that this natural ecumenical dimension to the project is one of its most important features.

I am not going to deny that by dealing in this way with students still in process of growing to maturity we may be running some risk. This is the kind of risk involved in every work of faith in which, like our father Abraham, we must 'go out, not knowing where we are to go'. Christian men and women being prepared for the realities of life deserve more of us than to have their faith artificially protected, kept to the ignorances of childhood. We have each to realise that other christians differ from ourselves for good reasons, not foolish ones; those who trust in God emerge the stronger from such an encounter. Reasonable safeguards could be made, however. The most important would be for each student to have a tutor of his own denomination, preferably a member of the department, to whom he can go regularly for discussion on those points of difference that he is discovering. But where this is not possible, as a result of university requirements, the existence of a chaplaincy will solve many of the difficulties.

In conclusion, if these ideas are felt to be reasonable, how can they best be put into practice? Of course the answer to this cannot be laid down in general terms; it will depend on the existing structure of particular university theology departments. But to take a not un-common example, where teachers acceptable to the university are drawn from theological colleges of various denominations, we believe that it would be useful from every point of view to form a Roman Catholic institute on the same lines. It would have a life of its own— and here I would ask you to remember all I began by saying about the need for research, the need for a permanent library, the need for a living community of people thinking and working together. At the same time it would be a place to which the university could naturally turn when looking for men to teach within the theological depart-ment. Such an institute should, then, be set up under the presidency of a scholar acceptable to the Bishop of the diocese, and begin to draw to itself other such men prepared to take part in the enterprise. There may well be an existing Catholic foundation of high academic standing within the diocese, on which to build. If it is to represent the whole Church it must clearly be made up of clerics and laymen working together in equality of partnership; this principle must ex-tend to its governing body, and be written into its constitution. It is no part of this paper to go further into detail about such a con-stitution, which must depend upon the actual situation as it is met in any particular place.

May I conclude on a personal note? As John Coulson and I have worked together on this project, with the willing collaboration of so many friends, Catholic and non-Catholic alike, and not least with that of the Abbot of Downside; as we have gradually watched what seemed almost insurmountable obstacles disappear before our eyes, and the goal come closer into view, it has been impossible not to feel the very real working of the Holy Spirit of God within human affairs. Our project, as it must be, is a modest one; yet it could have the most far-reaching consequences for the future not merely of our own country, but of the whole world.

Index

APOLOGETICS distinguished from theology, 35[1], 37, 40
ART (*see also* POETRY)
    and other creative disciplines, analogy between, 217
    distinction between form and content, 197, 210 ff.
    reaction to, 195
AUTHORITY
    abuses of, and its consequences, 39–41, 87, 102
    and scriptural interpretation, 138[1]
    ecclesiastical (*see* CHURCH)
    functions of, 92, 102, 123, 138[1]
    true and false within Church, 92, 102, 267
AUTONOMY
    of government of departments of Theology, examples of, 75–85
        of proposed department of Theology, 279
    of studies, fundamental to University, 31, 58, 73, 75, 81, 85–6, 169
        how reconciled to ecclesiastical authority, 4, 5, 158 f., 167–8, 182 f., 185, 278
    within the Church, 90–1

BELIEF (*see also* FAITH)
    dead, and breakthrough to living, 252
    in God, compatible with Science, 246
BIBLE
    basis of Christian thinking, 128, 266–7
    basis of theology course, 147 ff.
    character of authority of, 136
    dependence of dogmatic theology on, 125 ff.
    distinctive substance of doctrine, 140
    interpretation, problems of, 129, 138[1]
    possibility of single authoritative version, 135
BIBLICAL LANGUAGES
    how far necessary for lay theologians, 5, 95, 103, 166, 274[1]
    in proposed university theology course, 274[1]
BIBLICAL THEOLOGY
    collaboration in, 21
    life-giving to theology, 266
    need for, as being basic, 99
    special character of, 125
    teaching of, to laymen, 99, 274 ff.

CATHOLIC UNIVERSITY (*see* UNIVERSITY, Catholic)
CENTRE, Creative (*see* CREATIVE CENTRE)
CHAPLAINCIES, in Universities, 14, 38 ff., 279
CHRISTIAN LIFE
    in secular situation, need for living theology in, 262 ff.
    in University, 43
CHRISTIAN UNITY (*see also* ECUMENISM)
    challenge to Christianity, 16, 22
    Secretariat for, 16

CHURCH, THE
  authority of, and university autonomy (*see* AUTONOMY)
    inimical to university life?, 36, 58, 59, 70, 72
    in sincerity of witness, 92, 102, 267
  duties of, to teach all nations, 2, 14, 92
    towards laity, 47, 54–6, 115
  ecumenical dimension in, as 'Call of God', 83
  freedom in, rediscovery of, 90
  fullness of, in partnership of priests and laity, 8, 55
    to be effected by revivified theology, 265
  ghetto mentality in, and results of, 56, 59, 96, 110, 259 (*see* ISOLATIONISM)
  theology of, to be subordinate to corporate faith, 123
COMMUNICATION
  general problem of, 255
  within the Church, necessity for, 83, 255
COMMUNITY
  response to, as laying foundation for theological maturity, 46 n., 267
  the Church as, 43, 82, 256
  the University as, 42, 53, 55
CONSCIENCE
  personal, supremacy of, 22
CREATIVE CENTRE
  Church no longer at, 256
  in the University, 115, 141
  role of the layman in, 116, 251 ff.
  theology's need to be at, 108, 263 ff., 276
CULTURE (*see* CREATIVE CENTRE)

DIALOGUE
  between professional theologian and layman, necessity of, 103
  ecumenical, 14
    experiences in, in departments of theology, 157, 180
    necessity for, 17, 119, 132, 269 ff.
  need to distinguish essential from non-essential as prerequisite in, 275
DIASPORA
  Church of the new, 9, 92, 267
  situation: mission is sincere witness and personal example, 266
DOCTRINE (*see also* THEOLOGY)
  existential character of, 181, 183 ff.
  lack of comprehensiveness in modern formulations of, 266
  methods of teaching (*see also* EDUCATION, RELIGIOUS), 36, 157, 174, 182, 278
  relation with Dogmatic Theology, 174

ECCLESIOLOGY
  differences in Catholic and Protestant, equivalent to differences in respective
    theologies, 129, and in attitudes to scriptural interpretation, 138[1]
ECUMENISM, 1, 2
  English opportunity in, 104
  great work of the Holy Spirit, 119
  in Biblical theology, 21
  movement of, 15
  necessity for, in theology, 83, 100, 110, 118, 132, 277–9
  Newman's attitude to, 60
  not a clerical luxury, 20
  participation by priests and laity in, 17, 18, 119, 277
  preserves essential differences, 4, 5, 278
  unique opportunity for, by collaboration in departments of theology, 4, 104, 140, 158, 167, 277–8

EDUCATION, RELIGIOUS (*see also* THEOLOGY, TEACHING OF)
  aims, 7, 25, 38, 42, 251 ff.
  in Catholic schools, 36 ff.
    attitudes produced by, 25–36, 38–9, 258
    lack of qualified teachers, 37
    possible substitute for, 260 ff.
    syllabus of, 36
  liberal, Newman's ideas on, 49 ff.
  methods of (*see also* UNIVERSITY; THEOLOGY, TEACHING OF)
    on Continent, 48 ff.
    in England, 36, 133–90
    proposed, 274
  possibility of learning from non-Catholic world, 73
  practical examples of non-Catholic methods, 133–73
  problem of, in real situation, 254
EMPIRICISM, Philosophic (*see* PHILOSOPHIC EMPIRICISM)
ENGLISH (*see also* ART, LANGUAGE, LITERATURE, POETRY)
  importance of studies in for theology, 259 f., 276
ENVIRONMENT (*see also* CREATIVE CENTRE)
  as affecting man's development, 257
  secular, need for theology, 7, 251 ff., 263
  theology must respond to, to be living, 109, 259
FAITH
  and reason, wrong attitudes to, 54, 150, 194, 247
  as encounter between God and man, 252
  character of, 97–8, 194
  danger of losing, by fearing new ideas, 112
  necessity of distinction between substance, and formulation of, 98, 275
  relation to the real world, 121, 252 ff.
FREEDOM (*see* AUTONOMY, AUTHORITY)
GREEK (*see* BIBLICAL LANGUAGES)
HEBREW (*see* BIBLICAL LANGUAGES)
IMMATURITY, religious, dangers of, 31 f.
IMAGINATION, not special faculty, but life coming to consciousness, 217
INTELLECT, development of, 54
ISOLATIONISM, religious, dangers of, 56, 59, 68, 83, 89, 96, 102, 110, 259
LAITY, 47 ff.
  as teachers of religion, shortage of, 37
  definition of, 63 (*see also* PRIEST AND LAY)
  ecumenical dialogue at level of, 18, 118, 263 ff., 277 ff.
  theological literacy of, 5, 47 ff., 94, 99, 103, 264
    necessity of, both for sake of laymen and of the whole church, 55, 91,115,
      161, 263, 279
  training as theologians (*see also* THEOLOGY, TEACHING OF), 5, 42, 47 ff.,
    81 ff., 99, 133–90, 267, 268 ff.
LANGUAGE
  biblical (*see* BIBLICAL LANGUAGES)
  contemporary, need for theology to be presentable in, 99, 102, 259–60
LIBRARY
  importance of, 82–3, 270
  as form of Catholic contribution to university, 270
LITERACY, theological (*see* LAITY)
LITERATURE (*see also* ART, ENGLISH, LANGUAGE, POETRY)
  imaginative insights of, not a faculty, but life coming to consciousness, 217
  judgements concerning, their nature and relation to theology, 197, 205–9,
    218–19, 259 ff., 276–7
  value of to student of theology, 6, 111, 193–219, 254 ff.

LITURGY
  discussion of, in course of theology, 274
  fossilised, as one cause of gulf between people and Church, 256

MASS, THE (*see also* LITURGY, TRANSUBSTANTIATION)
  as a meal, ignorance of, 45, 274
  representation of one's neighbour at, as part of Christian life, 265

MATURITY
  breakthrough to, in the encounter between God and man, 253
  growth towards, and artificial protection of faith, 279
  link between social and theological, 46
  religious, need for in the Church, 97

MORALITY
  false ideas of, as abstract, legalistic, and largely irrelevant, stemming from
      inadequacies in teaching, 32, 34, 258
  more meaningful in context of sound theological training, 266, 274

NATURE AND GRACE, not opposed, 53 ff.
NATURAL THEOLOGY (*see also* THEOLOGY)
  and poetry, 193 ff.

PHILOSOPHIC EMPIRICISM, 221–2
PHILOSOPHY
  of Hume, and theology incompatible, 222
  modern trends in, 222–3
  need for theologians to be acquainted with modern methods of, 21, 99,103,
      129, 150, 160, 184, 224, 247
  relation to theology, 6, 21, 129, 141, 150, 177, 184, 220 ff.
    example of (Transubstantiation), 225 ff.
    in proposed department, 276
  violence to nature of, and its effects, 72

POETRY (*see also* ART)
  and knowledge, 194 ff., 208 ff.
  and meaning, 198, 210, 214
  and natural theology, 193 ff., 207 ff.
  as self-revelatory, 197, 207, 208, 211
  in development of responses and feelings, 261
  symbol in, 217[1]; its relation to natural theology, 205

PRIEST AND LAY (*see also* LAITY; PRIESTHOOD), 9, 55, 62, 251, 277
  distinction one of sacramental function, not that between ordained and
      unordained, 63
  distinction in its present form, not the only one conceivable, 65
  partnership between, necessary, 9, 55, 61–5, 251
    effected by theology, 62
    in Catholic University, 55, 75
    in proposed department of theology, 277–9
    in theology, necessity for, 116, 118

PRIESTHOOD (*see also* LAITY; PRIEST AND LAY), 63
  and celibacy, 64
  and clericalism, 277
  does not confer monopoly of theology, 118

RELIGION (*see also* EDUCATION, RELIGIOUS; THEOLOGY)
  and science, compatibility with, 236 ff.
    logical relation with, 245 ff.
  Departments of, alternative to Theology, 74[1], 171, 188, 189

SEMINARIES, dangers of confining theology to, 114, 144
SCIENTIFIC
  theories, account of, 244–5
    compatibility with morality and religion, 236 ff.

SCIENTIFIC—*cont.*
thought, deductive unification of experience, 242 ff.
and non-scientific thought, relation between, 238, 245 ff.
SCRIPTURE (*see* BIBLE)
SECULAR (*see also* CREATIVE CENTRE)
activity often deeply theological, 258
environment (*see* ENVIRONMENT)
University (*see* UNIVERSITY)
SUPERNATURALISM, false, 266, 277
SYMBOL
in poetry, 217[1]
and relation to natural theology, 205

THEOLOGY
defined, 51, 82, 111, 116, 121, 122, 140, 159, 166, 173–5
and apologetics, 35[1], 37, 40
biblical (*see* BIBLICAL THEOLOGY)
dead, 89, 109, 111, 254, 258
departments of in University, 1, 4, 62, 78 ff., 140 ff., 146 ff., 173 ff., 268 ff.
contents of course, 133–90
twofold responsibility of, 150
proposals for, 188 ff., 268 ff.
contents of courses, 271 ff., 274 n.
proposed, ecumenical in character, 277
need for in secular University, 20, 49–53, 114, 144, 162 (*see* UNIVERSITY)
departments of, in University, participation by Roman Catholics, 165, 173 ff., 188, 268
distinguished from apologetics (*see* APOLOGETICS)
Dogmatic, must be ecumenical, 130
and Biblical theology (*see also* BIBLICAL THEOLOGY), relation between,133, 136 ff.
and Doctrine, 174
ecclesial, not individual matter, 131, 46 n.
and so subordinate to corporate faith of church, 123
ecumenical (*see also* ECUMENISM), 131, 176, 269
function of, 107, 251 ff.
to serve community of believers, 7, 132
liberal, problem of, 179 ff; excess prevents dialogue, 180
living, needs to be both given, and discovered, 271
modern interpretation of, need for, 99, 109, 251 ff.
moral, dogmatic, Biblical, relation between, 124 ff.
must transcend division between speculative and practical, 82, 125, 273
natural, and poetry (*see* POETRY)
need for, in secular environment, 7, 251 ff., 263
needs laity (*see also* LAITY), 116, 118, 161, 251 ff.
non-collaboration in England, effects of, 96, 114, 270
option in general degree course, 172, 271
other disciplines, bearing on, 172, 251 ff., 276
their relevance to, 111, 167, 251 ff., 276
place in University, 1, 51, 59, 62, 114, 144, 162, 268 ff.
'Queen of the Sciences'—outworn metaphor, 1, 58, 159
relevance of philosophy to, 150
superficial, implications of, 219
task, nature of, 122
teaching of (*see also* EDUCATION, RELIGIOUS)
dangers and inadequacies in some forms of, 99, 254, 265
Continental experience:
institutions, 78 ff.

THEOLOGY
  teaching of, *cont.*
    methods, 78 ff.
    necessity for collaboration in, 83
    to laymen, 99–101 (*see also* LAITY)
    for pluralist society, 101, 251 ff.
    proposals for, 268 ff., 274 n.
  in real situation, problem of, 254
  no one Roman Catholic solution, 95, 272
  student commitment to?, 154 ff.
  violence to nature of, and its effects, 72
TRANSUBSTANTIATION
  as example of use of philosophical principles in theology, 225 ff.
TRUTH
  existential character of, 120–1, 177
  guiding principle of theology, 61
  infallible possession of, by whole church, 83
  of 'divinity', 154 ff.

UNDERGRADUATES, CATHOLIC (*see also* UNIVERSITY)
  academic record of, 27
  attitudes, defensive and offensive, 39
  education, criteria of, 25
    inadequacies in, 28, 40, 45–6
  environment, effect of, 40
  lack of commitment in, 33, 34
  morality, attitudes to (*see also* MORALITY), 32–4
  theology, unfamiliarity with, 41
  vocation of, 30, 33, 42
UNIVERSITY
  Catholic, grounds for and purpose of, according to Newman, 52, 53 ff.
    conditions for success of, 57, 59, 61, 86
    distinguished from 'open' university, 69, 73 ff.
    American experience of, 66 ff., 75
      history, 66
      views on, 68
      inadequacies in, 69–70
      need to integrate into national academic community, 71
    European experience of, 81 ff.
    Louvain, 86
  catholics in, history of, 13, 56 ff., 173 ff.
    Newman's views on, 3, 47, 60
    as theologians, necessity for, 20, 114 ff.
  community, 42, 43, 46, 271
    as image of the church, 43
  creative centre, 114 ff., 133–90, 270
  departments of theology in, 1, 4, 62, 78, 140, 146, 162, 173, 268 (*see also* THEOLOGY)
  dialogue in, opportunities for, 20, 167, 269 ff.
  freedom in (*see also* AUTONOMY), 74–6, 146 ff., 169, 279
  life, understanding of, 44
  secular, attitudes of Catholics towards, 74
  theology in, 1, 4, 51, 52, 59, 78, 114, 140, 144, 146, 172–3, 160–5, 188, 270–2
  theology's need for, 114 ff.

WITNESS, as mission of the diaspora situation, 266
WORD OF GOD (*see also* BIBLE)
  witness to, function of whole church, 82
WORLD COUNCIL OF CHURCHES
  membership of, 15